NEW YORK HISTORY

VOLUME 100, NUMBER 1

SUMMER 2019

New York History (ISSN 0146-437x) is a peer reviewed journal published two times a year by Cornell University Press in partnership with The New York State Museum. Postage is paid at Ithaca, NY 14850 and additional mailing offices. POSTMASTER: Send all address changes to Cornell University Press, 512 East State Street, Ithaca NY 14850.

New York History is available in print and electronically Project Muse (http://muse.jhu.edu). Cornell University Press does not assume responsibility for statements of fact or opinions made by contributors. Unlicensed distribution of all materials (including figures, tables, and other content) is prohibited. Communications about subscriptions, back issues, reproductions and permissions, and other business matters should be sent to Cornell University Press (nyhjournal@cornell.edu). Digital and print subscriptions, for individuals and institutions, may be ordered via Project Muse (https://www.press.jhu .edu/cart/for-sale?oc=3729). Single print copies and print back issues are available for $20.00. For subscriptions and individual issues, inquiries and orders may be made by email, nyhjournal@cornell.edu, or by mail: *New York History* Journal, Cornell University Press, 512 East State Street, Ithaca NY 14850.

Submitted articles should address, in an original fashion, some aspect of New York State history. Articles that deal with the history of other areas or with general American history must have a direct bearing on New York State history. It is assumed that the article will have some new, previously unexploited material to offer or will present new insights or new interpretations. Editorial communications, including article submissions, should be sent to the Editorial Board via email (NYHJ @nysed.gov) Suggested length is 20-30 double spaced pages (or between 6,000 and 9,000 words), including footnotes. All submitted articles must include a 100-word abstract summarizing the article and providing keywords (no more than 10). Authors must submit articles electronically, with all text in Word and all tables, figures, and images in formats supported by Microsoft Windows. Provision of images in proper resolution (no less than 300 dpi at 5" x 7"), securing requisite permissions, and the payment of any fees associated with images for articles are all the responsibility of the author. *New York History* employs, with some modification, footnote forms suggested in the *Chicago Manual of Style*. More detailed submissions guidelines are to be found on the research and collections page of the New York State Museum: http:// www.nysm.nysed.gov/research-collections/state-history/resources/new-york-history-journal

Cover art: "The Great Fire of the City of New York, 16 December 1835." Lithograph showing the burning of the Merchant's Exchange Building during the Great Fire of New York, December 16–17, 1835. Courtesy of the New York State Museum Collections.

CONTENTS

Volume 100, Number 1

BOOK REVIEWS

EXHIBIT REVIEWS

LETTER FROM THE EDITORS

Robert Chiles, Devin R. Lander, Jennifer Lemak, and Aaron Noble

Welcome to the second century of *New York History!* This new century marks several changes here at the journal, all of which will ensure its continued success for another 100 years and beyond. *New York History* is now under the proprietorship of Cornell University Press and edited by the New York State Museum staff members Jennifer Lemak, Chief Curator of History, and Devin Lander, State Historian, along with the University of Maryland's Robert Chiles. State Museum Senior Historian Aaron Noble is the new Reviews Editor. Over the years the State Museum has worked to bridge the gap among historians across New York – academic historians, museum professionals, municipal historians, public historians, and students – and we expect the journal will augment those efforts. To this end, we anticipate expanding offerings pertaining to public history, digital scholarship, museum studies, and new standing features such as Artifact NY and Community NY, while continuing to feature more traditional academic essays and maintaining a rigorous process of peer review. The journal will also begin volume 100 by transitioning to semi-annual publication and will once again be available in both print and digital formats.

Begun in 1919 as the *The Quarterly Journal of the New York State Historical Association*, the journal came into existence the same year that the New York State Legislature passed the law giving every village, town and city the legal power to appoint a historian responsible for preserving the history of his or her locality and fostering a local interest in history. The journal has always been connected with the idea that a proper understanding of history is a necessary good of public life. Indeed, the first two editors of the journal were the State Historians James Sullivan (1919–1924) and Alexander Flick (1924–1939) and, with the current State Historian acting as a co-editor, the journal is returning to its roots connecting public and academic history.

We are indebted to Professors Thomas D. Beal, D.L. Noorlander and Susan Goodier from the SUNY Oneonta Department of History for much of the material present in this issue, for which they began the editorial process. From 2012-2019, these historians acted as editors and stewards of *New York History* and gave countless hours of tireless dedication to ensuring the continued success of the publication. Their work left a lasting mark on *New York History* and we are honored that they have joined the journal's Editorial Advisory Board. A sincere thank you to Thomas, D.L. and Susan for all of their hard work.

We would also like to thank the members of the journal's Editorial Advisory Board. This is a diverse group of academic and public historians from across New York State who bring decades of experience and professional qualifications to their role as advisors. Their collective vision and understanding of the complexities of New York State history will help guide the journal forward into its second century. We would especially like to acknowledge the continued participation on the Editorial Advisory Board of Patricia U. Bonomi, who has served as a member of the journal's board since 1974 and continues to offer insightful guidance to the editors.

And finally, we would like to thank Cornell University Press for their dedication to ensuring that *New York History* thrives into its second century. Without the Press taking over publication duties for the journal, it would have faced an uncertain future. We are particularly, thankful for the dedication and hard work put forth by Senior Editor Michael J. McGandy.

The Empire State's history is rich and diverse; full of triumph and tragedy. It is our goal to ensure that *New York History* continues to represent the best that the field of New York State history has to offer. We take this task and responsibility extremely seriously and look forward to beginning the next chapter of the journal's history.

CONTRIBUTORS

LEE BERNSTEIN

SUE BOLAND

LAURIE KOZAKIEWICZ

Professor of History at SUNY New Paltz, where he has taught since 2004, Lee Bernstein is the author of *America is the Prison: Arts and Politics in Prison in the 1970s* (University of North Carolina Press), *The Greatest Menace: Organized Crime in Cold War America* (University of Massachusetts Press) and *African Americans and the Criminal Justice System* (Schomburg Center for Research in Black Culture). Recent articles have appeared in *American Nineteenth Century History* and *The Journal of American Culture*. He is a member of the PEN American Center's Prison Writing Committee and the Sing Sing Prison Museum's Academic Advisory Board.

Local Historian for the Matilda Joslyn Gage Center for Social Justice Dialogue in Fayetteville, New York, Sue Boland has worked with Dr. Sally Roesch Wagner, founding director of the Center, since 1999. Sue wrote a biography of Gage and the most extensive bibliography to date for the *Dictionary of Literary Biography: American Radical and Reform Writers, 2nd Series*, published by Gale/Cengage Learning. She is a 2017 graduate of the Master's Public History program at the University at Albany and also holds an MS in Public Communications from Syracuse University.

Lecturer in History at the University at Albany, State University of New York, Lauren Kozakiewicz also serves as History liaison for Albany's University in the High School Program, a statewide collaboration with selected high schools to develop advanced history offerings for university credit. She received her Ph.D. from the University at Albany in 2006. Her research focuses on women politicians and political culture in 19th and 20th century America, with special attention New York State politics. Her current research project is a New York State-centered history of women legislators from 1919-1992.

D.L. NOORLANDER

CHRISTINE L. RIDARSKY

NANCY J. ROSENBLOOM

With a Ph.D. in history from Georgetown University (2011), D.L. Noorlander is currently an assistant professor of history at the State University of New York at Oneonta, where he teaches colonial American history, the Atlantic world, and European expansion. His most recent work is *Heaven's Wrath: The Protestant Reformation and the Dutch West India Company in the Atlantic World* (Cornell University Press, forthcoming fall 2019), and his published essays and book reviews have appeared forums such as *The Sixteenth Century Journal, The Journal of Early American History,* and *Itinerario.*

The officially appointed Historian for the City of Rochester, NY, and Historical Services Consultant at the Rochester Public Library, Christine L. Ridarsky manages the Local History & Genealogy Division at the library. She has B.A.s in Journalism & Mass Communication and Political Science from Kent State University, an M.A. in American History from the State University of New York, College at Brockport, and is ABD toward a Ph.D. in American History at the University of Rochester. Christine is Editor of *Rochester History* journal and Co-Editor of *Susan B. Anthony and the Struggle for Equal Rights* (University of Rochester Press, 2012).

Professor of History at Canisius College, Nancy J. Rosenbloom is teaches a variety of courses in American social history. She has published articles on film censorship in the early twentieth century, most recently "From Greenwich Village to Hollywood: The Literary Apprenticeship of Sonya Levien" in the *Journal of Gilded Age and Progressive Era* (January 2015). Her academic interests also include Holocaust studies and she has twice participated in the Silberman Seminar at the United States Holocaust Memorial Museum as well as in the Summer Institute on the Holocaust and Jewish Civilization at Northwestern University.

MARK STURGES

Assistant professor of English at St. Lawrence University in northern New York, Mark Sturges teaches courses about early American literature and environmental literature as well as a creative writing course in the college's Adirondack Semester. His research interests include American agricultural history and the regional literature of the Adirondacks. Most recently, he has published a pair of articles about the cultural history of maple sugaring in early America.

DON WILDMAN

The host of *Travel Channel's* long-running hit, *Mysteries at the Museum*, as well as many other programs in the history/adventure realm, Don Wildman's advocacy for museums and historic sites keep him active throughout New York State. His company, Archivist Media, was founded to assist institutions here in New York and elsewhere in producing better media. Don resides with his wife in Westchester County, New York.

The Sing Sing Revolt
The Incarceration Crisis and Criminal Justice Liberalism in the 1980s

Lee Bernstein

As 1983 began, New York's prisons reached a chokepoint: in the past decade the inmate population went from 12,444 to 27,943. Mario Cuomo, who would become the nation's most prominent liberal politician after delivering the keynote address at the 1984 Democratic National Convention, prepared to take the oath of office to become the state's fifty-second governor.[1] Corrections officials scrambled to find beds for four hundred new people each week in crumbling facilities and repurposed public buildings. This overcrowding occurred, to different degrees, throughout the system—city and county jails, juvenile facilities, and in state-run facilities variously classified minimum, medium, and maximum security. Multiple factors converged to create this overcrowding, including the war on drugs, the victims' rights movement, and new "truth in sentencing" laws.[2] In addition, declining tax revenues and the economic struggles of the state's voters limited the state's ability to fund new prison construction and to accommodate the educational, therapeutic, and social needs of its burgeoning prison population. Access to basic needs like warm clothing, blankets, and mail became constrained. The Department of Correctional Services (DOCS) was characterized by laughably inadequate grievance procedures, insufficiently staffed facilities, anemic responses to ongoing labor-management disputes, rifts between uniformed and civilian employees, and failure to address racist and sexist barriers to fair treatment for employees and the incarcerated population.

Recent memory generated a foreboding sense of where all this would lead. In 1971, increasing frustration with inhumane treatment led directly to the Attica Correctional

This research benefited from insight gained from Joe Britto, Lisa Gail Collins, Andy Evans, Judith Weisenfeld, participants in Princeton University's American Studies Workshop Series, and feedback from the anonymous reviewers for New York History.
1. New York State Committee on Sentencing Guidelines, *Determinate Sentencing: Report and Recommendations* (Albany, NY, 1985), 15.
2. Michelle Alexander, *The New Jim Crow: Mass Incarceration in the Age of Colorblindness* (New York: New Press, 2010).

Facility rebellion. Governor Nelson Rockefeller's decision to replace peaceful negotiations with the murderous retaking of the facility led to ghastly results: 128 men shot, 10 hostages dead, 29 prisoners killed. In the years that followed, the state failed to prosecute a single state official or employee, instead charging 63 prisoners with over 1,200 separate crimes.[3] The state implemented some reforms following Attica, but more notable was the state's spearheading a national shift toward the use of lengthy prison terms with the 1973 passage of the Rockefeller Drug Laws, which set then-unheard-of sentences of fifteen years to life for selling or possessing narcotics.[4] By the time the state's prisons began to buckle under the pressure of new entrants, Rockefeller decamped Albany to serve as Gerald Ford's post-Watergate vice president. Malcolm Wilson, his lieutenant governor and successor, lost the 1974 race to Hugh Carey, a Democrat who would face the exploding prison population amid fiscal struggles that impeded the state's ability to borrow funds necessary for new prison construction.[5] Under Carey, mid-1970s cost-cutting led to further erosion of the state's prison reform tradition, which led to yet another uprising. In 1977, forty people incarcerated at Coxsackie Correctional Facility, a medium-security facility near Albany founded as a New Deal–Era vocational reformatory, took three hostages in protest of increasing violence by correctional officers and a reduction in the facility's unusually expansive vocational training and programming. This incident ended quickly and peacefully but failed to have a meaningful impact on the Department of Correctional Services; nor did it impede the legislative push for continued use of long-term incarceration for a wide range of offenses. Instead, as historian Joseph Spillane notes, the incident served as a fitting coda to the reformatory era.[6]

In 1983 the uprising would take place at Sing Sing, one of the oldest and most infamous prisons in the world. After many months of using peaceful means to change inhumane practices and conditions—including the state's own grievance procedures and nonviolent protest—failed to create change, inmates in Sing Sing's B Block took control of the block and held nineteen employees hostage for three days. Thirty years later, Lawrence Kurlander, who served as the state's director of criminal justice during the revolt, noted, "nobody remembers that prison riot, because we handled it very differently from the Attica prison riot."[7] Attica cast a long shadow throughout the Sing Sing ordeal. People

3. Heather Ann Thompson, *Blood in the Water: The Attica Prison Uprising of 1971 and Its Legacy* (New York: Pantheon, 2016). Governor Hugh Carey vacated the few successful prosecutions of Attica's prisoners.

4. Julilly Kohler-Hausmann, "'The Attila the Hun Law': New York's Rockefeller Drug Laws and the Making of a Punitive State," *Journal of Social History* 44 (September 2010): 71–95.

5. Kim Phillips-Fein, *Fear City: New York's Fiscal Crisis and the Rise of Austerity Politics* (New York: Metropolitan Books, 2017), 194–95.

6. Joseph Spillane, *Coxsackie: The Life and Death of Prison Reform* (Baltimore: Johns Hopkins University Press, 2014). Coxsackie is now classified as maximum security. There was another uprising at Coxsackie's Special Housing Unit (SHU, or solitary confinement) in 1988. See Bert Unseem, Camille Graham Camp, and George M. Camp, *Resolution of Prison Riots: Strategies and Policies* (New York: Oxford University Press, 1996), 107–20.

7. Lawrence Kurlander, quoted in Owen Lubozynski, "Lawrence Kurlander '64: Looks Back on Three Careers (and Counting)," *Cornell Law School Spotlights*, http://www.lawschool.cornell.edu/spotlights/Lawrence-Kurlander-64-Looks-Back-on-Three-Careers-and-Counting.cfm, accessed August 16, 2017.

incarcerated in B Block chanted "Attica!" just hours prior to overtaking the block, indicating that a takeover was imminent and perhaps also as an expression of solidarity with the previous decade's prisoners' rights movement. During the takeover, the inmates hung a banner in full view of the assembled media on which they wrote "We Don't Want Another Attica," expressing their memory of the violent retaking of that prison.[8]

To be sure, DOCS and inmate negotiators should be remembered for not repeating the mistakes of Attica. They reached a relatively peaceful resolution despite the improvised weapons of the inmates, heavily armed state forces, intense scrutiny of the New York news media, and grandstanding politicians. But there are other reasons why we should remember the Sing Sing revolt of 1983. The Sing Sing revolt broke the chokehold. It pushed elected officials, especially the governor and his director of criminal justice, to rapidly expand the state's prison capacity. Seeing the revolt as primarily the product of overcrowding, they convened a blue-ribbon sentencing commission that barely questioned the sentencing practices that were the central cause of the overcrowding in New York's prisons. Their actions guaranteed continuation of the upward trajectory of the prison population through the final decades of the twentieth century. Furthermore, the revolt served as the catalyst to shift the priorities of the Urban Development Corporation, created in 1968 to bring jobs and economic development to underdeveloped areas of New York City.[9] The doubling of the size of the state's prison system would be achieved through funds meant to support the very communities that sent its sons, brothers, and fathers to Sing Sing.

The state's response to the Sing Sing revolt demonstrates the aftereffects of what historian Elizabeth Hinton calls the transition "from the war on poverty to the war on crime." Rather than solely the product of clichéd "tough on crime" conservatism that led to the initial surge in incarceration, the prison-building boom of the 1980s and 1990s was also the product of "criminal justice liberalism." Under Cuomo's leadership, New York's liberal politicians and corrections officials built dozens of new prisons in order to address long-standing complaints by correctional officers and incarcerated people about dangerous and inhumane conditions. The state's leaders did not typically argue in favor of more punishment, and they even proposed some alternatives to incarceration, but they did not heed calls to roll back the relatively recent sentencing practices that led to the overcrowding. Rather, they implemented new determinate sentencing practices they hoped would prevent racial bias from influencing sentencing disparities but which also contributed to the overall rise in the size of the prison population. In order to fund this expansion, they transformed programs initially created by antipoverty liberals of the late 1960s and 1970s into a funding tool to build these prisons. This combination of liberal means and goals disassembled antipoverty liberalism and refashioned it as criminal justice liberalism. This, as much as

---

8. Sydney H. Schanberg, "Attica on Their Minds," *New York Times,* January 11, 1982, A19.
9. Mario Cuomo, quoted in Susan Chira, "Budget Proposes Space for Additional 2,300 Prisoners," *New York Times,* February 1, 1983, B5.

anti-government conservatism, had a chilling effect on the antipoverty and urban renewal programs as state resources went from housing and job creation for the residents of the impoverished neighborhoods to building new prisons in more rural parts of the state.

Thus, if Sing Sing's inmates revolted to address longstanding unresolved grievances, they also unwittingly left behind state-level evidence for how the apparatus of postwar liberalism was instrumental to the development of mass incarceration. We are increasingly aware of the way that mass incarceration was made possible as much by the rise of postwar liberalism as by the tough on crime rhetoric typically associated with the New Right's effort to discredit New Deal and War on Poverty programs. As Julilly Kohler-Hausmann noted, if 1980s criminal justice policies served to undermine welfare programs, they also "built upon the welfare state."[10] Republicans and moderate Democrats may have been the loudest voices driving mass incarceration, but the structures and programs of pre– and post–World War II liberalism facilitated the transformation of antipoverty programs into prisons. On the federal level, conservatives and moderates dismantled welfare programs while expanding funding for crime control. Elizabeth Hinton found that though the War on Poverty and the War on Crime were both products of Johnson-era liberalism, by 1980 the former had been eclipsed by the latter. Even before Reagan's 1981 inauguration, funding for "federal crime-control measures ballooned from $22 million in 1965 to approximately $7 billion."[11] Rather than combat racism, support education, end poverty, provide nutritional security, or build housing, federal policy and dollars increasingly supported militant policing and long-term incarceration.

This represented a transformation of liberalism as much as a dismantling of the welfare state. In the 1980s and 1990s, moderate Democrats, including Senate Judiciary Committee chair Joe Biden and President Bill Clinton, championed three-strikes laws, mandatory minimums, and the use of federal dollars to fund local police forces. Clinton couched his support for the expansion of policing and prisons in the language of liberalism. According to Naomi Murakawa, Clinton saw his crime bill as a compassionate effort to free poor people from crime-ravaged communities.[12] These policies, he hoped, might also neutralize conservative talking points that successfully targeted Democrats like Mike Dukakis as "card-carrying liberals" who were soft on crime.[13] What has perhaps been less well understood in the critique of New Democrats like Clinton are the ways that leading liberals of the 1980s like Ted Kennedy and Mario Cuomo contributed to mass incarceration

10. Julilly Kohler-Hausmann, "Guns and Butter: The Welfare State, the Carceral State, and the Politics of Exclusion in the Postwar United States," *Journal of American History* 102, no. 1 (2015): 89.

11. Elizabeth Hinton, "'A War within Our Own Boundaries': Lyndon Johnson's Great Society and the Rise of the Carceral State," *Journal of American History* 102, no. 1 (2015): 111. See also Hinton's *From the War on Poverty to the War on Crime: The Making of Mass Incarceration in America* (Cambridge, MA: Harvard University Press, 2016).

12. Naomi Murakawa, *The First Civil Right: How Liberals Built Prison America* (New York: Oxford University Press, 2014).

13. Hinton, "A War within Our Own Boundaries," 113

by promoting policies and practices they believed would make the criminal justice system more fair, more humane, and less racist. Liberal efforts like Kennedy's Sentencing Reform Act of 1984 sought to address racially disproportionate sentencing but ultimately contributed to across-the-board lengthening of prison sentences and an escalation in the use of the death penalty. Furthermore, these efforts to level punishments across race and class backfired when, in 1986, as Murakawa notes, "Congress established the infamous 100-to-1 ratio, giving a five-year mandatory minimum for trafficking 500 grams of powder cocaine or five grams of crack cocaine."[14] African Americans would soon account for 88.3 percent of all crack cocaine convictions, while 75 percent of all those who reported powder cocaine use were white.

Previous New York governors tried and failed to address the growing incarceration crisis. The economic crisis of the 1970s prevented construction of new facilities from regular tax revenues even as elected officials pushed for an increasing reliance on long prison sentences for a broad range of convictions that would not have resulted in significant prison time in prior generations. If the money had been available, construction and state procurement logistics made it nearly impossible to keep up with the rate the prison population was growing without bringing other state operations to a standstill. Early in the 1970s, New York operated 21 facilities holding just over 12,000 men and women. By the early 1980s, the state's prison population stood at over 30,000. It would more than double again, to over 60,000 by the mid-1990s. According to DOCS estimates, the system received 400 new admissions per week in 1982. These 20,000 new admissions per year would be offset by only 12,000 annual releases. In response, the state converted some drug treatment and mental health facilities to prisons during the second half of the 1970s, but these steps could not keep pace with the accelerated rate of prison population growth. This solution also meant that the state offered fewer facilities for treatment and rehabilitation at a time of rising demand for these services. It is reasonable to conclude that the conversions of rehabilitative alternatives to prisons would, before too long, intensify the problem of overcrowding as people with mental illnesses or addictions wound up in the penal system.

Incarcerated people, correctional bureaucracies, and elected officials struggled to respond to the consequences of startling new laws that simultaneously made it easier to receive a prison sentence and harder to get out.[15] Nationally, there was a clear and persistent trend to incarcerate large numbers of people during the final decades of the twentieth

---

14. Murakawa, *The First Civil Right*, 122.
15. Todd R. Clear and Natasha A. Frost, *The Punishment Imperative: The Rise and Failure of Mass Incarceration in America* (New York: NYU Press, 2014). Clear and Frost identify a "relentless punitive spirit" and "grand social experiment" that gave shape to the post-1960s criminal justice system. See also Jordan T. Camp, *Incarcerating the Crisis: Freedom Struggles and the Rise of the Neoliberal State* (Berkeley: University of California Press, 2016). Camp contends that mass incarceration emerged specifically in response to the class anxieties resulting from the intense antiracist activism of the 1960s and 1970s; see also Alex Lichtenstein, "Flocatex and the Fiscal Limits of Mass Incarceration: Toward a New Political Economy of the Postwar Carceral State," *Journal of American History* 102, no. 1 (2015): 113–25.

century, from 200,000 in the 1960s to over two million in the early twenty-first century. The impact of large inflows of people, reduced rehabilitative services, and insufficient funding for new prison construction first emerged in New York City's Department of Corrections.[16] In late 1974 a federal judge ordered the city's Men's House of Detention—the infamous "Tombs" prison in lower Manhattan—closed due to inhumane conditions. In response, the city slated three detention centers for closure, including the Tombs, causing more over-crowding at the city's main prison complex at Rikers Island. In addition, the city's un-derlying financial problems led to cuts in civilian and uniformed staff, as well as to drug rehabilitation and other social welfare programs, including those that sought to alleviate housing and nutritional insecurity.[17]

Men and women in Rikers reported overcrowding, fewer opportunities to leave cells, and limited access to attorneys and visitors. In November 1975 men housed in Rikers rose up for the second time in less than six months.[18] Twelve hundred men participated in the revolt, armed with broomsticks and homemade weapons. The men wanted more access to phones, more frequent contact with visitors, more time outside of their cells, improved medical care, more correctional officers, cleaner cellblocks, and a reduction in overcrowd-ing. Most of these demands were already mandated by federal courts, but the city proved unable or unwilling to implement them.[19] The city quickly agreed to many of the demands, including a promise of amnesty for all men involved in the revolt, and the hostages were released.

As a stopgap, the city canceled the planned closure of the Bronx House of Detention so it could transfer several hundred men from Rikers. The continued high pace of prison population growth made clear that the city and state needed to either build more prisons or incarcerate fewer people. In 1981, Governor Hugh Carey sought voter approval for a $500 million bond issuance for new prison construction. But a majority of voters rejected the new debt, and lawmakers refused the alternative of releasing prisoners to make room for the newcomers, leaving the state DOCS needing to find some other way to deal with the problem of more people than cells. Additional pressure came from county officials and judges who wanted to avoid more revolts and demanded that "state ready" prisoners—those who had been convicted and sentenced yet remained in county and city jails awaiting room in the state system—be transferred out of overcrowded local facilities and into state correctional facilities. In March 1981, New York City alone held a thousand postconviction inmates awaiting transfer to state facilities. In protest, the city filed suit against the state

---

16. By the end of 1975, historian Kim Phillips-Fein notes, the city's main jail for men at Riker's Island reduced the uniformed correctional staff from 500 to 340. The New York City Department of Correction saw an overall reduction of 350 officers and 150 civilian employees—500 people from a total workforce of 4,400 (Phillips-Fein, *Fear City*, 202).

17. "The Rikers Revolt Was for Rights Already Won," *New York Times*, November 30, 1975, 6.

18. Phillips-Fein, *Fear City*, 211.

19. "The Rikers Revolt Was for Rights Already Won," 6.

and refused to take in parole violators due to lack of space, forcing the state to take in four hundred prisoners for whom it had no cells within forty-eight hours.[20]

While overcrowding was a problem throughout the state, the issue was particularly acute at Ossining Correctional Facility, the little-used name then assigned to Sing Sing Prison. After conviction and sentencing, adult men would be sent to Downstate Correctional Facility in Fishkill, New York, for classification. Classification involved evaluation and review of a newly convicted person's criminal record, educational and health history, current violation, and length of sentence. Classification determined whether a person would initially serve their sentence in a medium- or maximum-security correctional facility. When New York's prison population was smaller, transfer to the longer-term facilities would take place shortly after classification. But with people going from the city and county jails to the state system faster than others were released at the end of their sentences, DOCS came up with a new plan: postclassification prisoners would be sent to Sing Sing while awaiting open beds at another facility or until new cells could be constructed.[21] Predictably, Sing Sing's population went from 1,400 in 1980 to over 2,100 at the beginning of 1982, with over 1,200 people awaiting permanent placement housed in Blocks A and B, two massive cellblocks only recently slated for closure due to crumbling infrastructure. These conditions eerily mirrored those at Rikers five years earlier. Rather than solve the problems that led to the Rikers revolt, they were merely shifted from the city facilities to the state facilities.

Sing Sing designated postclassification inmates as "transfers" or "in transit" and treated them differently from the people in other blocks at Sing Sing or, for that matter, other facilities, on the grounds that their stay was temporary. First, people from all risk and security classifications were grouped together in Blocks A and B—young and old, violent and non-violent, short-term and long-term, crammed together while awaiting transfer. These massive cellblocks constructed on the "Big House" model during the 1930s each housed over six hundred people in single cells along tiers measuring the length of several city blocks. All inmates awaiting transfer remained locked in their cells for at least nineteen hours per day. If the count was delayed, their "lock out" time outside of their cells was shorter. When permitted to leave their cells, people congregated along the "flats," the lengthy, narrow passage along the bottom tier, or in an unheated garage, where they could watch one of two

---

20. Testimony of Thomas Coughlin, Commissioner of Corrections, New York State Joint Legislative Hearing, Senate Committee on Crime and Correction, Assembly Committee on Codes, *In the Matter of: A Joint Hearing on the Investigation of the Events Leading to the January Incident at Ossining Correctional Facility*, Proceedings, April 20, 1983, 229, hereafter cited as *In the Matter of*. In addition to the threat of additional uprisings, the city faced considerable pressure from the courts to reduce the Rikers population. Prison officials faced the threat of contempt charges when they failed to implement a court order demanding that they release or transfer prisoners held in deplorable conditions, including on barges and temporary buildings. See Morris E. Lasker. "Taking Stock of the Accomplishments and Failures of Prison Reform Litigation: Prison Reform Revisited: A Judge's Perspective," *Pace Law Review* 24 (Spring 2004): 427–30; Robert McFadden, "Morris Lasker, Judge Who Forced City to Clean Up Jails, Dies at 92," *New York Times*, December 28, 2009, http://www.nytimes.com/2009/12/29/nyregion/29lasker.html.
21. Testimony of Thomas Coughlin, Commissioner of Corrections, *In the Matter of*, 229.

televisions or hang out at picnic tables. Their visiting hours were restricted to weekdays, sharply curtailing access to family and friends who might be available only on weekends. They had virtually no access to parcels. Educational, vocational, religious, therapeutic, and cultural programming were virtually nonexistent. And the cellblocks were filthy: stagnant water and rotting food attracted vermin and roaches. In short, A Block and B Block were dirty, dangerous, and degrading human warehouses.

There was some bureaucratic logic to these restrictions: because their ultimate destination remained undetermined, the administrators reasoned that inmates should not start a program they would not finish. It was also logistically challenging to coordinate the delivery of mail and visitors to a continuously revolving population. There were also the usual snafus: construction of a new visiting room that could accommodate Sing Sing's ballooning population took longer than expected, resulting in a policy decision to limit visits for the transfer population in order to accommodate the general confinement population during the week. In addition, DOCS did not have a mainframe computer that could monitor and efficiently allocate available prison cells throughout the state.[22] By 1983 the length of time people awaited transfer to a permanent facility ranged from six months to one year: six months to one year without packages, programming, access to visitors, and with less than six hours per day outside of a cell.[23]

While the revolt at Sing Sing on January 8 was not foreordained, the actions of the correctional officers and prisoners offer insight into the fraught context of New York's prisons on the eve of its decade-long expansion. At 3:00 p.m. on January 8, Alexander Cunningham, the sergeant-in-charge temporarily assigned to B Block and understood by the inmates to be a heavy drinker, ordered the block's correctional officers to lock in the entire block.[24] While this reflected the facility's policy, the regular officers on the block knew this order might cause trouble. Of the twenty-five officers assigned to B Block that afternoon, fifteen had served as correctional officers for less than six months. Employee turnover and training protocols made it difficult to keep the facility fully staffed with experienced uniformed and civilian employees. DOCS needed to rapidly recruit, hire, and train correctional officers and civilian staff to meet its growing mandate. Among the nineteen initial employee hostages during the revolt, nine were trainees. Three arrived at Sing Sing two weeks prior to the revolt.[25] Among these new officers were a new generation of women and men not typically represented among correctional officers. In the wake of Attica, DOCS

22. Lawrence T. Kurlander, *Governor Cuomo's 1984 Criminal Justice Accomplishments* (Albany, NY: Office of the Director of Criminal Justice, 1984), 10.

23. Testimony of John Nelson, Inmate at Ossining Correctional Facility, *In the Matter of*, 62–64.

24. John Mack, "Inside Sing Sing: An Inmate Chronicles the Revolt," *Village Voice*, February 8, 1983, 9. This summary of events is based on the subsequent state investigation conducted by Lawrence T. Kurlander, *Report to Governor Mario M. Cuomo: The Disturbance at Ossining Correctional Facility, January 8–11, 1983* (Albany, NY: Office of the Director of Criminal Justice, 1983).

25. Table 14, Employee Hostages. Three hostages were twenty-one years old, a fourth was twenty-two years old (Kurlander, *Report to Governor Cuomo*, 131).

hired Allen Bush as the department's minority recruitment director. Bush succeeded in increasing the racial diversity among the uniformed and civilian staff. This was particularly true at Sing Sing, where 75 percent of the facility's staff, including the superintendent, identified as "minority" in 1983.[26] The correctional officers on duty felt strongly that Cunningham's order was a bad idea and let their superior officer know that it deviated from regular practice amid ongoing tension about declining "lock out" time. Typically, the officers noted, fully half of the prison population did not go back to their cells after the 2:30 count because of work assignments. It was simply a waste of time to lock them in at 3:00 only to have to release them at 4:00 to go to the mess hall or work assignments.

Cunningham insisted that the officers follow the procedure rather than concede to informal practice, further instructing the officers to issue reports on all prisoners not in their cell after the 2:30 count. Tensions mounted when Cunningham refused to allow prisoners returning from work assignments to shower, offering no explanation for departing from the custom of allowing people to wash after engaging in physical labor. During evening recreation, Cunningham ordered prisoners to either return to their cells or go to the unheated and near-freezing garage used for recreation. Again, while this was in line with procedure, correctional officers typically allowed men to congregate along the flats on cold days because many of the transfer prisoners had not been issued winter coats. When Lieutenant Lowell Way, Cunningham's superior, arrived on the block, he rejected a signed medical pass excusing an inmate hoping to stay on the relatively warmer flats from going to the garage during recreation. The inmate refused to return to his cell. Way ordered Cunningham and two officers to take the inmate to solitary confinement.

Attica was in the air. Several inmates began shouting "Attica!" but the block quieted down quickly and Way ordered the officers to continue with the routine releases for recreation. Seeking to change the tone from Cunningham's hard line, Way ordered all inmates still in their cells released for recreation, and those already in the unheated garage returned to the flats. Nevertheless, inmates began to voice broader grievances concerning limited access to mail, visitation, commissary, and programming. Sensing a shift in tone, several of the veteran officers quietly left the block.

As the afternoon wore on, Way continued to try to diffuse the situation, first by speaking with inmates and, according to one account, extending the recreation period amid Cunningham's vocal protests.[27] Way dismissed Cunningham from the block, but it was too late. As Cunningham left, inmates began covering their faces, barricading the doors, restraining officers, and ordering all officers to one end of the block.[28] Ultimately, nineteen of the thirty officers and civilian employees working in B Block were held hostage. Eleven, including Cunningham, made it out. In the immediate melee, a wall of Muslim inmates

---

26. Ibid., 36.
27. Mack, "Inside Sing Sing," 9.
28. Ibid.

risked their own safety by protecting eighteen of the nineteen hostages from the rest of the population. The nineteenth officer was hidden away by an inmate who is not identified in official reports.

Several members of the Inmate Liaison Committee (ILC)—which had the ability to move freely through the facility—arrived on B Block just before the takeover. Quddos Farrad, chair of the committee and part of the prison's "cadre" (prisoners who held key positions within the facility), arrived on the cellblock during the initial takeover. Since the beginning of his term on the ILC the previous March, Farrad repeatedly reported on the deteriorating conditions and tense climate in Blocks A and B to the Sing Sing administrators. Each month, the ILC met with the administration, detailing grievances. The administration ordered an investigation of each grievance, which invariably would not be completed before the next monthly meeting, where additional grievances would be added. "We tried," Farrad later noted, "to give the administration the things that were needed to alleviate the problems, and it was just a thing of hitting your head on the wall."[29] The prison's administrators refused to resolve major policy-directed grievances involving medical treatment, the visiting room, and access to packages.[30]

These problems led to several smaller actions before the 1983 revolt. The men on A and B Blocks mounted two collective direct action protests: a food strike on B Block in August 1982 and a mass refusal to lock in among the A Block population that December. Farrad successfully worked with the administration and the prison population to bring these to an end, but the underlying issues were never addressed. The grievances at the heart of those peaceful protests would eventually emerge as key negotiating points during the January revolt.

This is not to say that the revolt was premeditated. Rather, it rolled along on the energy of long-standing grievances and deteriorating conditions. The refusal to go to the garage happened between 7:20 and 7:30 p.m. The hostages were taken at around 7:40 p.m. The department's main office in Albany was notified at 8:00 p.m., which in turn notified Governor Mario Cuomo's secretary, who briefed Cuomo via telephone. Cuomo immediately established a command post at his New York City office on the World Trade Center's fifty-seventh floor. He would stay on an open phone line with Commissioner of Corrections Thomas Coughlin throughout the revolt.[31] Joining him were key advisers and staff members, including Lawrence Kurlander, the state's director of criminal justice; Michael J.

29. Testimony of Quddos Farrad, *In the Matter of,,* 9.

30. The facility's grievance officer acknowledged that the facility's procedure was designed to allow inmates to file and log their grievance but did not provide a mechanism to actually resolve the underlying problems. "My job was only to see that the procedure operated in respect that the inmate was allowed to file his grievance, have it logged, and that he would get an answer. That was my responsibility. Whether he would get what was asking for in a grievance was not my . . . [answer cut off]" (*In the Matter of,* 179).

31. Mario Cuomo quoted in "Thomas A. Coughlin, III, 'The Good Public Servant,' Dies at 63," New York State, Department of Correctional Services, Office of Public Information, August 24, 2001, http://www.doccs.ny.gov /PressRel/2001/coughlinpr2.html.

Del Guidice, the governor's secretary; Timothy J. Russert, Cuomo's press secretary; Fabian Palomino, his special counsel; and Cuomo's son and policy adviser, Andrew Cuomo. The governor had taken the oath of office only eight days earlier. As the state bureaucracy snapped into action, some inmates used whatever was at hand amid the debris of the cellblock—stray lumber, mop handles, a sharpened bit of metal, a procured nightstick—to overpower and restrain the officers. Others prevented immediate physical harm to the officers by escorting them to the flats. Fearing especially for the safety of Lieutenant Way, Farrad and an unidentified Spanish-speaking inmate escorted him to the mess hall gate, convinced several inmates to allow them through, and accompanied Way to Deputy Superintendent McGinnis's office.

The DOCS main office in Albany had already been notified of the hostage situation by the time Way made it to McGinnis's office. Several DOCS officials, including Commissioner Coughlin, flew from Albany to Westchester County Airport. So, within a few hours, inmates on B Block achieved the full attention of the state's executive and correctional authorities where the existing grievance policies had been ineffective. The same concerns that emerged as the central causes of the revolt had festered for many months, despite repeated efforts by inmates and guards to inform their superiors using procedures DOCS set up after Attica.

After the preventative measures failed to address issues that repeatedly led to inmate uprisings, the state's emergency response protocol would receive a key test of its effectiveness. In the years after Attica, DOCS instituted a two-pronged approach to regaining control of inmate uprisings. First, they created coordinated teams at all state and county facilities. The Correctional Emergency Response Teams (CERT)—dubbed the "Orange Crush" or "Crush Squad" by inmates—used force in order to achieve institutional goals. Starting in 1975, each facility sought volunteers from the uniformed officer staff to receive training in riot control and other emergency response measures.[32] Teams from each institution could be coordinated and mobilized in response to larger scale conflicts like the Sing Sing revolt. Almost immediately after the revolt began, three nearby facilities mobilized their teams. By the end of the revolt, nine different facilities sent teams to Sing Sing to contain the revolt within B Block. Aware of the tactics of the Orange Crush, inmates spent the early hours of the takeover fearing a violent invasion. As officers strengthened barricades leading from B Block, inmates used picnic tables to create barricades leading in.[33]

As CERT mobilized its forces, a second group made their way to the B Block mess hall. The revolt was the first major test of the Crisis Intervention Team. Known more generally as Situation Control (Sit-Con), this team was formed in 1977 to peacefully resolve crises ranging from the relatively common refusal to leave a cell to the rare hostage situations.[34]

---

32. Kurlander, *Report to Governor Cuomo*, 142; Mack, "Inside Sing Sing," 11.
33. Kurlander, *Report to Governor Cuomo*, 145.
34. James Feron, "Notebook: Hostage Talks a First for Crisis Team," *New York Times,* January 16, 1983, B12.

As with CERT, each facility had its own Sit-Con team for small-scale crises. When needed, teams from different facilities could come together to form a larger coordinated team. DOCS identified and trained several dozen people from throughout the system in the hope that they could bring a peaceful end to the conflicts arising from the state's growing prison population. They trained at a camp in rural Wilton, New York, where they learned to work as a team and studied the art of negotiating from a range of experienced hostage negotiators. Among the lecturers in Wilton was Frank Bolz, head of New York City's Hostage Negotiating Team and author of 1979's *Hostage Cop*. Bolz emphasized flexibility and ongoing conversation designed primarily to prevent harm to hostages. Bolz described the need to reassure people holding hostages that they would not be harmed and that he would help them resolve underlying demands.

Bolz identified the origins of his approach to hostage negotiation in his visceral response to the failures and violence of the Attica uprising in 1971 and the Munich Olympics in 1972.[35] In particular, Bolz came to believe that police agencies needed to take seriously the political or personal demands of hostage takers. He urged negotiators to talk with people who take hostages for as long as possible. Bolz believed that negotiators should meet demands where they could, with the expectation that those holding hostages would also make concessions in order to incrementally move toward resolution. Refusal to do so in both Attica and Munich had resulted in what Bolz saw as an unnecessary loss of life.[36] Time, Bolz believed, was on the side of the state. He felt that at Attica, the state arbitrarily cut off negotiations and unnecessarily used overwhelming force to retake the facility.[37]

In Wilton, Sit-Con training culminated in a role-playing exercise involving a prison uprising in which they had to negotiate the release of hostages using Bolz's signature technique. Bolz emphasized the great need for negotiators to stretch out the negotiations both to resist one's own "fight or flight" urges and to avoid aggravating the person or people holding hostages. He did not create a false impression of friendship, nor did he argue during negotiations. He recognized that those taking hostages do not typically want those in their control to die or be harmed. This lesson made the Sing Sing negotiations far different from those at Attica. If Sit-Con could demonstrate a willingness to resolve underlying grievances while meeting short-term requests in exchange for inmate concessions, they believed they could peacefully bring the revolt to a close.

Twenty-seven members of Sit-Con eventually served during the Sing Sing revolt, as compared to at least one hundred members of CERT. This was the team's first opportunity

---

35. Frank Bolz and Edward Hershey, *Hostage Cop* (New York: Rawson, Wade, 1979), 240. For a detailed discussion of the Attica negotiations, see Thompson, *Blood in the Water*.

36. The Black September group that held Israeli athletes in Munich demanded the release of over two hundred Palestinians held in Israeli prisons. Bolz believed that the hostage negotiators in West Germany were hampered by the Israeli government's refusal to negotiate, as well as the International Olympic Committee's wish that the games continue (Bolz and Hershey, 301).

37. This view is also reflected in Tom Wicker's account of his experience as an observer in Attica, *A Time to Die* (New York: Crown, 1980).

to prove that negotiation could succeed over brute force in a major hostage negotiation. The team included Sit-Con commander and chief negotiator Anthony "Kenny" Umina, who was himself a hostage in the takeover of Coxsackie Correctional Facility in 1977, when he served in that facility as a correctional officer captain. Most other members of Sit-Con came from civilian professions, including social workers, psychologists, and recording technicians.[38] Sit-Con's first task was to set up listening posts under and around B Block. Because DOCS lacked electronic equipment, they enlisted members of CERT and Sit-Con to physically staff the eavesdropping stations, radioing information back to Sit-Con's command center in the mess hall. Meanwhile, inmates sought to jam these efforts by spraying water on the negotiating team and demanding direct contact with the news media.[39] But in order to negotiate, inmates needed to first agree on what they wanted. Taking over an entire cellblock was not simple; maintaining a semblance of order and moving toward a peaceful resolution proved far more difficult. Inmates had a hard time agreeing on demands and creating a consistent negotiating team, but just after midnight they did agree to exchange one hostage, Officer Trainee Patrick Peryea, who had been at Sing Sing for about five weeks, for medication.[40] Peryea described deep divisions on the block, especially between those inmates who sought a peaceful resolution and others who seemed eager to inflict harm. Peryea confirmed that no officers had been seriously injured in the takeover and that the different inmate factions so far agreed on only two things: they would no longer accept Cunningham on the block and they wanted direct contact with the news media.

As dawn arrived, Sing Sing was shaping up to be a major test of the two-pronged approach. The exchange of Peryea for medication clearly showed the potential of Bolz's methods. But because Sit-Con grew concerned with the lack of organized leadership or clear demands that might facilitate future negotiations, they began to develop contingency plans.[41] Umina ordered the water shut off while the leadership of CERT began planning to use tear gas and lethal weapons to retake the block.[42] There was a realistic assumption that a CERT assault was imminent as conditions, negotiating positions, and perceptions remained in constant flux. At the same time, the news media, as well as family members of the hostages, began congregating outside the gates. To prevent the inmates from listening to or watching news broadcasts, senior DOCS officials cut off electricity to the block. When incarcerated leaders in the block urged solidarity and order, this intensification by the state was accompanied by renewed hope.

The state's corrections officials debated using force to resolve the crisis. This was more

38. Feron, "Notebook," B12; Spillane, Coxsackie.
39. Joe Britto, interview with author, July 15, 2015. Britto, who served as a member of Sit-Con and its successor, Special Operations, had his initial training in Wilton during the summer of 1982.
40. Kurlander, Report to Governor Mario M. Cuomo, 148.
41. Ibid., 154.
42. Ibid., 150; "Anthony 'Kenny' Umina," Obituary, Albany Times-Union, October 29, 2011, n.p.

than a tactical debate between Orange Crush and Sit-Con. It also reflected long-standing tensions between the uniformed and civilian employees of the Department of Correctional Services. These tensions were heightened during and after a correctional officer strike in April and May 1979.[43] Along with National Guard soldiers who filled in for the officers, many civilian employees, including members of the Sit-Con team serving during the Sing Sing strike, crossed the picket line and served as security personnel.[44] In the wake of the strike, residual lack of trust escalated to a dangerous and frustrating breakdown in communication and collaboration. This was still the state of affairs in 1983. Correctional officers held DOCS administration and, in some cases, civilian employees, responsible for poor work conditions that had been repeatedly reported to local and state officials for months—and in some cases years—by prison advocacy groups, inmate self-government, and the correctional officers union. Local 1413 of the Security and Law Enforcement Employees Council 82 (typically referred to as Council 82), representing Sing Sing's officers, noted low morale due to administrative reliance on mandatory overtime due to unfilled positions and the closing of the officers mess hall. James Burke, Council 82's executive director, pointed to the systemic problems uncovered as far back as the McKay Commission, formed in the wake of 1971's Attica uprising. Statewide, Burke testified, New York's facilities were at 113 percent of capacity. Sing Sing stood at almost 130 percent of its capacity. He attributed many of the problems his members faced to overcrowding: assaults on officers by inmates, assaults on inmates by inmates, and inmate psychiatric problems.[45]

These frustrations were felt even more acutely by women officers, who noted the absence of a women's locker room and a discriminatory pattern of being passed over for promotions in favor of male colleagues.[46] Men and women officers of color faced additional challenges. New black and Latino officers described the compounding challenges of facing racist colleagues and a prison administration and union leadership that did not stand up for their interests. Rudolph Graham, an African American correctional officer at Sing Sing, noted that white officers would not even talk to him, creating a double burden: "Dealing

43. The strike was called after the state and union reached a tentative agreement on April 5, 1979. Despite initially agreeing to the terms, the union asked the state to reopen negotiations. When the state refused, workers went on strike. The state received a court order prohibiting Council 82 from striking. When Hollis V. Chase, the union's executive director, refused to obey, the state imprisoned him in the Albany County Jail. The state's entire prison population of twenty-one thousand people remained locked in their cells for the duration of the fifteen-day strike. Richard Gooding and Gene Ruffini, "Prison Guards Walk Out, Inmates Face Long Lockup," New York Post, April 19, 1979, 2.
44. Britto interview.
45. Testimony of James Burke, Executive Director of Council 82, In the Matter of, 100–102. Burke largely concurred with the inmates regarding the causes of the revolt, arguing that lack of capacity, idleness, and limited educational or therapeutic programming contributed to unsafe working conditions and high risk of rioting. His solution was to expand the prison system and stop plans to close the Long Island Correctional Facility. He suggested that the state acquire surplus federal property and turn them into prisons (104).
46. Minutes, Ossining Correctional Facility Labor Management Meeting, January 9, 1980, M. E. Grenander, Department of Special Collections and Archives, University at Albany, State University of New York, Council 82, Security and Law Enforcement Employees, American Federation of State, County and Municipal Employees (AFSCME) Records, 1968–1989, Sing Sing Local 1413, Series 5, Box 1.

with inmates is tough enough, but when you've got to deal with the administration too, you've got a double load on your back."[47]

Amid these degrading and racist working conditions, officers formed the Minority Correctional Officers Association (MCOA) in 1977 in order to represent the interests of black and Latino officers throughout the system. MCOA expressed outrage when Larry Van Dyke, an African American inmate from Kingston, New York, who had done time in Attica, Clinton, and Green Haven correctional facilities between 1973 and 1977, revealed that he was recruited by white correctional officers at each of those three facilities and offered incentives, including cash and reduced time in solitary confinement, if he would frame black civilian and uniformed employees for drug dealing, carrying money out of the prison, and sexual molestation. Echoing Graham's experience at Sing Sing, a Green Haven officer noted, "our problems are not so much with the inmates but with immediate supervisors— the racism and bigotry of administrative officials."[48]

Thus, for reasons grounded in their specific experiences as members of Council 82 and their gendered and racialized experiences within DOCS, many of Sing Sing's correctional officers held an adversarial view of the administration. Officers reported the same lack of follow-up regarding grievances as the inmates. Robert Slattery, a white member of the executive board of Sing Sing's Council 82 chapter at the time of the revolt who had worked at Sing Sing for eight years, explicitly sided with the testimony of John Nelson, an inmate who testified at the joint legislative committee on the Sing Sing revolt: "I am echoing John Nelson's antagonism when he is just tired of hearing all the lip service that is being paid to our problems."[49] In order to emphasize this point, Nelson provided minutes and notes from a 1980 task force that highlighted problems of overcrowding and low employee morale. While this did not mean that Slattery identified with the incarcerated population, it did mean that many officers would not see the administration and its negotiating team as their allies and saviors during the hostage negotiations.

Sit-Con continued to try to use time to its advantage. During the mid-morning hours of January 9, nine ill inmates left the cellblock in two groups. They confirmed that the basic conditions had not changed since Peryea emerged: there were no injuries, the hostages remained guarded by Muslim inmates seeking a peaceful and just resolution, and that Cunningham was the catalyst for the unplanned takeover. However, in addition to reiterating the immediate demand of direct media contact, they added more specific concerns regarding policies affecting inmates with transient status that largely mirrored those already required but not followed: more visitation, recreation, commissary, and programs.

47. "Plot Alleged Against Black Prison Guards," *Poughkeepsie Journal*, December 18, 1979, Council 82 Papers, Sing Sing Local 1313, Clippings File.
48. The state confirmed Van Dyke's story, including that he served as an informant in exchange for cash and suspension of sixty days in solitary confinement ("Charge of Entrapment in 3 Prisons Under Inquiry by Albany and U.S.," *New York Times*, March 11, 1979, 38).
49. Robert Slattery, executive board member, Local 1413 (Ossining Correctional Facility), *In the Matter of,* 122.

To Sit-Con, this new information appeared to be a good opportunity to open up negotiations. But over the next several hours, a rotating set of inmate spokespeople and an unproductive back-and-forth between Sit-Con, CERT, and Commissioner Coughlin resulted in no real progress. Finally, on the evening of the ninth, five inmate negotiators entered the mess hall with six demands: permanent reassignment of Cunningham, increased time outside of the cells, increased access to programs, overhaul of transfer status designation, access to packages, and relief of overcrowding. In addition, they demanded media coverage when they released the hostages. These demands would become the cornerstone of the eventual agreement, but along the way both sides added additional ultimatums regarding amnesty and access to food and medicine.

Importantly, both Sit-Con and the inmates quickly agreed that CERT would be barred from engaging in the use of force. The inmates promised that all prisoners would return to their cells prior to the retaking of the facility, and Sit-Con promised that the facility's superintendent and DOCS inspector general would personally monitor CERT. According to Lawrence Kurlander, the state's director of criminal justice, who was present at the governor's command post throughout the takeover, Governor Cuomo and Commissioner Coughlin agreed to file criminal charges against members of CERT or any other corrections employees who violated this agreement when retaking the block. Furthermore, in a clear response to Attica, where the facility's own correctional officers, among others, beat and shot inmates and hostages as they retook the facility, the governor barred officers from Sing Sing in participating in the retaking of B Block.[50] While they did not agree to amnesty from any prosecution for the inmates as a condition of releasing hostages, they did agree not to retaliate.

A resolution seemed imminent but was soon sidetracked. As a show of good faith, the state authorities restored electricity to the block. As they did so, inmates who turned on the television were treated to a live interview with state senator Ralph J. Marino, a Long Island Republican who chaired the Senate's Crime and Correction Committee. Marino, along with his senate colleague James J. Lack, decided to swing by the prison on the way to Albany. When they arrived, a DOCS official barred them from entering the prison but nevertheless updated them on the status of the negotiations. Marino then spoke to a television reporter, who broadcast his comments to all viewers, including those within B Block. Marino noted that the state conceded to most of the inmate demands but falsely said they would not grant amnesty from prosecution. He also noted that Muslims were serving as guards for the hostages.

When they watched Marino on the 11 p.m. nightly news broadcast, inmates felt betrayed. Negotiators had, in fact, not ruled out amnesty; they decided only not to make it a condition of hostage release. Furthermore, the Muslim inmates who protected the guards

---

50. Kurlander, *Report to Governor Mario M. Cuomo*, 160. See also Thompson, *Blood in the Water*.

felt incensed that they were singled out. They protected the guards at great personal risk, including facing physical reprisals from other inmates, only to be identified on television.[51] The negotiations immediately fell apart as inmates did not buy Sit-Con's assurances that Marino did not speak for the state. Cuomo called Coughlin to the carpet for granting any access to Marino. As tensions escalated, calls for physical confrontation again emerged on both sides of the mess hall gate. Commissioner Coughlin cut off the heat. Additional CERT teams arrived on the scene to replace the sleep-deprived officers who had been on alert for the prior twenty-four hours. Within the block, according to officers at a listening post, there were calls to "throw out the bodies."[52] Just after midnight, an inmate was released who had been stabbed. After Marino's interview the next morning, both sides managed to restore order. Coughlin reiterated the state's consent to inmate demands, and inmate negotiators returned to the table. DOCS held a press conference, reassuring the media that the situation was under control. At the same time, the hostages began communicating directly with the media via a bullhorn. Officer Randy Gorr, a twenty-two-year-old trainee, noted that no one had been hurt. Berry Madden, a sergeant who had served at Sing Sing for seventeen years, reported, "the inmates are treating us well." More dramatically, Officer Barry Clark, an African American officer who worked at Sing Sing for a year, accused the state of "playing with our lives."[53] In contrast to the crosstalk and bungling by Marino, the prisoners provided a steady stream of updates to the assembled media via both bullhorn and bedsheet banner. The bullhorn updates would prove to be more reliable than the press conferences offered by state officials. *New York Times* reporter Robert Hanley first learned that a deal was imminent from an 11 p.m. bullhorn broadcast from the cellblock on the final night of the revolt.[54]

While there was nothing particularly unusual about this group of correctional officers vis-à-vis Sing Sing's overall staff, their backgrounds reveal some important factors in the lead-up to the revolt. It also helps explain their unexpected support for the incarcerated people who held them hostage. It would be a mistake to overstate the similarities between the officers and those held in the facility, but there were some striking commonalities: the officers and inmates were younger, more transient, and disproportionately from communities of color than in other parts of DOCS, as well as the overall population of the state and nation. By themselves these similarities probably would not be enough to overcome the most important difference—the bars, uniforms, and lines of authority that, at times, overwhelmingly defined their relationship. For example, some African American inmates held particular contempt for correctional officers of color, arguing that they were "allowed

51. Kurlander, *Report to Governor Mario M. Cuomo*, 163.
52. Ibid., 198–200. This was the only reported stabbing during the revolt.
53. Ibid., 169–70. One officer trainee, Marcus Mendez, also spoke, but he later reported that he had done so at knifepoint. For age, race, and length of service information, see ibid. 131.
54. Robert Hanley, "The Bullhorns of Cell Block B: Reliable Source of Information," *New York Times,* January 11, 1983, B4.

to become an integral part of the oppressive forces with the system."[55] They believed that these employees served to paper over the inherently racist characteristics of incarceration. At the same time that some African Americans could earn middle-class incomes via civil service, DOCS would use their presence to claim progress on post-Attica demands for a diverse correctional staff, while the underlying conditions for inmates remained deplorable and black communities were torn apart.

Finally, at 6:30 p.m. on January 11, after fifty-three tense and often frightening hours involving over a thousand inmates, state employees, and the probing eye of the New York media, the inmates of Sing Sing's B Block began releasing hostages in stages as they and state negotiators agreed upon conditions. At one particularly dramatic moment, four hostages, all correctional officers, emerged from the cellblock. Instead of embracing their freedom, Officers Barry Clark, Marcus Mendez, Randy Gorr, and Israel Romero rejected the advances of the negotiating team. One of the four yelled: "Don't touch me! You people are not doing anything, and you're going to get them all killed." Another officer shook hands with the *inmate* negotiators and offered to "go back inside if I have to" if the state did not deliver on their recent promises that the media would be available to the inmates.[56] Some of the members of Sit-Con attributed this fracas to Stockholm syndrome, a term used by hostage negotiators and psychiatrists to describe the tendency of some hostages to demonstrate support for their captors. Coined a decade earlier by a Swedish psychiatrist to describe what he theorized as a psychological malady afflicting hostages in a bank who refused the help of the government and defended their captors, Stockholm syndrome achieved additional attention in the United States when Patricia Hearst, a nineteen-year-old college student and granddaughter of publisher William Randolph Hearst, joined the Symbionese Liberation Army, the revolutionary group that abducted her in 1974.[57] A psychologist who later evaluated the hostages attributed their reaction to the fact that the officers had slept less than three hours over the previous three days.[58]

But the frustrations and expressions of support for inmate grievances were not, or at least not only, the product of misplaced loyalty resulting from trauma or sleep deprivation. Instead, they reflected the long-standing grievances with their working conditions, in addition to a rational distrust of state prison authorities and elected officials. Following the release of these four officers, things moved quickly. The state's negotiators sent in food, signaling continued cooperation. Between 11:00 p.m. on January 11 and 1:00 a.m. on January 12, the inmates released all hostages. Sit-Con and inmate negotiators achieved some of their key goals—all hostages were released without harm, several inmates directly communicated their grievances to the assembled media and statewide officials, and the

---

55. Mack, "Inside Sing Sing," 10.
56. Kurlander, *Report to Governor Mario M. Cuomo*, 171.
57. Ibid., 172; Britto interview.
58. Feron, "Notebook," B12.

remaining inmates returned to their cells on their own. With the negotiators' work done, Orange Crush moved in. In keeping with the agreement, officials held back Sing Sing's own CERT team. Teams from at least five other facilities proceeded to secure all cells and clear the cellblock of debris and makeshift weapons.[59]

Once CERT regained control of the block, a new struggle emerged, one that shaped the meaning of the revolt in ways that served competing agendas. Governor Cuomo, Commissioner Coughlin, and Sit-Con received praise for their handling of the revolt, including from prisoner and civil rights advocates.[60] The Civil Rights Division of the U.S. Department of Justice investigated conditions in Sing Sing for violations of the Civil Rights of Institutionalized Persons Act, but did not ultimately press charges.[61] To be sure, inmates complained that CERT team members destroyed property and voiced racist epithets as they retook the facility.[62] The only criminal charges grew from an inmate who accused other inmates of repeatedly raping him during the revolt. He requested transfer to a federal prison facility, noting that even though he was in protective custody—solitary confinement—he received ongoing threats and reprisals by inmates and correctional officers.[63]

In contrast, political leaders in Ossining saw the revolt as further evidence that the correctional facility hindered their town's economic development and tarred its reputation. They felt that the revolt highlighted the ways the prison detracted from the Hudson River charm of the village. Mere hours after B Block was retaken, the Ossining town supervisor urged the governor to close the facility so that the prime riverfront real estate on which it stood could be redeveloped.[64] Cuomo also received pressure from Richard Ottinger, who represented Ossining in the U.S. Congress, to close the facility. Ottinger reminded the governor that just prior to the revolt he had proposed that DOCS lease Rikers Island from New York City and convert it into a state correctional facility as a replacement for Sing Sing.[65] The governor noted that severe overcrowding throughout the system prevented consideration of closing the facility.[66] Ossining mayor Joseph Caputo retorted that the state should

59. Kurlander, *Report to Governor Mario M. Cuomo*, 177.
60. David Rothenberg to Mario M. Cuomo, January 11, 1983, and Ramsey Clark to Mario M. Cuomo, January 21, 1983, New York State Archives, Governor Mario M. Cuomo Papers, hereafter Cuomo Papers. Correspondence Files, 1983–84, Reel 43.
61. William Bradford Reynolds, Assistant Attorney General, Civil Rights Division, to Mario M. Cuomo, "Notice of Intent to Commence Investigation at Ossining Correctional Facility," June 20, 1983, Cuomo Papers, Correspondence Files, 1983–84, Reel 43.
62. Some inmates reported (this was denied by independent inspectors and correctional officers but corroborated by several inmates) that the subsequent shakedown of A Block, F Block, and 7 Building (none of which participated in the revolt) resulted in significant destruction of inmate property and physical intimidation by CERT (Mack, "Inside Sing Sing," 10–11).
63. Robert Arkin to Michael Del Giudice, secretary to the governor, April 19, 1983, Cuomo Papers, Correspondence Files, 1983–84, Reel 43.
64. Richard G. Wishnie to Mario M. Cuomo, January 11, 1983; Joseph G. Caputo to Mario M. Cuomo, January 17, 1983, Cuomo Papers, Correspondence Files, 1983–84, Reel 43.
65. Richard L. Ottinger to Mario M. Cuomo, January 4, 1983 and January 27, 1983, Cuomo Papers, Correspondence Files, 1983–84, Reel 43.
66. Mario M. Cuomo to Richard L. Ottinger, June 17, 1983, Cuomo Papers, Correspondence Files, 1983–84, Reel 43.

provide annual payments in lieu of taxes and close Tappan, a separate correctional facility adjacent to Sing Sing.[67] When it became clear that riverfront redevelopment was of secondary importance to what Cuomo saw as an ongoing crisis in the state's correctional facilities, the village of Ossining passed a resolution urging DOCS to change the name of the facility from Ossining Correctional Facility back to Sing Sing, "a name much more widely known and having a lesser impact on our Village."[68]

For his part, the governor distilled the meaning of the prisoners' demands to suit his goal of reforming and expanding the state prison system. The prisoners held hostages in immediate reaction to what they saw as the arbitrary and cruel actions of Sergeant Cunningham. As the revolt continued, negotiators on both sides focused on a range of other issues, most notably DOCS policies related to their transient status that restricted access to education, rehabilitation, and visitors. Less than three months after the revolt, Cuomo signed legislation ordering DOCS to raise the minimum age for correctional officers from eighteen to twenty-one.[69] In early 1984, Senator Marino, who had come so close to derailing the negotiations when those participating in the revolt viewed his off-the-cuff remarks on the evening news, coauthored new legislative recommendations in response to several days of hearings about the Sing Sing revolt. The recommendations included a series of reforms centered on shortening the time to transfer, reducing idle time, improving recruitment and training for correctional officers, and fixing the failed grievance process.[70] These proposals pointed to the sources of frustration among the inmates and responded to the interpersonal and professional missteps by correctional staff.

DOCS provided a modest increase to state funding for educational and vocational programs and some new funding for work assignments with Correctional Industries.[71] The state also increased funding to expand the size and improve the training of correctional staff. All told, the 1984–85 state budget included $10 million in new funding for improved programming and work placement for inmates, new correctional officers, and improved training.[72] While these small-scale changes reflected a reasonable response to the legitimate

---

67. Mayor Joseph G. Caputo to Mario M. Cuomo, February 23, 1983, Cuomo Papers, Correspondence Files, 1983–84, Reel 43.
68. The name was changed back to Sing Sing in 1985. Lester M. Kimball, Village Clerk to New York State Department of Correctional Services, September 28, 1983, Cuomo Papers, Correspondence Files, 1983–84, Reel 43.
69. Executive Chamber, Press Release, March 29, 1984, Cuomo Papers, Correspondence Files, 1983–84, Reel 43.
70. Ralph J. Marino and Melvin H. Miller, "After Ossining: A Legislative Response with Recommendations," report based on investigations and hearings conducted by the Assembly Codes and Senate Crime and Correction Committees, January 9, 1984, Correctional Association of New York Records, M. E. Grenander Department of Special Collections and Archives, Archives of Public Affairs and Policy, University at Albany Library.
71. The increased funding for Correctional Industries (CI) would be offset by increased profits. CI, now Corcraft, saw a 30 percent increase in sales, from $6 million to $8 million, in the first quarter of 1984. CI went from an operating deficit to achieving a small profit. Lawrence T. Kurlander. *Governor Cuomo's 1984 Criminal Justice Accomplishments* (Albany: Office of the Director of Criminal Justice, 1984), 27.
72. Ibid., 3–4.

concerns of the prisoners who revolted, they would come to be far less significant than the impending transformation and expansion of the state's correctional system in the coming years. Mario Cuomo, who would symbolize the great liberal hope to counterbalance the rightward march of U.S. politics during the Reagan years and who would periodically and publicly flirt with making a run for the White House, instead championed a kind of criminal justice liberalism that addressed the crisis in incarceration by building more prisons.[73]

Faced with a daunting $1.8 billion budget deficit, Cuomo declared, "If we're going to do cuts, every agency has to be cut. There's not going to be somebody safeguarded—well, except for prisons."[74] The crucial long-term impact of the Sing Sing revolt would develop over the following decade as the governor repeatedly invoked the Sing Sing revolt when urging the state legislature to allocate greater state resources to prison construction and staffing in order to house sharply rising prison populations. A round of investigations and blue-ribbon committees concluded that prison overcrowding and sentencing disparities were the underlying cause of the revolt. These were long-standing concerns that brought together a range of critics of incarceration, even if they did not always agree on what to do about it. Rather than seek ways to cut the size of the prison population, state officials rarely publicly questioned the reality that the prison population would continue to grow, even while the governor requested $30 million to support alternatives to incarceration to try and slow the growth of the prison system.[75]

In particular, the New York State Committee on Sentencing Guidelines (NYSCSG) sought to reduce disparities in prison sentences but did not consider reducing the state's reliance on incarceration. It recommended, among other things, predictability in prison terms through a sentencing grid and a phased elimination of parole boards.[76] The committee's report candidly noted, "had the Committee interpreted its mandate as requiring that it propose sentences that would allow the state to live within its planned capacity, the Committee would have had to recommend a reduction in the use of incarceration."[77] At a moment in the state's history when the prison population stood at 110 percent of capacity—and triple its population of a decade earlier—the committee predicted that its recommendations would result in continued explosive growth, to over fifty thousand by the early 1990s.[78]

---

73. Saladin Ambar, *American Cicero: Mario Cuomo and the Defense of American Liberalism* (New York: Oxford University Press, 2018), xi. Ambar believes that Cuomo "has been the most significant liberal politician to challenge Reaganism in the past thirty years," with his prison construction as a significant failure in his otherwise progressive vision (xiv).

74. Robert S. McElvaine, *Mario Cuomo: A Biography* (New York: Charles Scribner's Sons, 1988), 311.

75. Kurlander, *Governor Cuomo's 1984 Criminal Justice Accomplishments*, 5.

76. New York State Committee on Sentencing Guidelines, *Determinate Sentencing Report and Recommendations* (Albany, NY, March 29, 1985), 8.

77. Ibid., 14.

78. Ibid., 15. Fifty thousand underestimated the rise. In 1994 the state's prison population peaked at sixty-seven thousand. See William H. Honan. "Thomas Coughlin, 63, a Chief of Prisons in New York State," *New York Times*, August 25, 2001, http://www.nytimes.com/2001/08/25/nyregion/thomas-coughlin-63-a-chief-of-prisons-in-new-york-state.html.

They also knew that this population growth would have a continued and deepening disparate impact on African Americans, Latinos, and poor people of all backgrounds.[79]

The committee proposed a plan that would eliminate indeterminate sentences, a practice where judges set minimum and maximum terms within which parole boards set a release date. The parole board theoretically based its release decisions on the severity of the initial crime, behavior while incarcerated, and future risk of reoffending. The critique of indeterminate sentencing came from many quarters, with conservatives seeing as unrealistic the expectation of rehabilitation at the philosophical heart of indeterminate sentencing, while more-liberal observers arguing that the resulting disparate sentences for similar crimes was itself unjust and a leading cause of racial disparities in incarceration rates.[80] In the 1970s and mid-1980s several states and the federal government began eliminating parole and establishing relatively fixed "truth in sentencing" statutes, allowing for some time off for good behavior. New York tried and failed to move toward determinate sentencing on at least three separate occasions prior to the 1983 revolt. With the wind of the Sing Sing revolt at their backs, the state joined the national bandwagon for determinate sentences. In addition, the Fair Treatment Standards Act provided a greater voice for crime victims in the criminal justice system by creating guidelines for ongoing notification of judicial and corrections proceedings.[81]

The rhetoric around this new legislation focused on "truth in sentencing" and "victims' rights," but would not result in an end to racially disparate sentences or abuses of discretion. Rather, the end result was a shift of discretion away from judges and parole boards and toward prosecuting attorneys who brought charges associated with the new, harsher sentences. In addition, correctional officers and other prison officials retained significant sway over the awarding of "good time," one of the few remaining mechanisms for reducing

---

79. New York State Committee on Sentencing Guidelines, *Determinate Sentencing: Report and Recommendations,* 21. Key members of the committee went on the record to note that "it is intolerable for the state to consider implementing a plan to reduce disparities in sentencing without paying equal attention to the implementation of strategies to reduce the overrepresentation of minorities, a marked disparity, in the composition of its correctional facilities." The four members who noted the disparate economic and racial impact of incarceration included Austin Gerald Lopez, past president of the Puerto Rican Bar Association; Basil Paterson, former state senator and father of future New York governor David Paterson; Lynn Walker, who was part of the NAACP Legal Defense and Education Fund team that successfully halted the use of the death penalty in Furman v. Georgia (1972) and who then led the Ford Foundation's Human Rights and Governance Program; and Milton Williams, an administrative judge for New York City's criminal courts who had been the executive director of the McKay Commission investigating the Attica uprising and would go on to serve on New York Court of Appeals ("A Court Official Will Lead Panel on Sentencing," *New York Times,* October 17, 1983, http://www.nytimes.com/1983/10/17/nyregion/a-court-official-will-lead-panel-on-sentencing.html; David Stout, "Lynn Walker Huntley" Obituary, *New York Times,* September 6, 2015, https://www.nytimes.com/2015/09/07/us/lynn-walker-huntley-lawyer-in-prominent-civil-rights-issues-dies-at-69.html?_r=0).
80. Robert Martinson, "What Works? Questions and Answers about Prison Reform," *The Public Interest* 35 (Spring 1974): 25. For a broader discussion of the trend toward determinate sentencing, see Pamela Griset. "Determinate Sentencing and the High Cost of Overblown Rhetoric: The New York Experience," *Crime and Delinquency* 40, no. 4 (1994): 532–45.
81. Kurlander, "Criminal Justice Accomplishments," 20.

prison terms.[82] Kurlander and Cuomo had more in mind than reform: they developed a three-year plan for almost nine thousand new cells in anticipation of continued rapid growth in the prison population. In 1983 the state's prison population of 28,000 people was about 2,400 more than its stated capacity, and this expansion anticipated continued growth in the prison population.[83] DOCS managed to construct space for two thousand new prisoners at existing facilities in 1984, and the governor proposed repurposing five state facilities—three psychiatric centers, a facility for people with developmental disabilities, and a high school—as prisons.[84] Next, beginning with construction of a "Maxi-Maxi" facility adjacent to Wallkill Correctional Facility in upstate Ulster County, the state created facilities that reflected new architectural and regimental trends in penology emphasizing smaller facilities rather than large cellblocks like Sing Sing's B Block, implementation of surveillance technology, and a greater reliance on isolation. By 1987 the capacity of the prison system had grown by ten thousand inmates.[85]

In financing this new construction, Cuomo vowed to not repeat Carey's earlier failed bond issuance. At the governor's urging, the state legislature authorized the Urban Development Corporation (UDC) to finance the construction of new correctional facilities, which would then lease the prisons back to the state.[86] The UDC was part of a state-level War on Poverty, created in 1968 in order to address "substantial and persistent unemployment and underemployment" in New York's urban areas.[87] Although the 1968 legislation did not mention a criminal justice mandate, it did provide significant leeway for the UDC to bypass state spending limits, issue bonds without voter approval, and enter into agreements to acquire or develop large-scale economic development projects. Over the next two decades the UDC financed the construction of thirty-eight new correctional facilities under the logic that these were economic development projects for struggling upstate New York communities.[88] Cuomo proposed issuing UDC bonds within two weeks of the Sing

82. Griset, "Determinate Sentencing and the High Cost of Overblown Rhetoric," 539, 542. See also Clear and Frost, *The Punishment Imperative*, 31. Alfred Blumstein and Allen J. Beck attributed almost all the growth in the national prison population in the 1980s and 1990s to changes in sentencing guidelines and increased use of incarceration as a penalty for drug crimes. Alfred Blumstein and Allen J. Beck, "Population Growth in U.S. Prisons, 1980–1996," in *Prisons,* ed. Michael Tonry and Joan Petersilia (Chicago: University of Chicago Press, 1999), 17–61. The New York State Committee on Sentencing Guidelines argued against mandatory minimums for this reason but were not able to stop the shift to longer sentences with fewer opportunities for early release.
83. Chira, "Budget Proposes Space," B5.
84. Kurlander, "Governor Cuomo's Accomplishments," 2.
85. Jeffrey Smalz, "New York Criminal Justice Commissioner Resigns," *New York Times,* December 6, 1987, https://www.nytimes.com/1987/12/06/nyregion/new-york-criminal-justice-commissioner-resigns.html ?searchResultPosition=1.
86. Chira, "Budget Proposes Space," B5.
87. Urban Development Corporation Act of 1968, New York State Legislature, Laws of New York State, accessed August 16, 2017, https://www.nysenate.gov/legislation/laws/UDA. The UDC funded low-, moderate-, and middle-income housing projects until 1975 (Josh Barbanel, "Cuomo to Seek Bonds of U.D.C. for Prison Cells," *New York Times,* January 26, 1983, B4).
88. Ryan S. King, Marc Mauer, and Tracy Huling, *Big Prisons, Small Towns: Prison Economics in Rural America* (Washington, DC: The Sentencing Project, 2003), 4.

Sing revolt. Noting that voters rejected Governor Carey's attempt to issue bonds for prison construction as recently as 1981, the *New York Times* reported that administration officials lauded the "new form of financing mechanism" for its potential to create construction and correctional jobs. One aide hubristically noted that the facilities "would be designed so that they could be converted to housing or industrial parks if the prison population dropped."[89]

Several state and nonprofit organizations opposed Cuomo's plan. The Correctional Association of New York, which led the opposition to the 1981 bond issuance, noted the UDC scheme specifically and illegally overturned the outcome of bond referendum. In addition, the chairperson of the state assembly's Housing Committee meekly criticized the move as seeming to "go beyond the existing statutory authority" of the UDC.[90] The strongest opposition came from state comptroller Edward Regan, who vowed to "oppose it with all the authority of my office" on the grounds of fiscal irresponsibility.[91] Regan later argued that Cuomo's plan circumvented not only the will of the 1981 voters but also the state's constitution, which required voter approval for issuance of all nonrevenue generating bonds.[92] Cuomo responded quickly to Regan's challenge, urging the legislature to see prison construction as a state emergency: "There is simply no time left to debate the merits of increasing prison spaces and rebuilding old, outmoded facilities. We must act quickly and decisively with the resources available to us." Cuomo justified this shifting of resources from the War on Poverty to the War on Crime, in part, by saying, "the events at Ossining are still recent enough to impress on us all the crisis in our prisons."[93] One month later, the legislature authorized a UDC bond issuance of $150 million. These funds would be used to build five new medium-security facilities, in addition to the two maximum-security facilities already under construction.[94]

What changed because of the Sing Sing revolt? It is tempting to read the revolt backward: from the perspective of the second decade of the twenty-first century, the revolt served as a harbinger of the failure of mass incarceration itself. In this interpretation, a narrative arc that began with Mario Cuomo's criminal justice liberalism would fittingly conclude with his son, Andrew Cuomo, the state's fifty-sixth governor. Andrew was present in his father's office during the revolt as a twenty-five-year-old policy adviser. He began his own first term in 2011, entering office less than two years after the state legislature and his predecessor, Governor David Patterson, succeeded in easing the Rockefeller Drug Laws that had fueled the prison population crisis in the first place. Several decades of activism

---

89. Barbanel, "Cuomo to Seek Bonds of U.D.C. for Prison Cells," B4.

90. Ibid. See also Josh Barbanel, "A Reporter's Notebook: Between Budget's Lines," *New York Times,* February 5, 1983, 20.

91. Sydney H. Schanberg, "Now for the Hard Part," *New York Times,* January 29, 1983, 23.

92. Edward Regan, "A Proper Bond Issue Properly Proposed" (letter to the editor), *New York Times,* November 7, 1983, A22.

93. Susan Chira, "Budget Proposes Space for Additional 2,300 Prisoners," *New York Times,* February 1, 1983, B5.

94. Edward A. Gargan, "New York Prison Population Hits a Record 30,000," *New York Times,* May 15, 1983, 27.

culminated in a successful campaign by Drop the Rock, Mothers of N.Y. Disappeared, and the Hip-Hop Summit Action Network, among others, to publicize the extreme consequences and racist impact of the state's drug laws and to lobby elected officials.[95] The state reduced Rockefeller sentences of fifteen years to life for nonviolent drug offenders to eight years. People sentenced under the Rockefeller laws also gained the right to seek an adjustment in their sentences and early release. Even people with determinate sentences sought and received time off for good behavior. These changes in law and practice were accompanied by double-digit drops in the overall crime rate. The state's prison population, especially in the medium- and minimum-security facilities filled primarily with people sentenced under the Rockefeller laws, dropped quickly and dramatically, from a high of over 67,000 in the mid-1990s to 46,000 in early 2019. The state closed twenty-four juvenile and adult facilities during Andrew Cuomo's first two terms in office, but the incarcerated population remained at almost four times its pre-Rockefeller size.[96]

While tempting, this narrative arc obscures the role of criminal justice liberalism, including as practiced by Mario Cuomo. Cuomo ignored warnings about the human, moral, and economic costs of mass incarceration and instead saw the crisis of incarceration primarily in terms of overcrowding. In response to the revolt, he dismantled programs intended to provide jobs and housing and redirected resources to intensive policing and prison construction. The erasure of criminal justice liberalism is perhaps most clearly demonstrated by Andrew Cuomo's first State of the State address. Just three days after taking office, he announced, "an incarceration program is not an employment program. If people need jobs, let's get people jobs. Don't put other people in prison to give some people jobs. Don't put other people in juvenile justice facilities to give some people jobs."[97] His father's administration financed prison construction specifically and perversely using a War on Poverty–era jobs and urban redevelopment program.

Instead, we might remember the Sing Sing revolt from the perspective of those who rose up. Their actions demonstrate Robin D. G. Kelley's insight that for people largely disenfranchised from the political process or from social movements, "politics comprises the many battles to roll back constraints and exercise some power over, or create some space within, the institutions and social relationships that dominate our lives."[98] Those who took over the block gained increased access to visitors, saw their wait times until transfer cut in half, were able to go to the gymnasium instead of the unheated warehouse, and would

95. Dasun Allah, "Hiphop Takes Stock in 'Drop the Rock,'" *Village Voice*, May 13, 2003, https://www.villagevoice.com/2003/05/13/hiphop-takes-stock-in-drop-the-rock.

96. Press release, "Governor Cuomo Announces Comprehensive Reforms to Improve the Re-Entry Process for Formerly Incarcerated Individuals," March 5, 2018, https://www.governor.ny.gov/news/governor-cuomo-announces-comprehensive-reforms-improve-re-entry-process-formerly-incarcerated.

97. Andrew Cuomo, "State of the State Address," January 4, 2011, https://www.ny.gov/programs/2011-state-state-address.

98. Robin D. G. Kelley, *Race Rebels: Culture, Politics, and the Black Working Class* (New York: Free Press, 1994), 10.

be guarded by officers who were older and better screened by the state.[99] In addition, the state stayed true to its word to not take reprisals against the inmates. Importantly, in the months that followed, inmates and correctional officers reported a cooling of the everyday tensions that served as the immediate catalyst for the revolt. Clifford Bell, an inmate in B Block during the revolt and who remained at Sing Sing, noted that there was "an attitude of understanding between officers and inmates."[100] In this sense, the revolt was a success.

This short-term success would prove costly, however, both for the state's taxpayers and for the individuals and communities most directly targeted for incarceration. Some observers might understand Mario Cuomo's massive expansion of the state's prison system within the framework of what he considered "progressive pragmatism."[101] He was a liberal governing during the Reagan years. He inherited a ballooning prison population, one with roots in decade-old drug laws passed by a more conservative predecessor, and sought to make prisons safer places to live and work by reducing overcrowding. But the rapid expansion of New York's prison system was not simply a concession to criminal justice conservatives by an otherwise stalwart liberal who opposed capital punishment and proposed an expansion of home confinement for nonviolent offenders. Rather, Cuomo's response to the Sing Sing revolt forestalled other paths to criminal justice and instead facilitated the rapid growth in the prison population. At the same time, it participated in a pivot away from state anti-poverty efforts. With the momentum generated by the Sing Sing revolt, Cuomo articulated and enacted key goals of 1980s criminal justice liberalism, including reducing overcrowded conditions in state prisons by building more facilities, eliminating sentencing disparities through determinate sentencing, and generating economic opportunities by siting new facilities in impoverished rural areas. Criminal justice liberalism, in the case of New York, provided both the ideological fuel and the bureaucratic machine to double the size of the state's prison system. John Nelson, an inmate at Sing Sing, came closest to describing the long-term impact of the revolt when he insisted that its lesson lay in this underlying trend toward mass incarceration: "I'm 73B5147, but you said I'm a human being. Prison became

---

99. *In the Matter of* 345. Overcrowding remained a problem. Five months after the revolt the prison's population sat at 115 percent of capacity.

100. Bell quoted in Jim Bencivenga, "Return to Sing Sing Five Months After the Hostage Crisis," *Christian Science Monitor*, May 20, 1983, https://www.csmonitor.com/1983/0520/052039.html. Not all inmates agreed with this assessment. Prisoners' Legal Services of New York (PLSNY), founded in the mid-1970s in response to the Attica uprising, noted that while B Block's visitation and package rules did indeed conform to the rest of the facility, PLSNY received increased complaints regarding deficiencies in medical care and educational programming since the revolt (testimony of Adrian Johnson, staff attorney for Prisoners' Legal Services of New York, *In the Matter of,* 218). Incarcerated people and corrections officials in other states took a similar approach to the prisoners and officials in New York. Robert T. Chase tells the story of a 1985 Tennessee revolt that mirrored the trajectory of the Sing Sing revolt. See "We Are Not Slaves: Rethinking the Rise of Carceral States through the Lens of the Prisoners' Rights Movement," *Journal of American History* 102, no. 1 (2015): 73–86.

101. Ambar, *American Cicero*, 49.

a correctional facility. Now it's back. Why don't they change the name back to prison again, then, if it's a game? We've gone back to the philosophy of lock them up and throw away the key. We're just locking young guys up who end up in trouble the second time, and there's no more chances."[102] With the Sing Sing Revolt, antipoverty liberalism became criminal justice liberalism.

---

102. Testimony of John Nelson, *In the Matter of,* 58–60.

The Power of Women
Matilda Joslyn Gage and the
New York Women's Vote of 1880

Sue Boland

Matilda Joslyn Gage woke on the morning of Wednesday, October 13, 1880, knowing that the day would be an important one for the women of New York State. At the beginning of the year, the New York legislature had passed a bill allowing women to vote and run for positions on local school boards. When the governor signed the bill into law, Gage started nine months of hard work in preparation for the fall elections that would take place in rural school districts, including her own in Fayetteville (near Syracuse). Like an expectant mother, she approached the day with a mixture of fear, excitement, and nervous anticipation.

Gage had devoted her life so far to the cause of women's rights, focusing on the vote. As a top officer in the National Woman Suffrage Association (NWSA), she was well aware of the challenges of a radical and unpopular movement. She had been told that women were intellectually incapable of voting, that it was against God's plan for women to vote, that it would destroy the home, that politics was too dirty for women to participate in, and that women didn't want to vote. "When women ask for the vote, they shall get it," said the anti-suffragists. The apathy of millions of women in the United States and their reluctance to work for their own political freedom was frustrating for Gage and her co-leaders, Susan B. Anthony and Elizabeth Cady Stanton. "How can it be that every woman, *every* woman," Gage wrote, "does not rise in the might of her inherent inborn rights, and cry 'away with it!'"[1]

But now, the women of New York State had a chance to prove that they did want a voice in their government, even if it was only for running school districts. Suffrage leaders believed that school suffrage was a "foot in the door" to full voting rights; that New York as the birthplace of the movement could either lead the forward progress of woman suffrage or cripple it by proving that women would not come out to vote. As Gage walked across the

---

1. Matilda Joslyn Gage, "Old Times and New," *National Citizen and Ballot Box* (hereafter *NCBB*), May 1880.

street from her home to the schoolhouse to monitor the election, she wondered what the day would bring.

The Importance of School Suffrage

School suffrage is not usually mentioned by historians because they have focused on Anthony and Stanton and their work for a federal amendment, and school elections just aren't very exciting unless something controversial is being voted on.[2] When historians do mention school suffrage, it is usually in a list with other forms of partial suffrage[3] or in works about the efforts after 1880 in other states.[4]

However, the story of that vote in the autumn of 1880 is useful to us today as a microcosm of the nineteenth-century suffrage movement. The first wave of suffrage leaders endured "repeated failure" and didn't live to see national success, but a few victories were won at the state and local levels, giving them hope to keep working.[5] This account highlights a forgotten leader, Matilda Joslyn Gage, who was active at the national, state, and local levels and took it upon herself to prove that women would vote if they were educated and organized.[6] The story of school suffrage in New York simultaneously demonstrates the courage of ordinary women and the need for strong female leaders. Leaving their home to vote required women to go outside their traditional domestic sphere and take on a new public role under harsh circumstances.

Would women find the courage within themselves to vote and perhaps even run for office, despite their not having held *any* public office in New York until just a few years before?[7] Unfortunately, we only know the answer for white women—voting would have certainly required more courage for women of color. But the historical record is almost all about white women. So far, I have only found one instance, noted later in this article, about African-American women participating in school suffrage. There is undoubtedly more to this story.

---

2. One exception is Heidi Hemming and Julie Hemming Savage, *Women Making America* (Silver Spring, MD: Clotho Press, 2009), 151.

3. Linda K. Kerber, *No Constitutional Right to Be Ladies: Women and the Obligations of Citizenship* (New York: Hill and Wang, 1998), 117; Doris Weatherford, *A History of the American Suffragist Movement* (Santa Barbara, CA: ABC-CLIO, 1998), 142, 159; Corrine M. McConnaughy, *The Woman Suffrage Movement in America: A Reassessment* (New York: Cambridge University Press, 2013).

4. Gerda Lerner, ed., *The Female Experience: An American Documentary* (New York: Oxford University Press, 1977), 357–61.

5. Susan Goodier and Karen Pastorello, *Women Will Vote: Winning Suffrage in New York State* (Ithaca, NY: Cornell University Press, 2017), 13.

6. Information about Gage is taken from Sally Roesch Wagner, *Matilda Joslyn Gage: She Who Holds the Sky* (Aberdeen, SD: Sky Carrier Press, 1999); Sally Roesch Wagner, introduction to *Woman, Church and State*, by Matilda Joslyn Gage (Amherst, NY: Humanity Books, 2002); Sue Boland, "Matilda Joslyn Gage" in *American Radical and Reform Writers*, vol. 345, 2nd. Ser., ed. Hester L. Furey, *Dictionary of Literary Biography* (Detroit: Gale, 2009) 141-154; Leila R. Brammer, *Excluded from Suffrage History: Matilda Joslyn Gage, Nineteenth-Century American Feminist* (Westport, CT: Greenwood Press, 2000).

7. Josephine Shaw Lowell was the first woman to hold public office in New York. She was appointed Commissioner of the State Board of Charities in 1876. Elizabeth Cady Stanton, Susan B. Anthony, and Matilda Joslyn Gage, eds., *History of Woman Suffrage*, vol. 3: 1876–1885 (Rochester, NY: Privately published, 1886), 417 (hereafter cited parenthetically as *HWS* 3).

Most of the leaders of the suffrage movement and women who voted were privileged, with the advantages of race, class, and education, yet all women and girls suffered from their gender and what that implied in 1880 in New York. The chasm of time makes it difficult to understand the burdens carried by these women. To do so, we have to undo over a century of progress. To go back, I will first introduce you to Matilda Joslyn Gage and her role in the national and state societies. I'll explain why the woman suffrage movement was controversial and progressed slowly, and I'll explore the example of Massachusetts women voting in school elections. Then I will delve into New York's school suffrage story, beginning with the defeat of an anti-suffrage governor in 1879 and the February 1880 passage of the bill allowing women to vote, then onward to the spring elections in New York's cities, a difficult summer for the suffragists in national politics, and to the rural school districts that voted in the fall of 1880, including Gage's hometown of Fayetteville.

Unfortunately, school suffrage was limited to Upstate New York in 1880. (For simplicity's sake, I will refer to anything outside of New York City as "Upstate New York," even though women voted in downstate areas such as Staten Island, Brooklyn, Queens, and Long Island.) Voters living within New York City, which was primarily Manhattan at that time, had no control over their schools. The state legislature created a board of education in 1871 to be appointed by the mayor of New York City, who in turn appointed local trustees in each ward to run the schools.[8] Women in New York City gained nothing from the school suffrage law.

Gage was a principal leader for women's rights who was virtually written out of history. For forty years, she worked alongside Stanton and Anthony; for twenty years she was a top officer in the NWSA.[9] Anthony was the organizer, Stanton the philosopher, but Gage was both.[10] She usually served as chair of the executive committee, an important behind-the-scenes position from which she organized conventions, lobbied politicians, and devised the strategy of the NWSA. In 1869, Gage organized New York State[11] and was a top officeholder of the New York State Woman Suffrage Association (NYSWSA) until the late 1880s.[12] In addition, from April 1878 to October 1881, Gage wrote, edited, and published the monthly newspaper of the NWSA, *The National Citizen and Ballot Box.*

8. Diane Ravitch, *The Great School Wars: A History of the New York City Public Schools* (New York: Basic Books, 1974).

9. For a list of NWSA officers 1872–1880, see appendix B, *The Selected Papers of Elizabeth Cady Stanton and Susan B. Anthony*, vol. 3: National Protection for National Citizens 1873 to 1880, ed. Ann D. Gordon (New Brunswick, NJ: Rutgers University Press, 2003), 577–82.

10. I am indebted to Dr. Sally Roesch Wagner, Gage's principal biographer and founding director of the Matilda Joslyn Gage Center for Social Justice Dialogue, for teaching me this concept.

11. Matilda Joslyn Gage and Elizabeth B. Phelps, "New York State Woman's Suffrage Convention," *Revolution* (New York, NY), June 17, 1869, 377–78; Matilda Joslyn Gage, "Appeal to the Friends of Woman's Suffrage in the State of New York," *Revolution*, July 29, 1869, 49; "New York State Woman Suffrage Association," *Revolution*, October 7, 1869, 219; "Letter from Mrs. Gage," *Revolution*, December 9, 1869, 364; "Letter from Mrs. Gage," *Revolution*, January 6, 1870, 4; "Suffrage Conventions," *Revolution*, July 14, 1870, 26; "Woman's Suffrage," *Revolution*, August 4, 1870, 73.

12. Goodier and Pastorello, *Women Will Vote*, 14–21; Susan B. Anthony and Ida Husted Harper, eds., *History of Woman Suffrage*, vol. 4: 1883–1900 (Rochester, NY: Privately published, 1902), 846 (hereafter cited

New York wasn't just home to Gage, Anthony, and (at one time) Stanton.[13] The Empire State was the most populated and wealthiest state in the country and the nation's leader in commerce, society, the arts, and politics. Achieving suffrage in New York could spur change across the country.[14] While the NWSA's strategy was to work toward an amendment to the U.S. Constitution protecting women's right to vote, they knew states would have to ratify an amendment. States also controlled many aspects of women's lives through divorce, child custody, and property laws. However, for much of the 1870s and into 1880, Anthony was busy traveling across the country lecturing on women's rights and was unable to take the lead on a state or local level.[15] It was up to Gage and other suffragists to make a success of school suffrage, which they hoped would lead to municipal voting, taxpayer voting, and presidential voting. The legislature could create these forms of voting without having to revise the state constitution, which was a long and difficult process. Because women were seen as the natural caretakers of children and their education, the legislature was more likely to allow women to oversee schools through their vote. In fact, several states permitted it before New York.[16] But before we visit 1880, we have to go further back in time.

Woman Suffrage and Women's Rights

The first volume of the *History of Woman Suffrage* takes a long look at not only the origins of the woman suffrage movement but also the larger issue of women's rights and centuries of oppression.[17] By exploring the past and naming the many reasons for oppression, Gage and Stanton predict what will be needed to attain women's future enfranchisement, true equality, and freedom.[18] In her chapter, "Woman, Church and State," Gage lays the blame

---

parenthetically as *HWS* 4). For more details, see *HWS* 3:422n; "Woman Suffrage," *New York Times*, May 12, 1876; "New York State Woman Suffrage Convention," *Ballot Box* (Toledo, OH), June 1877, "Woman Suffrage Association," *New York Times*, May 25, 1878, 8; "The Governor and the Ladies," *New York Times*, March 13, 1884; "The Ladies Take Their Turn," *New York Times*, February 14, 1885; "For Woman Suffrage: Meeting of the Annual Convention at New York," *The Marion (OH) Daily Star*, April 22, 1887; "Clever Women Who Want to Vote," *New-York Daily Tribune*, March 23, 1888.

13. By 1880, Stanton was living in New Jersey, so she is not a part of the New York school suffrage story. See Lori D. Ginzberg, *Elizabeth Cady Stanton: An American Life* (New York: Hill and Wang, 2009), 141–42.

14. Goodier and Pastorello, *Women Will Vote*, 2.

15. Ida Husted Harper, *The Life and Work of Susan B. Anthony*, vol. 1 (Indianapolis: Hollenbeck Press, 1898), chaps. 21–29, 351–513.

16. Table A.17, "States and Territories Allowing Women to Vote in Elections Dealing with Schools Prior to Nineteenth Amendment," in Alexander Keyssar, *The Right to Vote: The Contested History of Democracy in the United States*, rev. ed. (New York: Basic Books, 2009), appendix.

17. The *History* contains six volumes in all, published from 1881 to 1922.

18. Most historians refer to Stanton and Anthony as the authors of the first three volumes of *History of Woman Suffrage*; I believe that Gage and Stanton were the primary writers, for the following reasons: (1) In the contract for preparing and editing a history of the woman suffrage movement, Stanton and Gage agree to write and collect the material while Anthony agrees to secure the publication of the work. See Ida Husted Harper Collection, mssHM #10563, The Huntington Library, San Marino, California. (2) In an obituary that Anthony's biographer and coauthor of the fourth volume wrote, Harper states, "The actual writing was done by Mrs. Stanton and Mrs. Matilda Joslyn Gage, with assistants in all parts of the country" while Miss Anthony gathered material, raised money, and took care of the publication of the *History*. See Ida Husted Harper, "Susan B. Anthony," *The Independent*, March 22, 1906, 676. (3) Anthony's inability to write is well documented. See

for "the universal degradation of woman"[19] upon Christianity's teaching that females were inferior to men and subject to their authority because the first woman, Eve, disobeyed God and caused the downfall of mankind (*HWS* 1:756–57).[20] Woman's subjection was especially true within marriage, which rendered a married woman into a nonperson in the eyes of the law, subject to her husband's authority and without the right to own property, control her body, or have custody of her children.[21]

In the early years of the movement, before the Civil War, women's apathy to their own condition was viewed as an obstacle to their freedom. Suffragists compared women who were comfortable with their low status and didn't feel a need for change to enslaved men who did not resist or attempt to become free. It's important to note that the blame was usually put squarely upon the *situation* that women and enslaved people were forced into—the involuntary ignorance and total subjection in law, religion, and society—rather than any defects within the persons themselves. Oppressed people became "demoralized" and hopeless, inclined to agree that they were inferior and subject to another's authority (*HWS* 1:18). At the first women's rights convention in Seneca Falls in 1848, Stanton said, "The most discouraging, the most lamentable aspect our cause wears is the indifference, indeed, the contempt, with which women themselves regard the movement."[22]

Before nineteenth-century women could believe themselves equal to men and deserving of the same rights, they had to undergo no less than a complete "transformation" (*HWS* 1:18). The first step was to realize there was a problem. In 1855, Lucy Stone called herself "a disappointed woman" and vowed, "It shall be the business of my life to deepen this disappointment in every woman's heart until she bows down to it no longer" (*HWS* 1:165). Stone's disappointment was from lack of a political voice; however, most ordinary women's

Elizabeth Cady Stanton, Susan B. Anthony, and Matilda Joslyn Gage, eds., *History of Woman Suffrage*, 1: 1848–61 (New York: Fowler & Wells, 1881) (hereafter *HWS* 1), 456*HWS*; Harper, *The Life and Work of Susan B. Anthony*, 1:25n, 187, 299–300; Ida Husted Harper, *The Life and Work of Susan B. Anthony*, vol. 2 (Indianapolis: Hollenback Press, 1898), 913.

For the roles of Stanton, Anthony, and Gage during the creation of *History of Woman Suffrage*, see Lisa Tetrault, *The Myth of Seneca Falls: Memory and the Women's Suffrage Movement, 1848–1898* (Chapel Hill: University of North Carolina Press, 2014) and Mary E. Paddock Corey, "Matilda Joslyn Gage: Woman Suffrage Historian, 1852–1898" (PhD diss., University of Rochester, 1995).

19. *HWS* 1: 13

20. *HWS* 1: 756-757. Gage later expanded this work into a full-length book by the same title, published in 1893 by Charles H. Kerr, Chicago.

21. For the status of women in the early and mid-nineteenth century, see Ellen Carol DuBois, *Feminism and Suffrage: The Emergence of an Independent Women's Movement in America, 1848–1869* (Ithaca, NY: Cornell University Press, 1971); Barbara Leslie Epstein, *The Politics of Domesticity: Women, Evangelism, and Temperance in Nineteenth-Century America* (Middletown, CT: Wesleyan University Press, 1981); Sara M. Evans, *Born for Liberty: A History of Women in America* (New York: Free Press, 1989); Suzanne M. Marilley, *Woman Suffrage and the Origins of Liberal Feminism in the United States, 1820–1920* (Cambridge, MA: Harvard University Press, 1996); Sally G. McMillen, *Seneca Falls and the Origins of the Women's Rights Movement* (New York: Oxford University Press, 2008).

22. Elizabeth Cady Stanton, *Address Delivered at Seneca Falls and Rochester, New York* (New York: Robert J. Johnson, 1870), quoted in *The Elizabeth Cady Stanton-Susan B. Anthony Reader*, ed. Ellen Carol DuBois (Boston: Northeastern University Press, 1992), 33.

disappointment and subsequent apathy was due to a lack of time and energy. Historian Sally McMillen writes that reformers' upper-middle-class status made them out of touch with how most American women lived:

> Female indifference or resistance to the women's rights movement stemmed as much from the demands of women's daily lives as from a rejection of radical ideas that few had the time or energy to contemplate.... [F]or the majority of American women, changing their status was a frightening and unwelcome concept.[23]

Publicly asserting one's rights required a thick skin and economic independence: "the fear of public ridicule, and the loss of private favors from those who shelter, feed, and clothe them, withhold many from declaring their opinions and demanding their rights" (*HWS* 1:17).

Susan B. Anthony, who told a convention audience in 1855 that "woman is the greatest enemy of her own sex," was more tactful in her public remarks in later years, as was Stanton.[24] During the resurgence of the women's movement after the Civil War and the controversy over the Fourteenth and Fifteenth Amendments—which added the word "male" into the Constitution for the first time and gave the vote to African-American men—the blame for woman's condition no longer rested upon women but instead was placed squarely upon the men who made laws and voted for them. However, Gage, who had a reputation for being honest to a fault, could not hold her tongue.[25] When she took over the *National Citizen and Ballot Box,* Gage wrote that "one of the principal aims of the *National Citizen* will continue to be to make those women discontented who are now content."[26] When a friend of hers thought this was going too far, she responded:

> Does he not know that the deepest depth of degradation is reached, when a person who is wronged is insensible of the wrong done him? ... The old saw recognizes the fact that to each person is left his own work to do, in "whoever would be free, himself must strike the blow." No blow is ever struck until discontent is felt.[27]

Anti-suffragists proved Gage's point about contentment, saying that was the reason women did not want to vote. A typical example comes from the *Geneva Gazette*: "They [women] are happier, better off, better protected, more highly respected, receive a great degree of deference, enjoy more advantages in all circles *without,* than with, the ballot."[28] Hearing a woman say she had "all the rights I want" made Gage furious. In a blistering

23. McMillen, *Seneca Falls and the Origins of the Women's Rights Movement,* 139.
24. Ibid., 138.
25. Katherine Devereux Blake and Margaret Louise Wallace, *Champion of Women: The Life of Lillie Devereux Blake* (New York: Fleming H. Revell, 1943), 115.
26. "Prospectus," *NCBB,* May 1878.
27. "What the Press Says of Us," *NCBB,* June 1878.
28. "What the Press Says of Us," *NCBB,* October 1878.

editorial in the *National Citizen*, Gage railed against such "poor, foolish, brainless women," citing state laws and stories of women whose husbands abused them, took their property, and even gave their children away, leaving the women with no legal recourse.[29] For Gage, the solution was self-respect:

> One great obstacle towards securing woman's freedom arises from the fact of her self-depreciation—her non-recognition of her primal right to herself. So long trained in contempt of herself,—so long held to believe that she and all her rights are secondary to man or the lightest of his whims, so long educated in self-sacrifice, woman as a class has lost courage and the conviction of her duty to herself.[30]

Nowhere was women's courage needed more than in demanding their right to vote. Even Anthony "laughed heartily at the novelty and presumption of the demand" when she first read the report from the Seneca Falls convention (*HWS* 1:456). It is well known that securing the elective franchise was the most controversial of the resolutions at that first meeting and Frederick Douglass's help was needed for its passage (*HWS* 1:73).[31] But why was suffrage such a male enclave?

The doctrine of "separate spheres," or separate areas of activity, kept white middle- and upper-class women in the domestic sphere and out of men's public sphere. Their activities were separate because society believed men and women were created to be opposite and to complement one another. One popular minister, Theodore Parker, described the differences in a sermon: "I think man will always lead in affairs of intellect—of reason, imagination, understanding—he has the bigger brain; but that woman will always lead in affairs of emotion—moral, affectional, religious—she has the better heart, the truer intuition of the right, the lovely, the holy" (*HWS* 1:281–82).[32] The dominant philosophy taught to girls in pre–Civil War United States was "the cult of true womanhood," which judged females by "four cardinal virtues—piety, purity, submissiveness and domesticity."[33] It was so much more than caring for a family and a house. Women were seen as having a "peculiar susceptibility" to religion that helped to keep them pure and gave them the power to lead their families to God, which would in turn strengthen society.[34] A married woman was best able to show her love of country by subtly influencing her husband's political choices, raising sons to be good citizens, and doing charitable works to help those less fortunate. It was unthinkable that pure, sheltered women would come down from their pedestals to

---

29. Matilda Joslyn Gage, "All the Rights I Want," *NCBB*, January 1879.
30. "Professed Friends," *NCBB*, August 1880.
31. *HWS* DuBois, *Feminism and Suffrage*, 40–41; McMillen, *Seneca Falls and the Origins of the Women's Rights Movement*, 93–94; Ginzberg, *Elizabeth Cady Stanton*, 59–63; Judith Wellman, *The Road to Seneca Falls: Elizabeth Cady Stanton and the First Women's Rights Convention* (Urbana: University of Illinois Press, 2004), 203.
32. *HWS* Theodore Parker, *A Sermon of the Public Function of Woman* (Boston: Robert F. Wallcut, 1853), http://transcendentalism-legacy.tamu.edu/authors/parker/parkeronwomen.html.
33. Barbara Welter, "The Cult of True Womanhood: 1820–1860," *American Quarterly* 18, no. 2 (1966), 151–74.
34. Ibid.

go to the polls, because that was where all classes of men were at their worst—drinking, swearing, and fighting.

The physical act of voting was much different in the mid-nineteenth century than it is today. Even though elections were open to the public, some polling places, such as saloons or livery stables, were considered off-limits to respectable women. According to Richard Franklin Bensel, "The polling place was usually congested with milling throngs of men waiting for their turn to vote or, having voted, simply enjoying the public spectacle."[35] The spectacle came from excessive drinking as political parties supplied free hard cider or whiskey, which often led to unruly behavior. "Violence was a common characteristic of Gilded Age elections and not at all limited to the South," writes Peter Argersinger.[36] (To be clear, violence in the North was not nearly as severe as in the South, where African Americans were terrorized and murdered.) In the rural area of central New York where Gage lived, elections were marked by "magnificent processions" and "excited electioneering, and plenty of strong drink, and it was a tame one indeed that had not a fight thrown in."[37]

Voting rates were often as high as 80 percent, fueled by bribery from the political machines that dominated the Republicans (Upstate) and the Democrats (New York City). Representatives of political parties swarmed the polls, handing out preprinted ballots or "tickets," which were color-coded so everyone could see who you were voting for. Voters had to jostle their way through the crowd, step up onto a platform, and address the election officials on the other side of a wall through a "voting window." The voter would state his name so it could be written down or checked against a registration book. Any citizen standing nearby could challenge the eligibility of a voter; sometimes challengers were stationed by a political party. It would be up to an election official (also supplied by the political parties) to decide whether a voter was legitimate by such means as asking the voter to swear on the Bible that he was eligible according to the law.[38] If the voter was eligible, he would hand over his ticket through the window. The wall was there to keep the officials safe as "almost anything was permitted" in the public area, and election officials had no authority there if chaos ensued.[39] The standard to differentiate between jostling and violence was whether a "man of ordinary courage" could get to the window. If the environment was decided to be violent, the election results were invalidated.[40] Things were worse in New York City during the Tammany Hall era, when the boss would hire "shoulder hitters" and thugs to intimidate voters.[41]

---

35. Richard Franklin Bensel, *The American Ballot Box in the Mid-Nineteenth Century* (New York: Cambridge University Press, 2004), x.

36. Peter H. Argersinger, "New Perspectives on Election Fraud in the Gilded Age," *Political Science Quarterly* 100, no. 4 (1985–86): 669–87.

37. "Early Elections," *The Recorder* (Fayetteville, NY), October 27, 1893.

38. Bensel, *The American Ballot Box in the Mid-Nineteenth Century*, 18–19.

39. Ibid., 11–13.

40. Ibid., 21.

41. Tracy Campbell, *Deliver the Vote: A History of Election Fraud, an American Political Tradition 1724–2004* (New York: Carroll & Graf, 2005), 18–19.

Suffragists were proposing that women who had never entered a bar or spoken in public should, at best, submit themselves to the gaze of the men of their community, and, at worst, make physical contact with drunken partiers. Of course, the emotions of a presidential or gubernatorial election are rarely aroused in school elections, but in 1880 everyone knew that school elections were the first step to full suffrage. Historian Marc Wahlgren Summers calls nineteenth-century politics "America's most popular participatory sport."[42] He likens politics to war, which at that time was no place for women.[43] The male combatants were filled with a lust to win, ready to use any means to gain power: "Hoopla, hype, trickery, bribery and fraud were as natural to the process as a torchlight parade."[44] Is it any wonder that women were reluctant to participate or that men were reluctant to let them?

Throughout 1879, Gage and her fellow New York suffragists read about school suffrage in Massachusetts in the *Woman's Journal,* a newspaper edited by Lucy Stone and others in Boston for the American Woman Suffrage Association (AWSA), the rival organization to the NWSA (*HWS* 3:287).[45] The *Woman's Journal* made a big push to get women registered and voting, because they hoped school suffrage would "establish the precedent for Woman Suffrage generally."[46] One problem was the convoluted process women had to go through in order to register; another was the two-dollar poll tax.[47] (Two dollars in 1879 is equivalent to about fifty dollars in 2019.)[48]

Even if a woman could pay two dollars, it was not certain that she would have the courage to attend a school meeting and vote for the first time.[49] Suffragist Harriet Robinson handed out circulars at an election a few years earlier and recalled the "terror" and "repugnance" expressed at the "rash act for a woman to appear at the polls in company with men" (*HWS* 3:282). Registration, which for some women required a visit to the tax assessor's office, seemed "very formidable, like having a tooth drawn or being placed on the witness stand."[50] Middle- and upper-class white women were so concerned with decorum and modesty that they didn't even want their first name used in public:

> It was rather startling to hear one's name called in full, before such an audience; some
> ladies object to voting simply on that account, they are so used to being called "Miss So

---

42. Marc Wahlgren Summers, *Party Games: Getting, Keeping, and Using Power in Gilded Age Politics* (Chapel Hill: University of North Carolina Press, 2004), 34.

43. Ibid., 33.

44. Ibid., 4.

45. *HWS*The "Massachusetts" chapter is credited to Harriet H. Robinson.

46. T.W.H. [Thomas Wentworth Higginson], "Voting for School Officers," *Woman's Journal,* January 10, 1879.

47. L.S. [Lucy Stone], "Registration of Women Voters" and "Instructions for Women Voters," *Woman's Journal,* August 28, 1880. See also T.W.H., "School Suffrage Laws," March 6, 1880; L.S., "Anniversary Meeting," May 29, 1880; L.S., "School Suffrage," September 4, 1880; M.A.L. "School Suffrage in New York," September 18, 1880; "The Massachusetts School Suffrage Law," December 11, 1880; C.F.B., "Why One Woman Did Not Vote," December 18, 1880; all in *Woman's Journal.*.

48. Inflation Calculator, https://www.officialdata.org/1879-dollars-in-2018?amount=2·

49. "The Women Who Vote," *Woman's Journal,* June 12, 1880; L.S., "School Suffrage," *Woman's Journal,* June 19, 1880.

50. T.W.H., "The Political Ignorance of Women," *Woman's Journal,* September 20, 1879.

and So," or Mrs. John or Mrs. William Somebody, that they shrink from hearing the old familiar baptismal, Harriet, or Martha Jane.[51]

One letter writer to the *Woman's Journal* explained that women care much more than men about public opinion and their reputation: "No woman relishes the name of 'Amazonian,' 'obtrusive,' 'unladylike.'"[52] The implication is that voting was masculine, something no lady wanted to be.

Writers in the *Woman's Journal* often used the word *timid* and tried to reassure women that they could overcome their timidity. Stone told women to "never fear" because public sentiment was growing in favor of women voting on school topics.[53] However, there was much concern about the "rowdy" element and if it would show up at the caucuses, meetings, and polls as it had in the past, along with jostling, spitting, liquor, tobacco smoke, disorder, and confusion.[54] Most of the women who went to meetings and/or the polls went in groups of other women or with their husbands or fathers, such as the famous author Louisa May Alcott, who went with her father, Bronson Alcott.[55]

In December 1879, Boston women voted for the first time, and women in the rural/town districts of Massachusetts voted in March 1880. The turnout was disappointing, but suffragists were glad to see that even a couple thousand women voted "under all these difficulties."[56] After voting in Concord, Louise May Alcott concluded that "when the timid or indifferent [women], several of whom came to look on, see that we still live, they will venture to express publicly the opinions they have held or have lately learned to respect and believe."[57] The *Woman's Journal* reassured readers that those who voted "were the best women intellectually, morally, and, in many cases, socially"[58] and that no woman "met anything at the polls which weakened her sense of dignity or offended her delicacy."[59]

Suffragists reading about the school vote in Massachusetts would conclude that a dose of courage was necessary to get large numbers of everyday women to the polls. Gage had already proved her courage and leadership. In 1877, William N. Emerson, a New York senator from Rochester, introduced a bill authorizing women to serve on school boards, and it passed the legislature by a large margin (*HWS* 3:417).[60] However, Governor Lucius Robinson vetoed it, stating, "The God of nature has appointed different fields of labor, duty and

---

51. H.H. [Harriet Hanson] Robinson, "Malden Town Meeting," *Woman's Journal*, March 27, 1880.
52. "Importance of School Suffrage," *Woman's Journal*, June 26, 1880.
53. L.S., "Defending Their Rights," *Woman's Journal*, October 9, 1880.
54. "Women at the Ward Caucuses," reprinted from the Boston *Advertiser*, *Woman's Journal*, September 13, 1879.
55. L.M.A., "Letter from Louise M. Alcott," *Woman's Journal*, April 3, 1880.
56. "School Suffrage: Report of Abby W. May," *Woman's Journal*, January 10, 1880; "School Suffrage: Report at the Annual Meeting," *Woman's Journal*, February 7, 1880.
57. L.M.A., "Letter from Louise M. Alcott," *Woman's Journal*, April 3, 1880.
58. Massachusetts School Suffrage Association, "The Women Who Vote," *Woman's Journal*, June 12, 1880.
59. "School Suffrage: Report at the Annual Meeting," *Woman's Journal*, February 7, 1880.
60. *HWS* "Legislature of New York—Senate—Enlarging Woman's Sphere." *Albany Evening Journal*), February 15, 1877.

usefulness for the sexes. His decrees cannot be changed by human legislation. . . . Few, if any, of the intelligent and right-minded among women desire or would be willing to accept the change which such a law would inaugurate" (*HWS* 3:418).[61]

Fast-forward to the fall of 1879, as the state was preparing for November gubernatorial elections (at that time, governors served three-year terms). Gage called upon the women of New York to work against Robinson's reelection (*HWS* 3:422n). Gage and several members of the New York City and State societies spoke at rallies and handed out thousands of leaflets (*HWS* 3:423), and Gage wrote editorials about the importance of defeating Robinson in the *National Citizen*:

> What we demand is justice, and justice will consist in the paying of obedient attention to the voice of women citizens . . . as to the voice of men citizens. Neither chivalry or justice will compel this attention, but fear will. When men begin to *fear* the power of women, their voice and their influence, then we shall secure justice, but not before. When we demonstrate our ability to kill off, or seriously injure a candidate, or hurt a party, then we shall receive "respectful consideration." . . . We must be recognized as *aggressive*.[62]

After Robinson lost on Election Day, Gage wrote, "In this defeat, the women of New York have aided much. Three cheers for our success thus far!"[63] Several years later, Gage and Stanton wrote in the *History of Woman Suffrage* that "from this moment the leaders of the woman suffrage movement in New York regarded themselves as possessing some political influence" (*HWS* 3:423).[64]

The new governor, Alonzo B. Cornell, had promised to sign a school suffrage bill. In his inaugural address, he claimed, "Women are equally competent with men for this duty."[65] It is difficult to know how committed he was to women's rights because his papers include little about woman suffrage.[66] Alonzo's father was Ezra Cornell, who made a fortune in the telegraph industry and used it to start Cornell University in 1865. Ezra Cornell and his cofounder, Andrew Dickson White, intended to educate female students alongside men in the same courses of study. Among U.S. colleges, Cornell was far ahead of the times.[67]

A new bill allowing women to vote and run for school boards was guided through the legislature by Senator Edwin G. Halbert of Binghamton, Senator Loren B. Sessions of

61. *HWS* "Veto, Senate Bill No. 61, to Authorize Election of Women to School Offices," *Public Papers of Lucius Robinson, Governor of the State of New York. 1877* (Albany, NY: Argus, 1877), 42–43.

62. Matilda Joslyn Gage, "The Political Outlook," *NCBB*, September 1879 (emphasis in the original).

63. Matilda Joslyn Gage, "Robinson's Defeat," *NCBB*, November 1879.

64. *HWS* I believe the women had a minimal impact upon this election and the Republicans won because the Democratic vote was split, but that is much too long of a story to tell here.

65. *HWS* *Public Papers of Alonzo B. Cornell, Governor of the State of New York, 1880* (Albany, NY: E. H. Bender's Son, 1881), 7–8.

66. Alonzo B. Cornell Papers, 1830–1904, #773, Division of Rare and Manuscript Collections, Cornell University Library, Ithaca, NY. Examined by the author in August 2017.

67. Morris Bishop, *A History of Cornell* (Ithaca, NY: Cornell University Press, 1962).

Chautauqua, and Assemblyman James W. Husted of Westchester (*HWS* 3:424),[68] "who has always gallantly upheld the Woman's Rights cause."[69] The bill passed easily on February 11, 1880, and Governor Cornell signed it the next day.[70] On Friday, February 13, the Syracuse afternoon newspapers buried the news in a list of proceedings from Albany. That same day was the last day to register to vote for Syracuse's charter election on Tuesday, February 17. Despite the late notice, nineteen Syracuse women registered and thirteen voted. Gage noted in *History of Woman Suffrage* that her old friend Lucy Brand, a school principal, was the first woman to legally vote in New York state, casting her ballot "in silence and with a joyous solemnity well befitting the occasion" (*HWS* 3:424n).[71]

Women may have used some personal influence behind-the-scenes. When a second, expanded, woman suffrage bill, introduced by Assemblyman Charles S. Baker of Rochester, was passed on February 16,[72] a brief notice in an Albany newspaper read, "Among the ladies present on the floor of the House last evening were Mrs. Governor [Esther] Cornell and Mrs. C. S. [May] Baker."[73] Later that year, the *National Citizen* listed Mrs. Ezra [Mary Ann] Cornell as a member of the New York Woman Suffrage State Committee.[74] Using her name was premature, as a letter from Mrs. Cornell was read at the next state suffrage convention, saying that due to her age she could not work actively but that "my good wishes for your success in your undertaking are with you."[75]

Spring 1880: Difficulties for Women in New York's Cities
After Syracuse, the next women who could vote were those who lived in cities (except for New York City) that usually held their school board elections on the first Tuesday of March. Almost immediately, the poorly written law caused problems. It read: "No person shall be deemed to be ineligible to serve as any school officer, or to vote at any school meeting, by reason of sex, who has the other qualifications now required by law."[76] The simplicity of the law ignored the structure of the public school system in upstate New York—school meetings only took place in rural or town districts, while cities voted on school commissioners in general elections. A minor distinction, but it had ramifications for thousands of New York women. The New York State Constitution specifically required that voters be male; however, the constitution only covered general elections, not school meetings. Attorney

68. *HWSJournal of the Senate of the State of New York at Their One Hundred and Third Session* (Albany: Weed, Parsons, 1880), 82, 108, 110, 117; *Journal of the Assembly of the State of New York at their One Hundred and Third Session* (Albany, NY: Weed, Parsons, 1880), 210, 212.
69. "School Suffrage Established in New York," *Woman's Journal*, February 14, 1880.
70. *Laws of the State of New York passed at the One Hundred and Third Session of the Legislature*, vol. 1 (Albany, NY: Weed, Parsons, 1880), vi, 3.
71. "Women Voting," *Standard* (Syracuse, NY), February 17, 1880.
72. *Journal of the Assembly of the State of New York at Their One Hundred and Third Session*, 238.
73. "Capitol Notes," *Albany Evening Journal*, February 17, 1880.
74. "New York Woman Suffrage State Committee," *NCBB*, December 1880.
75. "Mrs. Ezra Cornell," *NCBB*, March 1881.
76. *Laws of the State of New York passed at the One Hundred and Third Session of the Legislature*, 1:10.

General Hamilton Ward Sr. rendered a decision stating that the new law was unconstitutional (*HWS* 3:425). In his opinion, which was not binding, women who lived in rural school districts could vote but women in cities could not.[77] Since the turnout of women voters in Syracuse had been small and did not affect the results, that election was still valid.[78]

Why question the constitutionality of this law when even the most conservative people agreed that women were well suited for managing the education of children? Because school suffrage was a step on the slippery slope of women's full voting equality. "I lament already the enactment of the school law, but may we be preserved from sustaining the shock, which will certainly follow, when our mothers and daughters take their standpoint with men upon all political matters," wrote a concerned citizen to the *Rochester Democrat and Chronicle*.[79] A few politicians did try to use whatever momentum school suffrage had created to expand women's voting rights, such as the aforementioned Assemblyman Baker, who tried to fix the mistakes of the school suffrage bill. His bill declared women eligible to serve in any capacity and vote for any school office in "towns, counties, cities and school districts of this State."[80] On February 19, Assemblyman Alexander Andrews of Binghamton introduced a bill permitting women to vote in presidential elections, which was a right that state legislatures could grant. Senator Halbert introduced an amendment to the New York Constitution securing the rights of women to vote upon all questions. But none of these bills would make it through the legislature.[81] The *Albany Evening Journal* advised women to change their slogan to "No Ballot, No Baby."[82]

The secretary of the NYSWSA, attorney James K. H. Willcox, quickly put together a legal brief that he submitted to the Judiciary Committee of the New York State Legislature on February 19. He then spoke at a public hearing before the governor and legislators, where he proved that the legislature had the power to create new voters and had done so in the past. Willcox advised women to register and vote in the upcoming elections in Cohoes, Ithaca, Newburg, Oswego, Rochester, Troy, Watertown, Flushing, and other cities. If election inspectors refused their votes, he would take the matter to court.[83] His efforts were needed in Albany, where women were refused registration in several wards of the city; however, in other wards women were duly registered, suggesting that election officials interpreted the new law for themselves.[84] A reporter was surprised that suffrage appealed to

---

77. "The New School Law," *Albany Evening Journal*, February 17, 1880.
78. "A Little Premature," *Syracuse Daily Journal*, February 17, 1880.
79. Citizen, "The Woman Question," *Rochester Democrat and Chronicle*, February 28, 1880.
80. *Journal of the Assembly of the State of New York at Their One Hundred and Third Session*, 238.
81. *HWS* 3:426. Volume 4 of the *History* tells us that until 1917, when full suffrage was finally granted, suffragists made almost yearly appeals to the New York legislature (*HWS* 4:853).
82. "Women and the Legislature," *Albany Evening Journal*, March 13, 1880.
83. "Wilcox [sic] Report," *Rochester Democrat and Chronicle*, February 20, 1880; *HWS* 3:426, 441–42, 959–61; "Work at Albany," *NCBB*, April 1880.
84. "Women Registering," *Albany Evening Journal*, March 23, 1880; *NCBB*, September 1880 (untitled thank-you to J.K.H. Willcox from the Albany County Woman Suffrage Society).

the conservative "Knickerbocker ladies, whose pride it is to honor and revere the traditions of the past two hundred years."[85] The largest registry was in the Fourteenth Ward, home of "the first families of this ancient bailiwick."[86] The new opportunity led to the creation of the Albany County Woman Suffrage Association. Out of the twenty-five to thirty women who cast a vote, the first was Kate Stoneman,[87] who in 1886 became New York's first female lawyer and lived to see U.S. women get complete suffrage in 1920.[88]

Albany is the only place, so far, where this historian has found a record of African-American women registering to vote in 1880, which caused "a stir."[89] A newspaper article, reprinted in the *National Citizen*, reported that six black women, led by Mrs. C. Mary Williams, a vice president of the County Woman's Suffrage Society, registered in the Eleventh Ward. The newspaper noted that Mrs. Williams "is a stately mulatto, of considerable education and refinement."[90] The women were followed by a crowd of white and black people who cheered when they were registered.[91]

The suffragists of Albany were braver than the suffragists of Rochester, who initially had been thrilled by the new law and had made plans to vote in their March election but didn't know what to do after learning the attorney general's decision.[92] Susan B. Anthony was out of town on speaking engagements at the time.[93] Without her strong leadership, the ladies met and decided that "there would be a lack of dignity in the women of Rochester to go and register when it was uncertain whether they could vote or not."[94] Amy Post and Mary S. Anthony, Susan's sister, both longtime suffragists with abolitionist backgrounds, tried to get the women to assert their rights, but they were outnumbered. The group passed a resolution that women would wait and prepare themselves for their rights and duties if the legislature changed the law.[95]

There was good news from the Hudson Valley. In Middletown in Orange County, Dr. Lydia Sayer Hasbrouck[96] had written to the local newspaper, saying the issue was not the constitutionality of the new law but how the people would improve their school system.[97] That spring, there were five openings on the nine-person board of education, whereas most years there were only three. The political parties in Middletown had long ago agreed not to

85. "Woman's Rights," *Evening Telegram*, March 27, 1880, reprinted in "Work at Albany," *NCBB*, April 1880.
86. Ibid.
87. "City Elections in this State," *New York Times*, April 14, 1880.
88. Katheryn D. Katz, "Kate Stoneman: A Pioneer for Equality," *Pioneering Women Lawyers: From Kate Stoneman to the Present*, ed. Patricia E. Salkin (American Bar Association, 2009).
89. "Registration in Albany," *Woman's Journal*, April 3, 1880.
90. "Woman's Rights," *Evening Telegram*, March 27, 1880, reprinted in "Work at Albany," *NCBB*, April 1880.
91. Ibid.
92. "To the Ladies of the Ninth Ward," *Rochester Democrat and Chronicle*, February 19, 1880; "Getting Ready to Vote," *Rochester Democrat and Chronicle*, February 20, 1880.
93. "The Ladies Who Vote," *Rochester Democrat and Chronicle*, February 15, 1880.
94. "Women's Work," *Rochester Democrat and Chronicle*, February 24, 1880.
95. Ibid. See also "Would-Be Voters," *Rochester Democrat and Chronicle*, February 29, 1880.
96. Hasbrouck is known as the editor of the *Sibyl*, a journal devoted to dress reform.
97. "How the Women Conquered," *New York Sun*, March 16, 1880.

let politics enter into school elections. However, the local Republican Party couldn't resist the opportunity to gain a majority on the board. They put forth a full slate of male candidates, which also prevented women from having any spots on the ticket. The suffragists, led by Hasbrouck, made their own ticket of five Republican women, which the Prohibition and Democratic Parties supported in retaliation, even creating a false list of possible male nominees and keeping the women's ticket secret.[98] Despite a "driving storm of snow and sleet,"[99] 114 women came out to vote, and all five women were elected with majorities greater than 114.[100] "The men elected us," said Mrs. Hasbrouck, "and it is certain we could not have been elected without the aid of the Democratic party."[101] One woman did not qualify for office; making the remaining four—Persis A. Marvin, Harriet B. Morgan, Mary A. Moore, and Lydia Sayer Hasbrouck—the first women elected to public office in New York State, that we know of.

Anthony and Gage looked forward to the summer of 1880 with hope that in this presidential election year, woman suffrage would receive some support from the Republican Party—a party that had given the vote to African-American men and was the more liberal of the two major parties. The Democratic Party was primarily the conservative party of the South and states' rights, although it was gaining strength in the North. The NWSA planned to rally hundreds of women to a great "mass meeting" in Chicago on the first day of the Republican National Convention on June 2. Then Gage and Anthony would travel for three weeks in the "terrible" summer heat to regional conventions throughout the Midwest, finishing at the Democratic National Convention in Cincinnati on June 22 (*HWS* 3:175–84).[102] Gage would even miss the high school graduation of her youngest daughter, Maud, in Syracuse.[103] "Susan B. Anthony, Matilda Joslyn Gage and their co-laborers in the cause of Woman Suffrage, are the best examples of dogged, downright, determined 'clear grit,' that the present age furnishes," said the *Chicago Evening Journal*.[104]

Despite a huge attendance of women at the mass meeting in Chicago and thousands of penny postcards sent by women across the country demanding suffrage, the Republicans refused to give seats to NWSA representatives or put any friendly words for women's rights in their platform, as they had done in the past. Belva Lockwood, the well-known

---

98. Ibid.

99. M., "Women Voting in New York State," *Woman's Journal*, March 20, 1880.

100. "Middletown Women School Trustees," *NCBB*, April 1880; "Middletown: A Retrospective of the Years," *Fifty Years: Commemorating the Fiftieth Anniversary of Middletown, New York as a City*, n.p., 1938, Middletown Thrall Library Digital Initiative, http://www.thrall.org/retro/1.htm.

101. "How the Women Conquered," *New York Sun*, March 16, 1880.

102. "National Woman Suffrage Convention," *Fayetteville (NY) Weekly Recorder*, June 10, 1880; "The National Woman Suffrage Association and the National Republican Nominating Convention," *NCBB*, June 1880; "Chicago Mass Meeting, *NCBB*, June 1880; "Woman Suffrage among the Greenbackers," *NCBB*, June 1880; "Grand Rapids Convention," *NCBB*, June 1880; "Woman and the Democratic Nominating Convention," *NCBB*, June 1880; "Dives and Lazarus," *NCBB*, June 1880; "The Woman Suffragists at Cincinnati," *Fayetteville (NY) Weekly Recorder*, July 1, 1880. See also Harper, *The Life and Work of Susan B. Anthony*, 2:517–20.

103. *Fayetteville Weekly Recorder*, June 17 and June 24, 1880.

104. "Editorial Notes," *NCBB*, May 1880.

Washington, D.C. attorney who, just a year earlier, had become the first woman member of the U.S. Supreme Court bar,[105] managed to get only ten minutes for Susan B. Anthony to speak in front of a subcommittee. The previous presidential election in 1876 had been excruciatingly close and the Republican Party couldn't risk associating with a radical reform. Gage was furious and expressed herself in the *National Citizen and Ballot Box*. The party that she and reformers had identified with since its start, the party of Lincoln that had freed the slaves, now "put itself upon record as woman's foe . . . living only for spoils and plunder. Its work is done, its hour is past, it is a dead party, and the more quickly it is buried the better for progress and humanity."[106] (Having thus burned her bridge to the Republican Party, in 1884 Gage supported the National Equal Rights Party and Lockwood's candidacy for president.[107])

The Democrats treated the suffragists much better, as several members of the platform committee supported women's rights, but decided there could be no plank due to "the objection of the extreme Southern element which feared the political recognition of negro women of the South."[108] "We cannot make either of the parties . . . believe recognition of political equality for women will help them to votes," Anthony wrote to a friend. "On the other hand all are afraid such recognition would lose them votes."[109] Rubbing salt into the wound, Gage came home to criticism from Republican women—fellow suffragists—for deserting their party and going to the Democrats. She responded:

> From men, we expect abuse and misrepresentation, but not from women. The woman who believes in herself, believes also in freedom for her sex. . . . When woman loves freedom for freedom's sake, she will not ask the name of that party which secures it to her.[110]

After the disappointing summer, suffragists needed a win. Anticipating the fall town/rural elections, the NYSWSA faced the challenge of informing tens of thousands of women scattered across back roads that they were eligible to vote. There were eleven thousand country school districts holding elections in October, representing about half of the state's one million children who attended public schools.[111] School districts typically elected one or two trustees to the school board plus a clerk, librarian, and tax collector. There were usually

---

105. Jill Norgren, *Belva Lockwood: The Woman Who Would Be President* (New York: New York University Press, 2007), 80–83, 107.
106. "The National Woman Suffrage Association and the National Republican Nominating Convention," *NCBB*, June 1880.
107. Norgren, *Belva Lockwood*, 137.
108. "Woman and the Democratic Nominating Convention," *NCBB*, June 1880.
109. Susan B. Anthony to Frederic A. Hinckley, July 23, 1880, *Selected Papers of Elizabeth Cady Stanton and Susan B. Anthony*, 547 (emphasis in the original).
110. Matilda Joslyn Gage, "Professed Friends," *NCBB*, August 1880.
111. Neil Gilmour, *Twenty-Seventh Annual Report of the Superintendent of Public Instruction of the State of New York* (Albany, NY: Weed, Parsons, 1881), 5, 7.

five trustees on a board; their terms were rotated so that the board was not elected all at once. Some elections would be held on October 12, the same day as the school meeting; others would be held the next day, as was the case in Fayetteville.

The president of the NYSWSA in 1880, Lillie Devereux Blake, canvassed the area surrounding New York City and the lower Hudson River Valley. Helen M. Slocum, chair of the State Executive Committee, was in charge of Long Island and counties east of the Hudson; James Willcox worked Ulster and Dutchess Counties, while Susan B. Anthony spoke in nine counties in central and western New York.[112] The NYSWSA sent out an appeal in the *National Citizen* and local newspapers across the state for suffragists to tell other women about the school vote, hold meetings to discuss the issue, write letters, sponsor speakers, do whatever they could to get the word out.[113] Finding women to run for office was a welcome plus. Blake and Gage stressed the importance of this vote beyond the election, saying that women's presence "will do much to convince the public of the importance of doing away with this unjust and unconstitutional disfranchisement. Show that you can value and use political freedom, and so help New York lead the world to full liberty and civilization."[114]

The situation looked bad at the end of September, just two weeks before the election, despite encouraging news from Long Island, where women voted in August, and Binghamton, where hundreds of women voted for school commissioners on September 21.[115] The state superintendent of schools, Neil Gilmour, had issued a circular, saying that women had to own large amounts of taxable property in order to vote in school elections. The penalty for voting unlawfully was "not less than six months' imprisonment" (*HWS* 3:428). Gage was outraged by what she saw as illegal intimidation, calling it "Ku-Klux-ism" and "treason of the very worst character."[116] The NYSWSA immediately issued its own circular, telling women about the legal qualifications for school voters, as Gage had already done in the *National Citizen*.[117] But the damage was done. In Knowersville (now Altamont, near Albany), a school trustee went through the village, reading Gilmour's circular to women to frighten them from voting. At Fulton (Oswego County), Lowville (Lewis County), Saratoga Springs, and even in Fayetteville, there was much talk of Gilmour's circular.[118] Gage knew that women were going to be challenged at the polling places and gave them a ready answer: "If her vote is challenged, she has simply to swear it in, and under section 13 of title vii, of the general school laws, if she does so her vote must be received."[119] To be fair to

112. "School Suffrage Campaign in New York," *Woman's Journal*, September 4, 1880.
113. "School Suffrage Letters," *NCBB*, October 1880.
114. "Address of the New York State Woman Suffrage Association," *NCBB*, August 1880.
115. Matilda Joslyn Gage, "Woman's School Suffrage," *Fayetteville Weekly Recorder*, September 30, 1880.
116. "Intimidation of New York Women," *NCBB*, October 1880. Of course, this intimidation was *not* equivalent to that of the Ku Klux Klan, but this is an example of the hyperbole that Gage, Stanton and Anthony used in their rhetoric.
117. "Address of the New York State Woman Suffrage Association," *NCBB*, August 1880.
118. "Intimidation of Voters Punishable by United States Laws," *NCBB*, November 1880.
119. "Address of the New York State Woman Suffrage Association," *NCBB*, August 1880.

Gilmour, he did try to explain his actions in the next year's annual report, saying that he was simply trying to hold women to the same laws as men, which were much more complex than the legislature had realized.[120] "Not claiming to be infallible," Gilmour decided to accept the proceedings of any school meeting where women voted in 1880. In fact, the following year, he said, "There are already good results from this law."[121] Gilmour had a much bigger problem on his hands than women voting, having spent the summer of 1880 in a very long and bitter dispute with the Cortland Normal School.[122]

On October 1, Gage called a meeting of women in the parlors of the Fayetteville Baptist Church, near the schoolhouse where the election would take place.[123] Thirty women enthusiastically talked for two and a half hours. They decided to canvass the village door-to-door to inform the two thousand residents of the new law and assure them of its legality. But not all women could walk to the polling place. There were several elderly widows living along the steep Genesee Street hill—their beautiful Greek Revival and Italianate homes still grace the National Historic District neighborhood. These women, whose fortunes had been made in the heyday of the Erie Canal, had been paying taxes for years and some relished the idea of voting. The suffragists worked out a system to transport them to the polls. Nine women volunteered their horses and carriages, including a special "low carriage" that made stepping in and out easier.[124]

The group met again on October 9 to discuss strategy. Deciding to be cautious, they asked for one woman to be put on the men's ticket. They made an excellent choice in Frances Carr, a well-respected woman who was married to an attorney, had an eight-year-old daughter, and was head of the Baptist Church Sunday School, the largest in Onondaga County.[125] There was no need to campaign—in a community of this size, everyone knew everybody else. Throughout Fayetteville, men were talking about Edward Gaynor as a possible candidate. He was an Irish immigrant[126] who had worked his way up to co-owner of the Bangs & Gaynor Lime and Plaster Works, which shipped cement for construction across the state via the Erie Canal.[127] Gaynor was forced to issue a circular saying that he

120. Neil Gilmour, *Twenty-Seventh Annual Report of the Superintendent of Public Instruction of the State of New York*, 25–28.

121. Neil Gilmour, *Twenty-Eighth Annual Report of the Superintendent of Public Instruction of the State of New York* (Albany, NY: Weed, Parsons, 1882), 27.

122. Gilmour, *Twenty-Ninth Annual Report of the Superintendent of Public Instruction*, 29–47; Paula Baker, *The Moral Framework of Public Life: Gender, Politics, and the State in Rural New York, 1870–1930* (New York: Oxford University Press, 1991), 113–18.

123. M. J. Gage, "To Women Voters," *Fayetteville Weekly Recorder*, September 30, 1880.

124. "School Officers," *Fayetteville Weekly Recorder*, October 21, 1880; "School Suffrage in Fayetteville," *NCBB*, October 1880.

125. Ann L. Moore, "Frances P. Carr," *People and Places: Fayetteville, Manlius, Minoa, and Neighbors* (Manlius, NY: Manlius Historical Society, 2002), 3:151–56.

126. 1880 United States Federal Census, State of New York, County of Onondaga, Town of Manlius, Enumeration District #181, p. 25, enumerated on June 10, 1880, accessed August 30, 2005, Ancestry.com.

127. Walter Pendergrast Jr., "Industries," *People and Places: Fayetteville, Manlius, Minoa, and Neighbors* (Manlius, NY: Manlius Historical Society, 1986), 1: 38, 84–87. Bangs & Gaynor advertised in the *National Citizen and Ballot Box*, a vital source of income for Gage.

was not interested in being a school trustee. He wrote, "I understand that the women of this School District actually pay more than half the taxes, and they are justly entitled to at least one member of the Board of Trustees, for which they ask."[128]

On October 12, the usual men and about fifty women gathered at the schoolhouse at 7 p.m. to hold a nominating caucus, a procedure required by law. They would nominate one trustee for the school board as well as a clerk, tax collector, and librarian. A woman stood up and nominated Frances Carr for trustee. Suddenly the moderator adjourned the meeting, with the men abruptly leaving and giving no indication of their candidates. As the women wondered what was going on, Gage invited them to her nearby home to discuss the situation.[129] The election tickets with the names of the nominees had to be printed that night, so they decided to print their own tickets with Frances Carr for trustee, leaving the other positions blank. Since the vote didn't start until noon, there would be time in the morning to find more nominees.[130]

The next morning, the men's faction, led by the incumbent male trustee, presented an all-male ticket. Gage was probably not surprised at the underhandedness—after all, a similar scenario had occurred in Middletown. The Fayetteville women responded the same way as the women of Middletown. They decided to write in the name of Gage's daughter, Helen Leslie Gage, for clerk and a young schoolteacher, Frances E. Ecker, for librarian. Later in the day, Mary M. Mathews agreed to run for tax collector and the suffragists had an all-female ticket.[131]

Fayetteville was not the only place where women faced opposition to their new civic duty. In the weeks to come, Gage would receive letter after letter, detailing the intimidation, and in some cases, violence, that women faced from election officials, family members, and the influential men in their small communities.[132] At Port Jervis, Orange County, women were kept from getting to the ballot box, and those who did had their votes challenged: "the election [was] held in a small room crowded with men, who amused themselves passing remarks about the ladies until the police were called in."[133] Lillie Devereux Blake reported that in several districts "certain men went early and locked the doors, filling the room with smoke and even put tobacco on the stoves to make it as disagreeable for the women as possible" (HWS 3:223). In Long Island City (now part of Queens), men threw stones in the street at Emma Gates Conkling, the suffragist who was rallying new voters. From Albany, Gage received reports of women being threatened with violence or expulsion from their homes by their husbands if they dared vote. In many areas, election inspectors refused to

128. "Personalities," Fayetteville Weekly Recorder, October 21, 1880.
129. 1874 Map of Fayetteville, New York, on the Fayetteville Free Library website, http://www.fayetteville freelibrary.org/images/pdfs/fymap3.pdf. The Gage Home is now a museum, the Matilda Joslyn Gage Center for Social Justice Dialogue, http://www.matildajoslyngage.org.
130. "School Election in Fayetteville," Fayetteville Weekly Recorder, October 21, 1880.
131. Ibid.
132. Gage, "Woman School Voting," Fayetteville Weekly Recorder, October 28, 1880.
133. Ibid.

register qualified women or take their votes (*HWS* 3:427–30). All over New York State, men insulted, ridiculed, shunned, and threatened women with arrest in their communities.

If the most common response to the idea of woman suffrage was "women don't want to vote," then the second was "when women ask for the vote they will get it." Men's reaction to school suffrage proved that they would never willingly hand over full voting rights. Gage stated it bluntly, "As a whole, men are not willing women should govern themselves."[134] Given the obvious objection by many men, would women come out to vote? Gage had lived in her adopted hometown of Fayetteville for twenty-six years; if she couldn't get her neighbors to vote, how would she convince women across the country to fight for their rights?

When Gage arrived at the schoolhouse on the morning of October 13, the election inspectors refused to let her have a seat at the inspection table so she could monitor the election. She stood her ground until they let her assume her post. Several women were there to volunteer—handing out ballots, encouraging the timid, and helping the new voters with the process. Everyone was bustling with excitement. When the polls opened, carriages started arriving as planned, each from the section of the village assigned to them. One of the ladies driving a carriage was married to a candidate on the male ticket."[135] At first the inspectors challenged every woman's vote, but with Gage's encouragement and strength each woman swore in her vote, and eventually the inspectors gave up. Gage greeted many elderly women who came on crutches and canes to vote. One woman, "an invalid, had not been upon the main street of the village in ten years," but she made it to the polls, "eager to use her one chance of self-government before she died."[136] The wealthiest lady in town came in to vote and told Gage, "I feel as if I was somebody now."[137] One man, whose wife was crossing the street to the schoolhouse, yelled to her, "Don't make a fool of yourself, there are fools enough over there already," but she ignored him and cast her vote.[138]

As the afternoon wore on and women kept coming to cast their historic first ballot, Gage's mood turned from anxious to ecstatic. Not only were woman suffragists voting as expected, so were "ladies who had stood on the woman suffrage fence" and "those who apparently were entirely upon the other side."[139] By 4 p.m., when the polls closed, 102 women had voted and the 3 women on their original ticket had won by clear majorities. Frances Carr, for trustee of the school board, received 189 votes out of 252 total votes. If all of the women present voted for Carr, that meant at least 67 men also voted for her, more than the 63 votes that her opponent received. Gage's daughter, Helen Leslie, won the clerk position, 161 to 66. Frances Ecker earned 162 votes for librarian to the male ticket's 63. Only Mary

---

134. Gage, "Woman School Voting," *FayettevilleWeekly Recorder*, October 28, 1880.
135. Gage, "School Election in Fayetteville," *FayettevilleWeekly Recorder*, October 21, 1880.
136. Gage, "School Suffrage in Fayetteville," *NCBB*, October 1880.
137. Ibid.
138. Ibid.
139. Ibid.

Matthews, whose name had been added late to the ticket, lost to incumbent Ira Morey for tax collector.[140]

Despite hateful and illegal intimidation, courageous women voted all over New York State in 1880. The *History of Woman Suffrage* commented, "The wonder is that against such a pressure so many women did vote after all" (*HWS*3:427). Women voted in Jamestown, Chautauqua County;[141] Penn Yan, Yates County; and Easton, Washington County. Women voted in the little hamlets of Carpenter's Point, Orange County, and Coffin's Summit, near Poughkeepsie, Dutchess County.[142] In Perry, Wyoming County, two women were elected to the board of education; two women were also elected as trustees in Nunda, Livingston County. Three women were elected in Johnsonville, Rensselaer County. In Wellsville, Allegany County, sixty women voted and two women were elected trustees. At East Chatham, Columbia County, and at Naples and Honeoye, Ontario County, women were elected. In Saratoga Springs, ladies ran eight carriages to bring in voters and elected three prominent women to the board of education. Women voted in West New Brighton and Port Richmond, Staten Island; Flushing, Queens County; Mt. Morris, Livingston County; Shelter Island and Patchogue, Suffolk County; Glen's Falls, Warren County; Belmont, Allegany County; Sing Sing (now Ossining), Peekskill, Yonkers, and Mount Vernon, Westchester County; Spring Valley and Haverstraw, Rockland County; Stamford, Delaware County; Connersville, Albany County; Middleport and Lockport, Niagara County. In central New York, women voted in Fulton, Oswego County; Rome, Oneida County; Hartsville (now Mycenae), Manlius, Skaneateles, and Baldwinsville in Onondaga County. Two hundred women voted in Geddes near Syracuse.[143] A woman from Oneida wrote that the twenty-seven women who voted were treated so courteously that "it was not half so trying as wearing a new hat to church the first time."[144] Emily Howland wrote from Cayuga County that women voted and were elected in Sherwood, Sempronius, Cayuga Bridge, Venice Center, and Poplar Ridge.[145] Women voted in one-half of the sixty counties of New York, and many were elected to school boards.[146]

Legacies

The first women's vote in New York State was a success, due to the efforts of Gage and her friends in the cause. Together, they proved that women did want to vote and would come out to vote despite the obstacles opponents threw in their path. The school elections were a step forward that encouraged suffragists to continue the struggle. Gage called the day of the

---

140. "School Officers," *Fayetteville Weekly Recorder*, October 21, 1880.
141. "School Suffrage in Chautauqua Co.," *Woman's Journal*, October 30, 1880.
142. Lucy Stone, "Women Voters in New York," *Woman's Journal*, November 20, 1880.
143. Gage, "Woman School Voting," *Fayetteville Weekly Recorder*, October 28, 1880.
144. C.M.F., "School Suffrage at Oneida," *Woman's Journal*, December 11, 1880.
145. "E. Howland, "School Suffrage in New York," *Woman's Journal*, December 18, 1880.
146. "Women Voters of New York," *NCBB*, November 1880.

Fayetteville election "the most gratifying day of my life."[147] The local newspaper said that she was "the happiest woman in America."[148]

It's satisfying to know that women dared to vote in 1880, but was school suffrage a long-term success in New York? There is much more to research, but we can get some tentative answers from work that has already been done. Historian Paula Baker takes a negative view. She discusses how school suffrage was used in rural areas in New York State in the 1890s: "Even suffragists and temperance activists had trouble mustering interest in school district elections"[149] because woman suffrage "seemed too drastic a change."[150] Likewise, Eleanor Flexner believes that partial suffrage supported the argument that women were not interested in voting, because most locales had low turnout.[151]

A few recent works are more positive. While noting the difficulties of looking at local suffrage (because of the wide range of activities and results), Lisa Tetrault decided that partial suffrage was "an important strategy"[152] and in reference to school suffrage, "its success was unmistakable."[153] Political expert Michael C. Pisapia believes that school suffrage helped prop open the door to full suffrage. He demonstrates how public education was "the original policy field through which American women became empowered as voters and political officials."[154] Gaylynn Welch's dissertation contains a section detailing the New York school elections of 1880. She believes it was crucial that women demonstrated their willingness to vote, that the topic of school suffrage is "obviously very important" and "has not received the attention it deserves from historians of the woman suffrage movement."[155]

More research is needed to see if local efforts influenced attitudes about women voting on other matters or if women serving on school boards impacted education. A recent paper published by the National Bureau of Economic Research concludes that full suffrage in 1920 "increased local education expenditures by 9 percent on average and corresponded with a rise in school enrollment," especially in southern areas with African-American residents.[156]

Historian Ellen Carol DuBois explains that we study the woman suffrage movement "to see how history creates and restrains the possibilities for people to intervene deliberately

147. Gage, "School Suffrage in Fayetteville," NCBB, October 1880.
148. "Personalities," Fayetteville Weekly Recorder, October 21, 1880.
149. Baker, The Moral Framework of Public Life, 75.
150. Ibid., 78.
151. Eleanor Flexner, A Century of Struggle: The Woman's Rights Movement in the United States (New York: Atheneum, 1974), 177.
152. Tetrault, The Myth of Seneca Falls, 84.
153. Ibid., 86.
154. Michael Callaghan Pisapia, "Public Education and the Role of Women in American Political Development, 1852–1979" (PhD diss., University of Wisconsin–Madison, 2010), 162.
155. Gaylynn Welch, "Local and National Forces Shaping the American Woman Suffrage Movement 1870–1890" (PhD diss., Binghamton University, 2009), 16.
156. Alia Wong, "How Women's Suffrage Improved Education for a Whole Generation of Children," The Atlantic, August 28, 2018, https://www.theatlantic.com/education/archive/2018/08/womens-suffrage -educational-improvement/568726/.

in it and change its course."[157] In other words, we study the past to find out how we can change our future, just as Gage, Stanton, and Anthony did when they produced *The History of Woman Suffrage*. In the nineteenth century, female citizens were slowly waking up to their political power and, for many, school suffrage was the first small step in using that power. Since long before suffrage was granted, girls and women have realized that voting is just one part of being active in their government and that paying attention, seeking information, discerning the truth, expressing their opinion, protesting wrong, and running for office are also important ways to use political power in a democracy. Every successive step that women have taken to use their power has required more courage, more organization, more education, and more encouragement from a long line of inspirational, strong leaders. After a century of progress, do the men in high offices fear the voices and influence of women? Maybe, maybe not—but the world has not yet seen the full strength of women's power.

---

157. Ellen Carol DuBois, *Woman Suffrage and Women's Rights* (New York: New York University Press, 1998), 68.

Suffrage's Second Act
Women in the New York State Legislature, 1919–1930

Laurie Kozakiewicz

We know much more about the struggle to win the vote than we do about those who first ran for and won elective office in New York. This essay assesses the impact of the first women in the New York State Legislature after suffrage. In the "long decade" of the 1920s (1919–30), five women won seats, all in the Assembly: Ida B. Sammis (R) 1919–20, Mary Lilly (D) 1919–20; Elizabeth Gillette (D) 1920–21, Marguerite Smith (R) 1920–22; and Rhoda Fox Graves (R) 1924–32. Graves would break the invisible barrier of the Senate, becoming the first woman elected there in 1934 and remaining until her retirement in 1947. Their experiences show us what it was like for the first cohort of women who entered the world of New York State electoral politics. Their political careers illuminate the new challenges women faced as they confronted a masculine political culture and parties reluctant to share power with women. Sammis, Lilly, Gillette, Smith, and Graves deserve recognition as pioneers in the second act of women's suffrage in New York.

Political and Cultural Dynamics
The main focus of this essay is on the experiences of the women as they became politicians—in particular how they had to learn how to work effectively within parties and with political leaders. Women had to learn how to campaign and govern at an accelerated pace. Until 1938 legislative terms were for one year, not two as they are now, so new legislators had a single session in which to seek reelection. Sessions in the 1920s were also shorter, running from January through April and not through the end of June as they do now.

Once elected, what was reasonable to expect in terms of achievements? Here normal political considerations about which party held power and whether each woman had the support of the leadership mattered. At the same time, the women politicians also contended with cultural expectations about what was or was not acceptable behavior for female office holders. Finally, these women struggled with how to represent women's interests given that so few women were elected to office during this period and that the interests of the state were anything but homogeneous. In the introduction to their 2001 book, *New York Politics:*

A Tale of Two States, Edward Schneier and John Murtaugh make the case that "social and economic cleavages in New York reinforce and confound each other." They see New York divided socially and politically.[1] They argue that the state's partisan, economic, and political divides "are so extraordinarily dualistic as to put traditional theories of government . . . to the test."[2] Parts of New York rank among the richest areas in the country and have a record of supporting policy innovations to expand the state's involvement in overall economic and urban development. But its status as one of the most urbanized states in the union over-shadows how thinly populated much of the state is. More than 50,000 people live within one square mile in Manhattan; yet there are just 3.1 per square mile in Hamilton County, an hour outside the city of Albany. While the urban areas of the state are ethnically and racially diverse, rural demographics show a more homogeneous pattern.[3] Those rural areas have historically taken a more reserved attitude toward an expansive state presence.[4] Democrats and Republicans each have their "centers of gravity" within the state: downstate and urban for the Democrats, and upstate and rural for the Republicans.[5] Women in politics have been no less affected by the existence of such differences than have men. Even when big issues like suffrage seemed unifying, women's attitudes and behaviors differed by party affiliation, region, socioeconomic background, and the gendered boundaries of society.[6] Additionally, whether women voted in larger or smaller numbers than expected reflected residual local sentiment on the suffrage question itself.[7]

The political tumult of the 1920s resulted in redrawing of boundaries regarding male and female roles in the political arena. Women gained access to new areas, like holding office and party appointments. However, in every case except one of those analyzed in this essay, male party leaders determined the limits of those opportunities.[8] The parties did not set women candidates up to fail per se, but their small numbers meant these women effected only incremental changes in how the parties and legislatures operated. Their voices on certain issues may not have been as strong as they would have liked, but their greatest achievement was their persistence in normalizing women as political actors, no small feat given that these female novices had to undertake and complete their political education on

---

1. Edward Schneier and John Murtaugh, *New York Politics: A Tale of Two States* (New York: M. E. Scharpe, 2001), xiii.

2. Ibid.

3. Schneier and Murtaugh, *New York Politics*, x, 20.

4. Paula Baker, "The Gilded Age," in *The Empire State: A History of New York*, ed. Milton Klein (Ithaca, NY: Cornell University Press, 2001), 474. Rural resistance to state-mandated school consolidation lasted into the 1930s. Paula Baker, in *The Moral Framework of Public Life: Gender, Politics, and the State in Rural New York 1870–1930* (New York: Oxford University Press, 1991) shows the slow pace of rural New York's shift to supporting active state intervention.

5. Schneier and Murtaugh, *New York Politics*, 21.

6. Susan Goodier and Karen Pastorello, *Women Will Vote: Winning Suffrage in New York State* (Ithaca, NY: Cornell University Press, 2017), 3.

7. Kristi Anderson, *After Suffrage: Women in Partisan and Electoral Politics Before the New Deal* (Chicago: University of Chicago Press, 1996), 68.

8. Anderson, *After Suffrage*, 2, 15, 150.

an accelerated schedule. Until now women's relationship to party politics and campaigning had been auxiliary. Not until the 1910s did the two main parties heavily utilize women during campaign seasons in support of male candidates. They had no experience as candidates or elected officials themselves. Nor did women necessarily appreciate the behaviors expected of elected officials, especially in terms of party responsibilities. Some scholars see women's slow progress at increasing their numbers in elected offices in this period as stemming from their lack of experience in both preparing to run and then negotiating the political environment once elected.[9] Still, it was significant that women elected officials "ceased to be a rarity" in the eyes of the public.[10]

An important impediment to knowing more about these women is the extremely thin paper trail. Only Graves amassed records of her public life, and only recently have they been identified and given over to the University at Albany M. E. Grenander Department of Special Collections and Archives, where the staff is working to preserve and inventory them.[11] There are no records of debates on legislation held in the Assembly chamber. There are no "legislative bill jackets" for the first years when women served. (Jackets were and are collections of supplementary material that are forwarded with passed legislation to the governor to provide background information on the bill.) We are left mostly with what has been said about the women in the media, the biographical information they submitted on themselves to the annual legislative summary, *The New York Red Book*, lists of the laws they introduced, and a few mentions in other sources. When woven with scholarship that takes a broad look at women entering politics immediately after suffrage and of women in individual state legislatures in this period, these sources allow us to gain an understanding of early New York women legislators' histories.[12]

Sometimes the absence of something can be meaningful in and of itself. In his book *Silencing the Past: Power and the Production of History*, Michel-Rolph Trouillot argues that certain voices have been silenced and thus marginalized at key points in the process of creating the historical narrative.[13] The stories of these early legislators illustrate how such "silences" have existed around what we know about women as politicians and how important it is to reorient the view of the past to include them in the narrative. The lack of archival

9. Kathleen Dolan and Lynne E. Ford, "Are All Women State Legislators Alike?" in *Women and Elective Office: Past, Present, and Future*, ed. Sue Thomas and Clyde Wilcox (New York: Oxford University Press, 1998): 75.

10. Stanley Lemons, *The Woman Citizen* (Urbana: University of Illinois Press, 1973), 102–4.

11. In the summer of 2016 I found the papers in the unventilated attic of the Gouvernour Museum in that town. They were lying on shelves, some in and some out of molding boxes, none labeled. I spent time looking through them there, but the collection will not be ready for scholarly research until after 2020.

12. In addition, these five women's experiences are part of a larger research project, a New York State–centered history of women legislators. My study looks at ninety women over a seventy-three-year period. The primary source material from and about women legislators improves markedly with time. The observations in this essay are thus based on the historical record about these specific women, albeit limited, compared with and augmented by these other sources.

13. Michel-Rolph Trouillot, *Silencing the Past: Power and the Production of History* (Boston: Beacon Press, 2015), 26, 46, 48–49.

Rhoda Fox Graves, 1932. (COURTESY OF THE AUTHOR'S PERSONAL COLLECTION)

materials on these early legislators may say something about how hard it was for political women to find their own voice in the decade after suffrage. Graves is the only woman who saved her records and the only one of the five to actively seek the nomination of her party, both for her campaign for the Assembly and, later, the Senate. This lack of attention to self may be a social element at work related to broader cultural expectations during a time when the presumed selfless nature of women made them uncomfortable with promoting their own political profiles. Also, political leaders looked for women who were not potential challengers to their control of party. Scholars generally agree that politicians may have initially sought out higher profile women from the suffrage movement as candidates but rapidly shifted over to what one historian has called "more docile party functionaries."[14] In this they may have paralleled the career trajectory of many of their male colleagues who also left very thin documentary records. The essence of being a functionary is that you do not cast too large a shadow of your own. Party leaders feared the potential power of a women's bloc to challenge their authority; an organized cohort of women outside party control might create women candidates who would prioritize issues over loyalty. Historian Anna Harvey has looked at New York Democratic and Republican Party behavior in the 1920s and found that the parties diffused the threat by aggressively bringing the woman voter into the existing system where the female leadership would be chosen by the party organizations.[15] Contemporary social scientist and activist Sophonisba Breckinridge

---

14. Anna Harvey, *Votes without Leverage* (Cambridge: Cambridge University Press, 1998), 66. See also Jo Freeman, *A Room at a Time: How Women Entered Party Politics* (Lanham, MD: Rowman and Littlefield, 2000), 163.
15. Harvey, *Votes without Leverage*, 155, 160.

connected those dots when she offered her opinion about why women seemed to have such limited success in gaining political power in the 1920s: "If, however, the voice of women in the parties is still perhaps faint, it should never be forgotten that many, if not most, men voters dwell likewise in dim remoteness from the center of party control. The women of the parties are not solitary in their isolation."[16]

The Republican Party in New York had one early encounter with a major suffrage figure that appears to have "soured" party leaders on cultivating better known women candidates. Mary Garrett Hay was head of New York City's Woman Suffrage Party and a past president of the New York State Federation of Women's Clubs.[17] Republican leaders eager to reach newly enfranchised women appointed Hay to the Republican State Executive Committee and offered her the chairmanship of the platform committee at the state convention in 1918.[18] At the national level, Hay became the treasurer of the Republican Woman's National Executive Committee, a campaign organization set up by the Republican National Committee to court the women's vote. A *New York Sun* piece from 1919 reported that thousands of women throughout the United States affectionately referred to Hay as "the big boss" in recognition of her work for women's causes.[19] It would appear Republican leaders were making the right choice by elevating Hay within the party. The problem was that Hay either did not understand the partisan nature of these commitments or chose to reject them. Partisanship could not simply be suspended, as Hay thought it should be, when a stand on a particular issue seemed more compelling than party loyalty.[20] In 1920 when Republican leaders in New York called for support of U.S. Senator James Wadsworth's reelection, Hay vigorously objected and pledged to campaign against him. Wadsworth had opposed woman suffrage; his wife, Alice Hay Wadsworth, had led the National Association Opposed to Women's Suffrage. It perplexed Hay that other party members, including many women, criticized her lack of partisanship and cheered when she was removed from party posts following Wadsworth's successful reelection. "Being a new voter," Hay commented to the *Chicago News*, "I cannot see how my opposition to the candidacy or election of a US Senator can have anything to do with being a delegate to the Republican National Convention [a position she had expected to be given but was not]."[21] Hay was an example of the downside of a nonpartisan tradition that scholars Linda Witt, Karen Paget, and Glenna

16. Sophonisba Breckinridge, *Women in the Twentieth Century: A Study of Their Political, Social, and Economic Activities* (New York: McGraw-Hill, 1933), 291.

17. Information on Hay comes from a biography from around 1920 found in the Mary Garrett Hay scrapbook, New York Public Library, New York City (NYPL). For a full discussion of Hay's short career as a Republican politician, see Elisabeth I. Perry, "Defying the Party Whip Mary Garrett Hay and the Republican Party, 1917–20," in *We Have Come to Stay* (Albuquerque: University of New Mexico Press, 1997), 97–107.

18. *New York Times*, July 19, 1918, 6. Hay was listed as a "compromise" candidate between rival factions.

19. *New York Evening Sun*, February 21, 1919, Mary Garrett Hay scrapbook, NYPL.

20. "Republican Club Resolution Calls Voters' League Non-American," *New York Times*, April 1919, 5. Republican women attacked the New York State League of Women Voters' nonpartisan focus. Hay's service as president of the organization is another indication of her nonpartisan frame of reference.

21. *Chicago News*, June 1920, Mary Garrett Hay scrapbook, NYPL.

Matthews say "lacked recognition of the importance of power."[22] The women who became active in politics at this time had their formative experiences in a distinctively female culture that prioritized character and virtue over power as its own goal. Women had to overcome their reluctance to see themselves as political figures.[23] Women thus faced a unique cultural hurdle associated with their politicization.

Hay's experience illustrates one facet of the challenges that all women faced as they entered politics. Women like Sammis, Lilly, Gillette, Smith, and Graves had to find their way within a political world created by, and embodying, the characteristics of the men who controlled it. Partisanship was shorthand for a political culture and operating system that demanded loyalty of the members. Nineteenth-century politics were built around validation of manhood through party rituals and shows of support, which allowed partisanship to be seen as a quintessentially masculine attribute.[24] But now women were expected to be partisan as well.

At the same time they were to embrace partisanship, these women politicians were judged by a set of gendered cultural standards that expected women to embody qualities associated specifically with womanhood. While men easily equated public activism with enrolling in a political party and declaring one's partisanship, women saw activism as a commitment to a vision of an improved, more moral society made possible through personal and group action. Women's embrace of partisan politics meant they had to conquer not only male skepticism about their suitability for politics but also women's distrust of behaviors that seemed to contradict deeply held ideas about womanhood. It was those ideas and not partisan allegiance that had initially engaged women on public issues. Historian Paula Baker has shown that women in the nineteenth century learned to wield their motherhood as a powerful tool. At first, it was used to justify women's private organizations providing social services that existing governments were not prepared to offer. Later, women used maternal arguments to pressure governments to assume those responsibilities.[25] Political Scientist Theda Skocpol goes further, suggesting women's organizations came tantalizingly close to achieving something like a maternalist welfare state in the Progressive Era.[26]

---

22. Linda Witt, Karen Paget, and Glenna Matthews, *Running as a Woman: Gender and Power in American Politics* (New York: Free Press, 1994): 30.
23. Anderson, *After Suffrage*, 27, 163.
24. The arguments and sources presented in this section on partisanship are taken from Lauren Kozakiewicz, "Political Episodes 1890–1960: Three Republican Women in Twentieth Century New York State Politics" (Ph.D. diss., University at Albany, 2006), chaps 1 and 2. In addition, see Richard McCormick, *The Party Period and Public Policy* (New York: Oxford University Press, 1986), 162–64, 201–4; and Michael McGerr, *The Decline of Popular Politics: The North, 1865–1928* (Oxford: Oxford University Press, 1986), 14.
25. Paula Baker, "Domestication of Politics," 629–30. Baker argues that government in the nineteenth century largely relinquished economic regulation to business and the courts. As for social legislation, there was little history of government leadership in this area. Governments in the nineteenth century had limited goals revolving around distributory activities. This position is reiterated by Seth Koven and Sonya Michel in "Womanly Duties: Maternalist Politics and the Origins of the Welfare States in France, Germany, Great Britain and the United States, 1880–1920," *American Historical Review* 95, no. 4 (1990): 1093.
26. Theda Skocpol, *Protecting Soldiers and Mothers: The Political Origins of Social Policy in the United States* (Boston: Harvard University Press, 1995), 2.

Nonpartisanship implied women were more virtuous than male politicians because they could not be corrupted by that system. It meant they were more interested in the well-being of society than in personal gain. Nonpartisanship held women's pre-suffrage political culture together just as partisanship defined the male political culture.[27] As historian Melanie Gustafson observes, "prominent women of the time argued that if principle and party loyalty were unbalanced, it was principle that had to be protected."[28]

Why These Women?

Three of our five legislators had been invested in this nonpartisan, issues-driven women's political culture. Sammis was a member of the Daughters of the American Revolution, had started the first suffrage club in Suffolk County in 1911, served as chair of the franchise department of her local Women's Christian Temperance Union, and been involved with the Red Cross during World War I.[29] Lilly was the recording secretary for the New York City Federation of Women's Clubs, president of the Knickerbockers Civic League, and vice president of the Society for the Aid of Mental Defectives.[30] Graves's list of women's organizations was the most extensive: also a DAR member, she was part of the New York Federation of Women's Clubs, the Shakespeare Club of Gouverneur, member of the Julia Ward Howe Tent of the Daughters of Veterans, member of the Marble Chapter of the Order of the Eastern Star, and a member of the Child Welfare Board of St. Lawrence County.[31]

Sammis, Lilly, and Graves all belonged to party organizations. That might have brought them to the attention of party leaders who would expect such women knew the meaning of party membership. Such commitment could be exhibited through recruiting and acculturating other women to how politics works. Sammis modeled her Huntington suffrage club on partisan organizing principles; her club conformed to the outline of her assembly district, and she was even referred to as the "Assembly District Leader" in a publicity piece that profiled her activities during the failed 1915 suffrage campaign.[32] The article followed Sammis's schedule on the day of the local school tax appropriations. New York's women had successfully won this form of partial suffrage in 1880. The none-too-subtle message of the article was that a woman could fulfill all her daily obligations as a woman and still vote. Along with voting, Sammis prepared family meals, cleaned the home, arranged for a Bible class at her local church, and spent the evening reading and listening to music. Another option to women was to join all of a political party's organizations. Lilly was an

27. Melanie Gustafson, "Florence Collins Porter and the Concept of the Principled Partisan Woman," *Frontiers: A Journal of Women's Studies* 18, no. 1 (1997): 10.
28. Ibid.
29. Jane Mathews, *The Woman Suffrage Movement in Suffolk County*, 10, 12, 16; biographical entry for Ida Sammis in *The New York Red Book: An Illustrated State Manual*, 1919 (Albany, NY: J. B. Lyon, 1919).
30. Biographical entry for Mary Lilly in *The New York Red Book*, 1919.
31. Biographical entry for Rhoda Fox Graves in *The New York Red Book: An Illustrated State Manual*, 1925 (Albany, NY: J. B. Lyon, 1925).
32. "Political Equality Notes," Wyoming County (NY) *Reporter*, April 21, 1915.

Ida Sammis, date unknown.
(COURTESY OF THE NEW YORK
STATE LEGISLATIVE WOMEN'S
CAUCUS)

active member of Democratic organizations in New York City and part of the Democratic club that covered her district, where decisions about nominations were made. Yet a third approach was to make oneself useful to the parties. Graves was an early organizer of Republican women in her county and was appointed vice chair of the Republican County Committee as a result.

Of the three possible ways for women to quickly take on political roles, success as an organizer of new party members was most important to the leadership. Both parties had begun seriously organizing women after the 1916 presidential election. At the national level, each created a women's division and named a woman as its leader. Those women became the vice chairs of the national committees. Each state party selected one man and, by the mid-1920s, one woman to sit on its national committee. Similar structures developed at the state level. A woman was named to "share" leadership of the state committee and held the title of vice chair. The heads of each of the county committees made up the membership of the state body. Each county committee also added a woman as vice chair; this is the position Graves held. It signified she was the leader of all Republican women in St. Lawrence County. In truth, by merely adding women onto existing committees party leaders guaranteed they would be too large and unwieldy to be effective. Real power in the state party was exercised by an appointed state executive committee with a majority male membership. In addition, this system institutionalized gender segregation within the parties. Women were shut out of chairmanships, positions that retained any real power. Party leaders controlled the women through their power to appoint them to these positions.[33] It was not until 1938 when the state's constitution was amended that New York's women won the right to be elected to the state committees directly by the party membership vote as men were. That victory aside, women nationally knew that, given the ways the parties organized, they would have to work harder to achieve real power and influence.[34]

The remaining two New York women, Gillette and Smith, had neither a strong résumé of women's club service nor party connections. They did share some common attributes associated with a type of so-called modern woman. They both lived in cities, Gillette in Schenectady and Smith in New York City. Both also had professional credentials and careers. Gillette was a physician and Smith an educator. Gillette received her medical degree from New York Medical College and Hospital for Women and began practicing in 1899. She listed herself as a surgeon at Mercy Hospital in Schenectady since 1900.[35] Smith was much younger, having just graduated from Teachers College at Columbia in 1918 with her master's and began teaching hygiene and physical training at the Horace Mann School.[36] When Smith stood for election in the primary, the *New York Times* had little else to report on other than her school activities, where she captained the baseball team and was president of the Athletic Association of Teachers College, and for her work at a summer camp for girls in Vermont.[37] The *Times* profile of her following her election in 1919 began with her skill as a tennis player and only later in the article reported on her views on issues. She was called a "progressive" but not a "suffragette," and no further information was provided on what these terms might have signified about her political philosophy. Smith did receive praise for her work during World War I raising funds for the United War Relief Fund, but again, the article stressed even more her success at organizing dances for the soldiers, "for if there is anything in this world which she likes more than anything in the way of athletics it is the art terpsichorean [love of dance]."[38] Over and over within the *Times* article Smith's youthfulness is referred to as a prominent feature.

Party leaders supported both Gillette and Smith despite their lack of political experience or demonstrated success at organizing women politically. In her study of women entering politics in the 1920s, Kristi Anderson argues that political parties intentionally steered novice women to unwinnable campaigns in a way that allowed parties to claim to support women without actually ceding power to them.[39] This is a fair criticism for

---

33. Harvey, *Votes without Leverage*, 155.
34. Anderson, *After Suffrage*, 105.
35. Biographical entry for Elizabeth Gillette in *The New York Red Book: An Illustrated State Manual*, 1920 (Albany, NY: J. B. Lyon, 1920).
36. Biographical entry for Marguerite Smith, ibid.
37. "Negro to Oppose Woman," *New York Times*, August 30, 1919, 18.
38. "Assemblyman Miss Smith of Harlem," *New York Times*, November 9, 1919, xxi.
39. Anderson, *After Suffrage*, 150; Jo Freeman, *A Room at a Time*, 230.

Elizabeth Gillette, date unknown.
(COURTESY OF THE SCHENECTADY COUNTY
HISTORICAL SOCIETY)

Marguerite Smith, date unknown.
(COURTESY OF THE NEW YORK STATE
LEGISLATIVE WOMEN'S CAUCUS)

congressional and statewide races, but women had their greatest success winning elections to state legislatures. By 1933, 320 women across the United States had served in their state legislatures; only Louisiana had not yet elected a woman legislator.[40] In the New York State cases examined here, a closer look suggests that local political considerations went into making nominating decisions and that the parties were not surrendering to the opposition by running any of these five women.

Sammis and Graves came out of Republican strongholds, and it was presumed they would win their elections. But Lilly, Smith, and Gillette all ran in districts with more complicated political dynamics. On its face, Gillette seems the most atypical candidate. She cast almost no public shadow, either as a physician or as an elected legislator from Schenectady. The limited information available suggests Gillette became politicized when she observed the injustices experienced by the working classes. She credits this awakening for her enrollment in the Democratic Party.[41] Republicans dominated politics in Schenectady County until the 1960s with the notable exception of George Lunn, who was elected mayor of Schenectady in 1911, making him the first Socialist mayor in New York State. Though he lost to a fusion candidate (combined Democrat, Republican, Progressive) in 1913, Lunn returned

---

40. Breckinridge, *Women in the Twentieth Century*, 324.
41. *Albany Times Union*, November 11, 1919, 5.

to office in 1915. In 1916, the Schenectady electorate sent him to Congress for one term and then again to the mayoralty in 1919 and 1921. Much of the credit for Lunn's victories went to the growing working-class population employed by General Electric and related businesses in the city.[42] In 1922, Lunn accepted the Democratic nomination for lieutenant governor and ran successfully with Al Smith, who won what would be the first of three consecutive terms as governor (1922–28). Smith had also been governor from 1919 to 1920.

That same electorate is almost assuredly what swept Gillette into office in 1919. Gillette's margin of victory was a narrow 636 votes, which left her little margin of error going forward.[43] Lunn appears to have moved toward the center and prospered, but in 1919 Gillette was a political newcomer with a razor-thin plurality. She had neither the mandate nor the political experience to expand that base during her one term in office. And Gillette's advocacy for perceived radicals may have made it even harder to woo an electorate that was becoming skeptical of such ideas. In the 1920 legislative session Gillette voted with a small minority of twenty-eight against expelling the five men who had been elected to the legislature from New York City as avowed Socialists.[44] She lost her reelection bid later that year. Her principled stand in the legislature against expelling her Socialist colleagues conflicted with the post–World War I Red Scare that dampened enthusiasm for radical groups across the country.

Smith was the second woman from a challenging district; she was young and popular and Republican in a district in Manhattan bordering Harlem that was represented by Tammany Democrats before her election in 1919 and after her defeat in 1921 (she was successfully reelected in 1920). Republicans already controlled the Assembly and could afford to take a chance on Smith in 1919. The fact that she faced a challenger in the 1919 primary, even though the party had already settled on her candidacy, suggests that at least some people thought the seat was winnable. Republicans had briefly taken it from Tammany in 1917 when they ran a black candidate, Edward Johnson, a former dean of Shaw University Law School. Tammany operative Martin Healey won it back in 1918.[45] Republican leaders in 1919 seemed set on a woman candidate to oppose Healey, perhaps hoping to maximize the turnout of new women voters.[46] The year 1919 was disappointing generally for Democrats; they lost eleven seats in the Assembly, including that of Democrat assemblywoman

42. Brian Keough, "George Lunn," in *The Encyclopedia of New York State*, ed. Peter Eisenstadt (Syracuse, NY: Syracuse University Press, 2005), 935.

43. *Albany Times Union*, November 11, 1919, 5. The *Brooklyn Standard Union*, November 5, 1919, 3, also reported that one of the female candidates was carried over the finish line by the Socialists.

44. *New York Times*, April 2, 1920, 1. The vote was 17 Democrat and 11 Republican to allow the legislators to take their seats.

45. Healey was a controversial figure in Harlem. He refused to admit black members to the Nineteenth District Democratic Club. His 1918 victory was only possible because he opposed Prohibition. Julie Gallagher, *Black Women and Politics in New York City* (Urbana: University of Illinois Press, 2012), 28; John C. Walter, *The Harlem Fox: J. Raymond Jones and Tammany, 1920–1970* (Albany: SUNY Press, 1989), 4.

46. Gallagher, *Black Women and Politics*, 28; "Assemblyman Miss Smith of Harlem," *New York Times*, November 9, 1919, xxi. Gallagher references an unofficial deal between the Nineteenth A.D. Republican Club and local leaders that slotted the assembly seat for a woman candidate and an aldermanic seat for a black candidate.

Lilly, one of the first two women elected to the legislature the year before. Conditions thus gave Smith a fighting chance. Her election was the result of a somewhat weaker Tammany presence, coupled with the novelty of a likable woman candidate.

Lilly's electoral experience in 1918 had demonstrated the efforts of the Democratic Party leaders to juggle a number of factors in choosing a candidate they thought would appeal to women voters. Lilly, like Smith and Gillette one year later, might have seemed a sacrificial candidate in a traditionally Republican district, but she was not. As noted earlier, Lilly was a lawyer, a clubwoman, and a party member. She graduated from Hunter College and New York University and was one of the first women admitted to the bar in New York State, in 1895. While we cannot infer too much from her *Red Book* biographical entry, she checked all the boxes that seemed to have feminine appeal. Lilly began by noting she was a lifelong Manhattan resident, then followed with a description of her early education and a vague mention of having taught for a number of years.[47] Only then did she list her law degree. The most space went to club and party organizational memberships.[48] Her background and experience helped her connect with all kinds of women: homemakers, professionals, and reformers. In sum, Lilly would have seemed a decent candidate who could and did win in 1918 even though the Seventh Assembly District seat had been in Republican hands for years and the Republicans controlled the Assembly. And it is also not totally surprising that she failed to be reelected in 1919 as the seat remained competitive. Republicans held on only until 1923 when Democrats won the district back and kept it going forward, even in the 1928 presidential election where Republicans dominated nationally and where Governor Smith saw his New York City support decline enough that he failed to win the popular vote in his home state.[49] Despite Smith's loss in the presidential contest that year, he had been responsible in the 1920s for an upsurge in Democratic registrations, particularly in New York City.[50] The increase in registered Democrats may have factored into the Democrats keeping control of that Seventh District.

Political leaders ran three women in districts where they did not normally have a majority, but in each case it could be argued that the party made reasonable choices. Some of these individual choices had to do with the perceived influence a particular woman might

---

47. There appears to be no set template for what went into a member's biographical statement. The lengths varied considerably as did the type of information provided. Some members also used the space to make political statements. Graves included a vignette from her 1924 campaign regarding her opponent. The one area where the editor likely made the choice on material was the listing of the members' occupation, which was in a separate section. In 1925, Graves's biography said she owned and operated a farm with her husband; yet she was not listed as a farmer in the occupation section (see note 56).
48. Biographical entry for Mary Lilly in *The New York Red Book*, 1919.
49. Robert Chiles, "Vanquished Warrior: Reconsidering Al Smith's 1928 New York Defeat," *New York History* 98, no. 1 (2017): 90, 92, 97. Smith's support weakened the most in those areas of Manhattan and Queens where Republicans had either gained electoral ground or were becoming more competitive.
50. Ibid., 101. In previous gubernatorial elections Smith had been able to capture progressive Republican votes. The 1928 presidential election loss represented a failure to hold that constituency rather than a failure to win Democratic votes.

have had in bringing this newly enfranchised group to the polls. In other cases, women candidates emerged out of a complex dynamic that took account of both the local political environment and the way a woman candidate might leverage that environment into victory. Still, in these three examples, male leaders controlled both the process of candidate selection and the subsequent party support provided (or not) to that candidate.

The Women in Office

Graves's campaigns and service set her apart somewhat from her female colleagues. From the start of her legislative career, Graves exhibited political skills that the other four did not have or did not possess as fully. As already noted, Graves solicited the nomination for the Assembly seat in 1924 and was considered the frontrunner from the outset.[51] She defeated a male primary challenger whose slogan was "there is no sentiment for a woman."[52] Located in what the locals called the North Country region of the state, St. Lawrence County was a long-standing Republican stronghold, so any primary winner was expected to win the general election.[53] Graves included the challenger's slogan in her official legislative biography in 1925; it stood out as a somewhat public rebuke to the idea that gender still precluded women from politics. During her campaign Graves had not relied on partisanship alone to win but had directly connected herself to the perceived women's responsibility for the home. "The state," she explained, "has entered the home and because woman's place is in the home, she must take an intelligent and active interest in state if she is properly to look after her home."[54] Graves could also accurately claim to understand the issues that most concerned a rural county. She and her husband, Perle, owned and ran a dairy farm, something Graves highlighted in her biography section of the *Red Book* for 1925.[55] They continued with the farm throughout her legislative career. An interesting side note is that the editors of the *Red Book* series struggled with how best to credit Graves with this occupational choice. Members' occupations were listed in a separate section, and in 1925 Graves had none listed. In 1926 she was listed as "interested in farming," while the editors reverted to giving her no occupation in 1927 and 1928. Finally, in 1929, Graves's biography and occupational listing matched.[56] During the time Graves served in the legislature, farming was still the most frequently listed occupations for legislators.

51. "Graves Announces for Assembly," *Ogdensburg Republican Journal*, July 5, 1922, 2; "Mrs. Graves to Enter Race," *Northern Tribune*, May 28, 1924, 1; "Enter the Woman," *Canton Commercial Advertiser*, May 27, 1924, 4; "Mrs. Graves Candidacy Booms," *Potsdam Courier Freeman*, June 18, 1924, 1.
52. Biographical entry for Rhoda Graves in *The New York Red Book, 1925*.
53. "Press Release Announcing Senatorial Candidacy," July 7, 1932, in the Papers of Rhoda Fox Graves, Gouverneur Museum, Gouverneur, NY (hereafter Graves Papers) specifies the "North Country" as Jefferson, St. Lawrence, Franklin, and Clinton Counties; "Pioneer Suffragette Wants to Be Sent to the Assembly," *Ogdensburg Republican-Journal*, May 26, 1924, 2.
54. Obituary, *New York Times*, January 26, 1950, 28.
55. Biographical entry for Rhoda Fox Graves in *The New York Red Book, 1925*.
56. Demographic listing of member's name, party, occupation, and address in *The New York Red Book: An Illustrated State Manual* for the years 1926, 1927, 1928, and 1929 (Albany: J. B. Lyon, 1926–29).

Graves had the advantage of being in the majority party, as did Sammis and Smith. In the 1920s Republicans solidly controlled the Assembly.[57] It is not surprising, then, that the first bill introduced by a woman and passed into law came from the Republican Ida B. Sammis.[58] In all, ten of the fifteen bills Sammis introduced became law. The 67 percent success rate of her legislation far exceeded overall legislative passage rate of 16 percent in 1919.[59] The first woman to win reelection was the Republican Marguerite Smith, and the first woman senator would be Graves. Gillette and Lilly, both Democrats, had much thinner records. Three of the fifteen bills Lilly wrote become law, while Gillette had no legislative accomplishments. She immediately returned to her medical practice and continued there until her retirement in 1959. Still, there are two small clues to suggest Gillette found some value in her single term, that she had progressed in her political education. She was the first to introduce legislation that would have required the election of one female for every male elected to the state party committee (the same issue that ultimately went to the constitutional convention in 1938). Her action suggests that she understood that women's political equality should mean equal treatment by the parties and that she was willing to advocate for that belief.[60] Though Gillette never again sought or held public office, she did join the National Order of Women Legislators, or NOWL. NOWL originated in Connecticut, where women legislators created a state organization in 1927; they issued a call to take the group national in 1938.[61] Former legislators were eligible for membership and the NOWL scrapbook for 1950–52 lists Gillette as second vice president.[62] The organization never enrolled a majority of the states or even a majority of the women from the member states, including New York. However, it seems fair to say that Gillette continued to feel connected in some way to her time as a woman legislator.

As Graves showed with her success at organizing women politically and her assembly seat, she was unique among the five women in this essay for her willingness to challenge party leadership and the existing political culture when she thought them wrongheaded. However, when she did so it was seen to be in the interest of her community and constituents and not for political self-interest. Graves's positive reputation may have helped

---

57. Democrats controlled the Senate during the 1923 and 1924 legislative sessions with a one vote majority 26–25.

58. *New York Times,* January 15, 1919, 7. It was also the first bill passed and signed into law in the 1919 session.

59. Original source, "The Legislative Orgy," *New York Times,* May 27, 1919, 14. Also cited in Jeremy Creelan and Laura Moulton, *The New York Legislative Process: An Evaluation and Blueprint for Reform* (New York: Brennan Center for Justice at the NYU School of Law, 2004), 37. https://www.brennancenter.org/publication/new-york-state-legislative-process-evaluation-and-blueprint-reform and https://www.brennancenter.org/sites/default/files/legacy/d/albanyreform_finalreport.pdf

60. *New York Times,* February 8, 1920, 12.

61. Introduction to *History of the National Order of Women Legislators,* ed. Emma R. Poeter (Las Vegas: Hanes Thomas, 1981). A statement by the NOWL's organizer and first president, Julia Emery, reported that eleven states participated in the first national meeting and eleven others expressed interest. New York State's women that year sent only a letter of support.

62. NOWL scrapbook 1950–60, National Order of Women Legislator Records, Box 3 85S-2, Sophia Smith Special Collections, Smith College, Northampton, MA.

her son, Paul, who announced his candidacy for her Senate seat as she announced her retirement in 1948.[63] He held it from 1948 to 1953, when he left for an appointment to the New York State Supreme Court. Beyond building a family legacy in politics, Graves can be credited with helping initiate a shift in the nature of political service itself. Women legislators' sustained emphasis on constituent service over time became a regularized part of the state legislator's portfolio. In her analysis of the emergence of the political woman, political scientist Jeanne Kirkpatrick argued that women legislators came from a background that predisposed them to be problem solvers for their constituents. Women's traditional roles focused their attention "on people, on duty, service, and the 'higher' aspects of life."[64] Bessie Buchanan would be the first black woman elected to the legislature. As Harlem's Assembly representative from 1954 to 1962, Buchanan would cite her service to her constituents as her primary achievement.[65] Such attention took the focus off her thin record of legislative successes, with only three bills becoming law during her tenure. Gerald Benjamin and Robert Nakamura's evaluation of the New York legislature's mid-twentieth-century modernization efforts emphasized that the style and organization of legislative life changed in significant ways during that period.[66] One change that stood apart from the general focus on increased professionalization and bureaucratization of the era was the opening of district offices beginning around 1966. Such offices increased constituent access and elevated constituent concerns. Modern studies suggest that women legislators around the country spent more time with constituents and helped with problems more often than male legislators, even after state differences get factored in.[67]

Graves championed numerous rural issues, including the creation of a commission to plan for a bridge over the St. Lawrence River into Canada, the right of rural school districts to have their votes counted when it came to making decisions on district consolidations, and the creation of a junior license for rural teens to drive at a younger age.[68] Her bill on rural licenses was so popular with constituents that she had to fend off colleagues who wanted to take away the privilege of sponsoring the legislation.[69] In 1928 she broke party ranks by refusing to help kill Governor Smith's water-power initiative, which would have

---

63. "It's a Man's World in Part of Albany," *New York Times*, May 19, 1948, 23. Paul Graves was serving as the Franklin County district attorney.
64. Kirkpatrick, *Political Woman*, 214–15.
65. "Only Woman Negro Legislature in State Guided by Brotherhood," *Tonawanda News*, February 16, 1961, 4.
66. Robert Connery and Gerald Benjamin, *Rockefeller of New York: Executive Power in the Statehouse* (Ithaca: Cornell University Press, 1979), 79-80, 101.
67. Anne Marie Cammisa and Beth Reingold, "Review Essay Women in State Legislatures and State Legislative Research: Beyond Sameness and Difference," *State Politics and Policy Quarterly* 4, no 2 (2004): 194.
68. "Extension of Bridge Commission," Legislative Jacket for Chapter 94 of the Laws of 1935, "An Act to Amend the Motor Vehicle Law," Legislative Jacket for Chapter 319 of the Laws of 1929, microfilm, New York State Library, Albany, NY; "Rural Areas Fight for the School Law," *New York Times*, March 30, 1939, 14; Rhoda Fox Graves to Mrs. Charles McArthur, February 1, 1931, on supporting rural school concerns, Graves Papers.
69. Rhoda Fox Graves to Mrs. Charles McArthur, February 1, 1931, on supporting rural school concerns, Graves Papers. The letter indicates that there may have been more than one version of the bill floating around the Assembly but that it was the bill sponsored by Graves that went to the governor.

created a state power authority to bring hydroelectric power to the region. She was the only Republican to vote for the Democrat-sponsored bills.[70] At the time, Republican leaders in the legislature were more interested in frustrating Smith's agenda than in the issues themselves. Legislative approval for both initiatives would come in the 1940s when Republican Thomas E. Dewey was governor.

Her popularity in her district contributed to Graves's decision to buck party leadership by running for the Senate in 1932. Republicans in St. Lawrence and Franklin Counties had agreed (no one remembered just when) that if the area's congressman came from one county then the state senator had to be from the other.[71] In 1932, Congressman H. B. Snell lived in St. Lawrence County. Graves boldly challenged Warren Thayer, the incumbent Republican state senator who lived in Franklin County, declaring, "I will not blindly follow the dictates of party bosses when . . . [that] works hardship on the taxpayers of the State." Her press release declared, "I am a firm believer in party regularity, but I cannot guarantee the right to hold public office in 1933 should be foreclosed against me by some ancient political deal. . . . The test of fitness alone should be the yard stick by which the candidate is measured."[72] With party organization support, Thayer bested Graves in the primary. But Thayer was forced to resign his seat in June 1934 after an investigation revealed he had taken money from parties that represented a conflict of interest.[73] Graves immediately declared her candidacy and won in the general election.

Still, women legislators continued to find themselves judged by two conflicting standards—one for politicians and one for women—which often meant they alienated some constituency or another. In 1918, Sammis ran with the endorsement of both the Republican and Prohibition Parties for the seat in a heavily Republican district.[74] But she lost the backing of her party during her 1919 reelection bid; leaders suddenly withdrew their endorsement and gave it to her male Democratic opponent.[75] Sammis said that the party betrayal was a result of her refusal to "supinely carry out the wishes of the men leaders."[76] The record, however, shows that she had indeed followed the party's lead. Ten of the fifteen

---

70. *New York Times*, March 3, 1928, 3; "Mrs. Graves, First Woman in the State Senate, Is Independent on Home and Other Issues," *New York Times*, November 7, 1934, 14.

71. "Press Release Announcing Senatorial Candidacy," July 7, 1932, Graves Papers; Ezra Carpenter, Franklin County Auditor, to Rhoda Fox Graves, April 22, 1938, Graves Papers. Carpenter expresses the opinion among politicians in Franklin County that the position should come back there if Graves decided not to run for reelection.

72. "Press Release Announcing Senatorial Candidacy," July 7, 1932, Graves Papers.

73. "Relieves His Party of Load," *New York Times*, June 12, 1934, 5. From 1926 through 1932, Thayer had received $27,000 from the Associated Gas and Electric Company, supposedly as compensation for his interests in a power company purchased by Associated Gas. In addition to irregularities in the arrangement itself, payments ceased abruptly when the Democrats won a Senate majority in 1932 and Thayer was no longer chair of the Senate Public Service Committee.

74. Jane Mathews, "The Woman Suffrage Movement in Suffolk County New York, 1911–1917, a Case Study of the Tactical Differences between Two Prominent Long Island Suffragists: Mrs. Ida Bunce Sammis and Miss Rosalie Jones" (master's thesis, Adelphia University, 1988), 82.

75. *Brooklyn Standard Union*, November 15, 1919, 3.

76. *Auburn Citizen Advertiser*, January 12, 1934, 2.

bills she introduced became law, the best record for this early period. During one contentious vote, the press noted she "joined [the Speaker], recognizing party obligation above any other."[77] Sammis did grow more critical of party politics after she fell out of political favor and by the 1930s was calling for women to "be freed from the dictates of party bosses and to have a voice of their own in the working out of policies."[78] But that does not answer the question of why the party not only abandoned her but supported her opponent in 1919. Sammis was the only Republican running in Suffolk County to lose her race.[79] One possibility is that her personal life affected her political career. Though nothing was made public at the time, her past played out in the papers in the 1930s when she married for the second and third times.[80] Sammis had run for office in 1918 as a widow, which at that time, along with being unmarried, lessened concerns for a woman candidate about balancing home and family, especially since she did not have small children. Women's responsibility to their families was considered their most important role, a tenet that Sammis may have violated. At one point it was suggested that her child from her first marriage might really have been fathered by the man who became her second husband in 1923. Both her second and third marriages would be of the May–December variety, which generated accusations of gold digging. These stories appeared after her time in the legislature; there is no evidence that conclusively proves this was the cause of her political downfall. But something pushed Republicans to back away from Sammis so late in the 1919 election cycle that she remained on the ballot as the Republican nominee. At the very least, her time in the legislature thrust her into the public eye in ways that were not beneficial for her. She never held elective or appointive public office again but remained someone worthy of newspaper coverage more than a decade after she left office, coverage that showed how gendered ideas about behavior persisted and became the basis for the harsh treatment she received from the press.[81]

On the other side of the aisle, another of the women in this essay faced a different kind of gendered criticism. During the 1919 elections, the Citizen's Union, a good government organization in New York City, charged Assemblywoman Lilly with holding a patronage job as director of women prisoners on Blackwell Island while still technically in office.[82] Whether it was legal to do so or not mattered less than how the accusation supported the

77. *Syracuse Post Standard*, April 20, 1919, 5.
78. "Women Must Organize New Party, 'Asserts Ida B. Sammis Satchwell,'" *New York Sun*, June 20, 1934, 27.
79. "Republicans Gain Eleven Seats," *New York Times*, November 5, 1919, 1.
80. *Huntington Long Islander*, November 10, 1933; December 8, 1933, II:5; January 19, 1934, II:1; August 10, 1934; July 27, 1935, II:6.
81. Anderson. *After Suffrage*, 25, cites the persistent association of women with piety and domesticity as a factor in women's slow path to electoral success; Kirkpatrick, *Political Woman*, 45–50 (chap. 3), observes women legislators mid-twentieth century and notes they have a history of mirroring traditional ideas about womanhood in their behavior and values; Daniel Hayes, "When Gender and Party Collide: Stereotyping in Candidate Trait Attribution," *Politics and Gender* 7 (2011): 135, begins a present-day assessment of the persistent gender stereotyping by citing a long line of research supporting the thesis that gender attributes had historically been regularly applied to women candidates.
82. "Citizens Union Hits Woman Candidate," *New York Times*, November 3, 1919, 1.

perception that Lilly was focused more on herself than on important issues. This followed the Citizens Union's negative evaluation of her first term. This private, good government group summarized New York City legislators' positions on a set of bills the group decided were important to the welfare of the city.[83] Lilly called the Union's complaint that "she was attentive to the duties" but had a "very poor record of votes" inconsistent and demanded the Union explain itself.[84] The Union alleged she voted against important bills it considered "in the public interest" and failed to oppose a series of bills the Union deemed "vicious" to the city's interests. The Union had leveled the criticism of a poor voting record against twelve of the eighteen Democrat legislators from Manhattan, which suggests that their comments were somewhat common. Voting with her fellow Democrats suggested to the Citizens Union that Lilly had failed to prioritize principle over party as the Union so noted in responding to her criticism of their evaluation.[85] The suggestion was that a woman should have been more nonpartisan. But the Union went even further and issued a press release the day before the election alleging that Lilly violated the state constitution by holding an elected position and a patronage job simultaneously, explaining that they believed "these facts . . . should be of interest to the voters."[86] Lilly's response appeared the next day in the papers, where she called the accusations "a low and unfair attack." She then made a legalistic argument by drawing a distinction between holding two public offices simultaneously and holding a public office whose obligation for the year was over while also accepting an appointment to another publicly funded job.[87] Despite her attempted explanation, the damage had been done. Lilly's was one of the eleven Assembly seats Democrats in the city who lost that cycle.[88] Historian Kristi Anderson believes that women's uneven success in the political arena in the 1920s was partly due to society's continued discomfort with seeing women in the political or public arenas, as opposed to their traditional place in the private sphere of the home. This discomfort reflected the persistence of nineteenth century ideas about woman's selfless, caring nature. One Progressive Era argument Anderson says was used to justify political participation for women was to presume they would enter politics as disinterested actors, meaning they would not exhibit overt ambition or pursue personal gain.[89] Lilly's dissembling might have played to concerns about politics as the proper place for women. Or it might have convinced voters that Lilly was somehow betraying her own gender.

In the 1920s the public showed little tolerance for women politicians thought to be using their position for personal gain. In 1925, Republican Florence E. Knapp was elected

83. "Analyzes Records of Assemblymen," New York Times, August 11, 1919, 7.
84. "Nine Candidates Out of Primary Fight," New York Times, August 16, 1919, 18.
85. "Union Answers Mrs. Lilly," New York Times, August 18, 1919, 14.
86. "Citizens Union Hits Woman Candidate," New York Times, November 3, 1919, 1.
87. "Mrs. Lilly Upholds Her Two Salaries," New York Times, November 4, 1919, 5.
88. "Republicans Gain Eleven Seats," New York Times, November 5, 1919, 1.
89. Anderson, After Suffrage, 31, 101-2, 104-5.

Mary Lilly, date unknown. (COURTESY OF THE NEW YORK STATE LEGISLATIVE WOMEN'S CAUCUS)

Rhoda Fox Graves, date unknown. (COURTESY OF THE NEW YORK STATE LEGISLATIVE WOMEN'S CAUCUS)

secretary of state in New York, which made her the first woman to hold statewide office after suffrage.[90] During her two-year term, 1926–27, she oversaw the last separately taken New York State census, where she managed a significant allocation for the hiring of census takers and enumerators. However, after she left office, accusations of malfeasance forced Governor Smith to order an investigation into the census process; this led to her indictment and subsequent conviction at trial on charges of forgery and grand larceny. Though several Republican political figures were also implicated in the scandal, only Knapp was indicted. At the start of the investigation a *New York Times* editorial had opined "[if the] charges are sustained, the situation will carry a peculiar irony for those who had looked to her to demonstrate what could be accomplished in public life by the woman with the broom!"[91]

Marguerite Smith worked well with fellow Republicans, which may account for her becoming the first woman legislator to win reelection. She won praise for her parliamentary skills during her first term when she briefly took over as speaker and successfully

---

90. After 1927 the position was constitutionally changed to be appointive. The arguments and sources presented in this section on Knapp's trial for graft in office are taken from Lauren Kozakiewicz, "Political Episodes 1890–1960: Three Republican Women in Twentieth Century New York State Politics" (Ph.D. diss., University at Albany, 2006), chap. 4.
91. "The Census Scandal," *New York Times*, October 4, 1927, 28.

mediated a heated dispute between two members.[92] She angered some women's groups in her second term, though, by entering into a public conflict with the Women's Trade Union League (WTUL), an organization of mainly middle-class women focused on supporting protective legislation for women in the industrial workforce. Smith had sponsored legislation to revise the Fifty-Four Hour Law so women could work more and later hours.[93] The WTUL accused Smith her of selling out to political leaders and abandoning women.[94] Here Smith experienced a division within the ranks of reform-minded women in the 1920s.[95] The WTUL continued to support a kind of protective legislation that had emerged in the Progressive Era whose goal was to prevent the exploitation of women in the workplace. But the National Women's Party formed by Alice Paul in 1916 favored a strictly equal-rights approach that would eliminate any gender-based distinctions in the workplace; its support of an Equal Rights Amendment, introduced in 1923, reflected that position. However, in 1921 the more traditional protectionist viewpoint still dominated. Two years earlier, in the 1919 legislative session, Sammis authored a law to limit the hours elevator operators—most of whom were women—could work, at the request of the Women's Joint Legislative Conference (WJLC) of New York State. It stipulated that no woman under eighteen could work as an operator and that every operator had to receive one day off out of seven worked.[96] Sammis's bill was one of three introduced that session that were intended to limit women's working hours; the other two focused on women office workers and women transportation workers. The WJLC lobbied for all three bills, with Mary Dreier, social reformer and member of the New York WTUL, testifying before a legislative hearing. Yet, women also organized in opposition, and by the time Dreier's supporters got to the chamber on the day of her testimony, the room was nearly full of women belonging to the Women's League for Equal Opportunity, an organization demanding the legislature reject the bills in the name of "industrial equality." Nora Stanton Blatch, granddaughter of Elizabeth Cady Stanton, was present to lend her support to the opposition.[97] Even after the transportation bill was signed into law, women employed by the Brooklyn transit system unsuccessfully lobbied

---

92. "Acting Speaker Smith," *New York Times*, April 23, 1920; April 1, 1920; April 26, 1920, 12. The article used the term *parliamentary* when referring to Smith's actions, suggesting her ability to use the rules to keep the other legislators in line.

93. New York approved a fifty-four-hour work limit per week for women and minors in 1912. The law also included a prohibition on late night work. Critics argued the prohibition on night work effectively barred women from certain, potentially more lucrative, kinds of employment. During this period the WTUL was pushing for a lower threshold with a forty-eight-hour bill. The forty-eight-hour bill would become law in 1927.

94. Assembly Proposal A190 to Amend the Labor Law on Women Workers and Chapter 489 of the Laws of 1921, New York State Library, Albany, NY; "League Would Defeat City Assemblywoman," *New York Times*, October 31, 1921, 2.

95. The divide is covered in Nancy Cott, "Equal Rights and Economic Roles: The Conflict over the Equal Rights Amendment in the 1920s," in *Women's America: Refocusing the Past*, ed. Linda Kerber, Sharon De Hart, Cornelia Dayton, and Judy Wu, 8th ed. (New York: Oxford University Press, 2015), 503–12.

96. *The New York Red Book*, 1919. Chapter 544 of the laws of 1919; *Watkins New York Express*, March 26, 1919, 1.

97. "Women Fail to Agree on Welfare Measures," *New York Times*, March 6, 1919, 7.

the governor to call a special session to repeal the measure, which they said would harm them economically.[98] In Smith's case, newspaper coverage of divisions among women on issues and the vocal criticism leveled against her by a significant organization like the WTUL may have contributed to her losing her bid for a third term in 1921.

The Limits of Their Influence

Although gender could lead to a double standard of higher expectations for women legislators, the women were not above turning assumptions of gender differences to their advantage. Some of their most effective arguments in this regard emphasized how they would improve politics and governance because they were elected to office as true outsiders. As noted above, women's politicization during the presuffrage era had proceeded along a separate track from men's. Now these five women came into the legislature with the expectation that they would make a difference *because* they were women, an expectation that was unformed in many ways. Acting on their difference could mean that women would fundamentally change the structure and process of politics and government, as much had been said about the corruption associated with a male-dominated political system that needed fixing. However, the idea that political parties would require women to conform to their system was not as seriously considered as it perhaps should have been considering that the price of entry was often unquestioning partisan loyalty.

New York's first two women legislators illustrated this point in the 1919 session, when the demands of party superseded support for each other. Democrat Lilly attacked Republican Sammis for failing to support a crucial set of bills that the press labeled a "feminist welfare program" and included the eight-hour day, minimum wage, and health insurance. "You have passed bills here conserving ducks, skunks and scallops," she said, "but you refuse to pass bills conserving the working power of the state.... I say it is unmoral to fail to provide a living wage for working women."[99] Sammis's first two pieces of successful legislation dealt with waterfowl and scallops. Even the press noted that in the confrontation on the floor "Mrs Sammis, Republican woman member, joined [the Speaker] in recognizing party obligation above any other."[100] Party pressure on legislators, women included, forced them to take positions that seemed contrary to what one would otherwise expect of the legislator. The pressure to follow party dictates only grew stronger when the leaders in the respective chambers gained greater control over the legislative process by midcentury.[101]

---

98. "B.R.T. Women Beg Smith for Aid," *New York Times*, May 25, 1919, 1
99. "Barely Retains Assembly Control," *New York Times*, April 17, 1919, 4.
100. Chapter 1 of the Laws of 1919, *Syracuse Post Standard*, April 20, 1919, 5.
101. For evidence of the growth of party control over voting regardless of issue, see David Hill, "Women State Legislators and Party Voting on the ERA," *Social Science Quarterly* 64 (June 1983): 318–26; Michelle A. Barnello, "Gender and Roll Call Voting in the New York State Assembly," *Women and Politics* 20, no. 4 (2001): 77–94.

However, even as early as 1919. Walter Lloyd George, an English novelist writing on women in politics for *Harper's Magazine*, predicted that "[party] loyalty will certainly be a feature of the woman legislator."[102]

Apart from systemic pressure to "toe the line," the very concept of "women's issues" was diffuse and hard to pin down. It was unclear whether those issues would be about women themselves or about various groups that women were "by nature" drawn to protect. At first, it was equally unclear whether the difference would come more from the power of a woman's bloc of voters or from women holding office and making those issues a priority, or both. By the mid-1920s, parties realized that women did not vote in a bloc even on "women's issues." Women, like men, filtered issues through their own personal lens, which included where they lived, their family backgrounds, and their economic needs.[103] Little had been discussed in the era before suffrage about how many women in office it would take for woman-led change to be possible. Though both parties supported women candidates, neither felt compelled to have a large number of them in the legislature. There was no cry of anguish when the legislatures of 1923 and 1924 had no women. It was Graves herself, not her political party, who opened the door of the Senate to women. Between 1934 and 1964 only one other woman, Janet Gordon (another Republican from a rural district deemed a party stronghold), served there. Graves's time in the Senate (1934–47) never overlapped with Gordon's (1958–62).

Scholars mostly agree that the presence of a critical mass of women in the legislature is an important component for accomplishing legislative goals important to women.[104] The early women who won these few seats exhibited characteristics of what political scientist Michelle Saint-Germain has called "tokenism." They were too few to challenge the status quo on their own so they fell back toward what she terms "invisibility."[105] Invisibility often meant avoiding the subject of gender, but Saint-Germain also notes that while most minorities pursued invisibility strategies because their numbers were so small, a few women instead opted for a strategy of overachievement; they took on the male-centered environment and beat the men at their own game. Graves might be said to have fit that description. Political scientist Drude Dahlerup argues that it is important to evaluate the progress

---

102. W. L. George, "Women in Politics," *Harpers*, June 1919, 85–92. He did hold out some hope that some women could overcome male prejudice against women politician and thus exhibit some independence.
103. Anderson, *After Suffrage*, 155, 157.
104. For support for the importance of the "critical mass" theory, see Michelle Saint-Germain, "Does Their Difference Make a Difference? The Impact of Women on Public Policy in the Arizona Legislature," *Social Science Quarterly* 70 (December): 956–68; Sue Thomas and Susan Welch, "The Impact of Gender on Activities and Priorities of State Legislators," *Western Political Quarterly* (1990): 447; Witt, Paget, and Matthews, *Running as a Woman*, 18. For analysis that suggests the critical mass theory should be modified or qualified by the addition of other factors, see Beth Reingold, *Representing Women: Sex, Gender and Legislative Behavior in Arizona and California* (Chapel Hill: University of North Carolina Press, 200), 3.
105. Saint-Germain, "Does Their Difference Make a Difference?" 958.

early elected women legislators made with balancing their independence of action with their effectiveness at advancing policies.[106] Using that metric, New York's first cohort of women legislators can be given at least some credit for asserting themselves by the very act of raising new issues specifically related to women, though they did not see great success in achieving a women's agenda at the time.

Politicians, members of the public, and many women had expected that female legislators would call attention to women's issues.[107] One can point to bills introduced by early woman legislative pioneers that clearly reflected a concern for women and families. Most bills failed, but they set precedents for the kinds of issues subsequent women legislators would champion successfully. Lilly, Sammis, Smith, and Graves all introduced legislation dealing with women and families that reflected their particular backgrounds and skill sets. Lilly's bills aimed to expand the rights of illegitimate children and clarify their legal status and to broaden protections for minors in the court system.[108] Sammis wanted to amend the state charities law in order to build a tuberculosis sanitarium specifically for children. Smith promoted legislation to require the establishment of kindergartens upon the petition of parents and guardians to their local school boards.[109] Graves succeeded in expanding the law on scholarships for training industrial teachers to include women.[110] She was less successful in extending equal legal guardianship of minor children to mothers.[111]

Still, it is important to appreciate how the efforts of these few, somewhat isolated early women members of the legislature laid the groundwork for larger changes in the future. Some of those changes would come in the form of opportunities for ever-larger numbers of women to have longer careers in the legislature or use their time there as training for higher office. Today in New York, women make up 32.4 percent of the legislature. That is slightly above the national average of 28.5 percent.[112] This is progress, especially when New York's first two women in the 1919 legislature represented 1 percent of a combined chamber of 201 elected officials. These early legislative women encountered a political system and culture

106. Drude Dahlerup "The Story of the Theory of Critical Mass," *Politics and Gender* 2, no. 4 (2006): 511–522, here, 514, 519.

107. Anderson, *After Suffrage*, 131–33; Nancy Baker Jones and Ruth Winegarten, *Capitol Women: Texas Female Legislators, 1923–1999* (Austin: University of Texas Press, 2000), 15.

108. *The New York Red Book, 1920.* Assembly Bill A425 would give the illegitimate child the right to the name of the father and to support by the father; Assembly Bill 106 would abolish the death penalty for minors in first degree cases; Assembly Bill 107 would expand the jurisdiction of the Children's Court from the age of sixteen to eighteen.

109. *The New York Red Book; An Illustrated State Manual,* 1921 (Albany, NY: J. B. Lyon, 1921). Assembly Bill A1272 to Amend the Education Law.

110. *The New York Red Book: An Illustrated State Manual,* 1925. Chapter 667 of the Laws of 1925.

111. *The New York Red Book: An Illustrated State Manual, 1930* (Albany, NY: J. B. Lyon, 1930). Assembly Bill 69 to make both parents joint natural guardians of minor children.

112. "Women in State Legislatures for 2019," National Conference of State Legislators website, published January 8, 2019, http://www.ncsl.org/legislators-staff/legislators/womens-legislative-network/women-in-state-legislatures-for-2019.aspx

that forced more adaptation than changes to the status quo. Yet, these five pioneers collectively blazed a trail that allowed women to become a permanent part of New York's politics. And, these women were themselves changed by their political experiences. They learned how to move within the political system, though not all of them were equally adept at doing so. They struggled with the challenge of articulating a woman's voice within that system, but credit can be given to these women for helping effect a shift in the legislative culture to make constituent service a much larger part of the modern legislator's portfolio. As the careers of these five women illustrate, change does not come overnight, but by midcentury it would be possible for one political scholar to definitively state: "there is no question that political woman exists"[113]

113. Kirkpatrick, *Political Woman*, 219.

The Lost Poems of Jacob Steendam

D. L. Noorlander

Jacob Steendam did not enjoy great advantages in life. Born in Germany, he moved to the Netherlands as a young man and mostly remained on the fringes of Dutch society, working in lowly positions his entire career. Perhaps in part because of the handicap or "deformity" of his feet, he never led men in battle, never served as governor or burgomaster, never served on any colonial council. Though he dabbled in trade, his skills and connections were insufficient to win much wealth or attention. Yet most students of New Netherland have at least heard his name because he wrote poetry, including a few poems about the colony that was his home from 1652 to late 1660 or early 1661. Most famously, he tried to entice other potential immigrants with his "Praise of New Netherland," published in Amsterdam after he left America.[1]

Steendam might have been happy to hear that at different times in the future he would be called "the first poet in New Netherland," "first poet of New York," and "first poet of the United States."[2] But he would have also been confused, because he could not have located two of those three place-names on any map available at the time. He was certainly not a New Yorker, nor was he an American, strictly speaking. Rather, he was a Germano-Dutch

1. The only biographical treatment of Steendam to this point is H. C. Murphy, *Jacob Steendam, Noch Vaster: A Memoir of the First Poet of New Netherland* (The Hague, Neth.: The Brothers Giunta D'Albani, 1861). Murphy republished the same material (along with new material on other poets) in *Anthology of New Netherland; or, Translations from the Early Dutch Poets of New York, with Memoirs of Their Lives* (New York: Bradford Club, 1865). See also Christine van Boheemen, "Dutch-American Poets of the Seventeenth Century," in *The Dutch in North America: Their Immigration and Cultural Continuity*, ed. Rob Kroes and Henk-Otto Neuschafer (Amsterdam: VU University Press, 1991), 114–30; Frans Blom and Henk Looijesteijn, "A Land of Milk and Honey: Colonial Propaganda and the City of Amsterdam, 1656–1664," *De Halve Maen* 85, no. 3 (2012): 47–56. Murphy did not know about Germany, and as far as I can tell, no one until now has known about Steendam's handicap. For the latter, see Stadsarchief Amsterdam, toegangsnr. 379, archief van de Classis Amsterdam, inv. nr. 157, ff. 35–36, June 25 and July 16, 1640. This essay is the first attempt to publish materials from a much larger, ongoing project on Jacob Steendam and the Dutch Empire in the seventeenth century.
2. For "New Netherland" and "New York," see Murphy, *Jacob Steendam*, 14; Wm. H. Carpenter, "Dutch Contributions to the Vocabulary of English in America: Dutch Remainders in New York State," *Modern Philology* 6, no. 1 (1908): 58; Van Boheemen, "Dutch-American Poets," 129. For "United States," see G. J. van Bork and P. J. Verkruijsse, eds., *De Nederlandse en Vlaamse Auteurs: Van middeleeuwen tot heden met inbegrip van de Friese auteurs* (Weesp, Neth.: De Haan, 1985), 545: "oudste dichter der Verenigde Staten." Two Steendam poems also appear in Nina Baym, ed., *The Norton Anthology of American Literature, Vol. A: Literature to 1820*, 6th ed. (New York: Norton, 2003), 276–85.

traveler, and over the course of his life he lived in Europe, Africa, America, and Asia. Ironically, the man who is mostly known today for his American poetry wrote far more about each of those other places. Compared against his three New Netherland poems, he wrote at least thirty-five poems about West Africa and the people he had known during his eight years as lay preacher on the Gold Coast, and at the end of his life he published a whole book of poems for the youth of Batavia in the Dutch East Indies. Many of the Batavian poems were on broad, universal topics like love and courage, but again, as he had done with America and Africa before, he also included poems about specific people, places, and events from his time in the East. In total, Steendam published at least 236 poems and a few short works in prose.[3]

The "Lost Poems" of this essay's title do not refer to Steendam's African and Asian poetry. Dutch historians are already aware of both, and even if they haven't done much with them, they have sometimes mentioned them or examined limited, individual poems in writing about New Netherland or the Dutch Atlantic.[4] By "Lost Poems" I am referring to four poems written in New Netherland (or in one case *about* New Netherland) that Steendam published in his Asian collection in the 1670s, much later than his three better-known New Netherland poems. In general, historians must use poetry with caution, of course, because any particular work might reflect the views of some nebulous, unnamed narrator, not necessarily the author. As Joanne van der Woude and Jaap Jacobs learned in studying Petrus Stuyvesant's unpublished poems, early modern writers also sometimes chose not to engage with their colonial surroundings or provide concrete historical, biographical details about their lives. But in Stuyvesant's poetical exchanges with Johan Farret, a Dutch official at Curaçao, van der Woude and Jacobs did still find subjects of great value. They could at least identify and analyze Atlantic friendship networks, spheres of influence, "male affect," and imperial ambition. Historians and literary scholars can both do more to include these kinds of sources in the corpus of colonial and early American literature.[5]

Because Steendam, unlike Stuyvesant, wrote about real places and moments, his poems are a useful window on his life and travels, as well as the ideas and culture of his time. So committed was he to the strengths and possibilities of poetry, he sometimes wrote even his correspondence in verse, using rhyming couplets, for example, to share with friends the details of a recent voyage or his initial impressions of a new and unfamiliar land.[6] When

---

3. Steendam published his African poems (and many others) in *Den Distelvink* (3 vols., Amsterdam, 1649–50). His Asian poems appeared as *Zeede-sangen voor de Batavische Jonkheyt* (Batavia, no date).

4. See Willem Frijhoff's use of Steendam's African poetry in *Wegen van Evert Willemsz: Een Hollands weeskind op zoek naar zichzelf, 1607–1647* (Nijmegen, Neth.: SUN, 1995), 535–39; and Jaap Jacobs, *The Colony of New Netherland: A Dutch Settlement in Seventeenth-Century America* (Ithaca, NY: Cornell University Press, 2009), 230.

5. Joanne van der Woude and Jaap Jacobs, "Sweet Resoundings: Friendship Poetry by Petrus Stuyvesant and Johan Farret on Curacao, 1639–1645," *William and Mary Quarterly* 75, no. 3 (2018): 508.

6. My favorite example of this phenomenon is his "letter" to Aafie Cornelis, published in *Den Distelvink*, 2:193–95. On the question of cultural value in colonial poetry, see also van Boheemen, "Dutch-American poetry," 115–116.

the voice or narrator is uncertain—even when Steendam is clearly adopting a different persona—the huge volume of his work allows us to identify the ideas and issues that concerned him most. More than anything else, in the four poems examined in this essay he revealed contemporary notions about families and their social, cultural significance. Less directly but still through suggestion and the coincidence of circumstance, living as he then was in America, Steendam communicated in the same poems the value of family relationships in planting colonies and building empires. He never wrote much about his own wife, Sara Steendam, yet he sometimes depended on her for his professional appointments and successes, such as they were, and even for his publishing.[7]

Marriage and families had been common themes for Steendam from the start of his writing career. He celebrated Christian marriage especially in his Africa collection (*Den Distelvink*), perhaps because he was living in a place without much European power and without all the trappings of Dutch society. In other words, he might have been lonely and homesick, and in that state he was extra sensitive to what he, in his limited and prejudiced perception, found lacking in Africa. Europe was "the best part of the world," Steendam wrote. There God had gathered his congregation, blessing them with reason, knowledge, learning, and truth.[8] God also gave them marriage, which Steendam placed at the heart of civilization, for marriage produced families, and families were necessary to form cities. Borrowing from an intellectual tradition that stretched from ancient Greece and Rome to seventeenth-century Europe and the urban Dutch Republic, Steendam maintained that cities sheltered the citizenry (*burgery*) and "the rights of citizenship" (*burger recht*).[9] He later suggested similar connections between domesticity and municipal, national strength— and similar connections between religion and strength—when he extolled America's virtues and colonial possibilities in "Praise of New Netherland." According to Steendam, all

---

7. Sara Steendam sometimes also appears as "Sara de Rosschou" or "Sara Abrahamsz" in various manuscript sources. On women in Dutch colonies, see Susanah Shaw Romney, "'With & alongside his housewife': Claiming Ground in New Netherland and the Early Modern Dutch Empire," *William and Mary Quarterly* 73, no. 2 (2016): 187–224; Susanah Shaw Romney, *New Netherland Connections: Intimate Networks and Atlantic Ties in Seventeenth-Century America* (Chapel Hill: University of North Carolina Press, 2014). For families in the Atlantic world (not just the Dutch world), see Julie Hardwick, Sarah M. S. Pearsall, and Karin Wulf, "Introduction: Centering Families in Atlantic Histories," *William and Mary Quarterly* 70, no. 2 (2013): 205–24. Like Romney, they (Hardwick, Pearsall, and Wulf) write about families claiming spaces and marking territories as culturally European (218). The entirety of the forum on families (the forum they are introducing) runs from 205–424.
On marriage under the Dutch West India Company, see Deborah Hamer, "Creating an Orderly Society: The Regulation of Marriage and Sex in the Dutch Atlantic World, 1621-1674" (Ph.D. diss., Columbia University, 2014).
8. Steendam, *Den Distelvink* 2:72, 3:76–79. Calvinist clergy like Steendam tended to condemn the behavior, but European men and African women did often have relationships and bear children in West Africa, sometimes even marrying each other. Those children, once grown, facilitated exchange no less than European families strengthened Dutch land claims in America. See Johannes Postma, *The Dutch in the Atlantic Slave Trade, 1600-1815* (Cambridge: Cambridge University Press, 1990), 68–71. For the potential advantages of these relationships to African women, see Pernille Ipsen, "'The Christened Mulatresses': Euro-African Families in a Slave-Trading Town," *William and Mary Quarterly* 70, no. 2 (2013): 371–398.
9. Ibid., 2:55–59. On citizenship, civitas, and ancient Rome, see Anthony Pagden, *Lords of All the World: Ideologies of Empire in Spain, Britain, and France, c. 1500–1800* (New Haven, CT: Yale University Press, 1995), chap. 1.

healthy societies needed truth and the word of God, "Through which a House, and City, and Country stand."[10]

Steendam included these themes in his forgotten New Netherland poems, three of which he wrote to celebrate specific weddings shortly after his arrival in the colony: the weddings of Isaac Bedlo and Elisabeth de Potter (1653), Pieter Jacobs Marius and Maria Pieters (1655), and Lucas Andries Sabyn and Eva Louwerens van der Wel (1655).[11] Steendam had written wedding poems in Holland and West Africa before, and he would do so again in other places in the future. In this case the people whose marriages he celebrated are noteworthy because they seem to have traveled almost as much as Steendam. They certainly came from the same set of transatlantic, global merchants and wanderers. Sabyn had the most experience locally in New Amsterdam because, according to the marriage register, he was born there, which would have put him among the earliest Dutch-American births. Three of the other five individuals came from the Netherlands—two from Amsterdam and one from the village of Hoogwoud in West Friesland. Bedlo and De Potter traveled the farthest, he "from Calais in France" and she all the way "from Batavia in the East Indies." We can only speculate about whether Elisabeth de Potter had enjoyed her time in the East Indies and whether Steendam, who had not yet traveled there in the 1650s, learned much about his future Asian home in conversation with her.[12]

Steendam's writing for these particular individuals and weddings suggests at least two interpretations. First, as a new colonist he did not yet have many friends or connections and was trying to make them through flattery and the flaunting of his talents. Second, he had already begun to establish those local connections, and the marriage poems, like Stuyvesant's poetical exchanges with Farret, reflect the economic networks and spheres of influence within which Steendam operated in New Netherland. The second interpretation seems more likely because of how he (and the three grooms) made a living. He no longer worked as lay preacher for the Dutch Reformed Church, as he had for so many years in West Africa. Instead he shows up in various American records as a tradesman and merchant: delivering upholstery, dabbling in tobacco and other agriculture, at one point asking to participate in the slave trade.[13] Steendam made enough money to purchase multiple homes and land in America, most of which he rented to others, and he twice contributed funds for New Amsterdam's defense. Although he never held any powerful positions or offices, he was sufficiently important for colonial authorities to consult about new taxes.

10. Murphy, *Anthology*, 66–67. The translation in this case is mine, not Murphy's.

11. For their marriage poems, see Steendam, *Zeede-sangen*, 86–93.

12. Samuel S. Purple, ed., *Collections of the New York Genealogical and Biographical Society, Vol. 1: Marriages from 1639 to 1801 in the Reformed Dutch Church, New York* (New York: Printed for the Society, 1890), 18, 20.

13. Berthold Fernow, trans., *The Records of New Amsterdam from 1653 to 1674* (Baltimore, MD: Genealogical Publishing, 1976), 1:158; 2:397, 401; 3:142. For the slave trade, see the New York State Archives, New York Colonial Manuscripts (hereafter NYCM), 9:322. For tobacco, see the Stadsarchief Amsterdam (hereafter SAA), 5033, 5:296; and SAA, Notarieel Archief, 2294:11–14.

The New Amsterdam court also sometimes appointed him as arbiter in legal disputes. Through commerce and land speculation he rose to become—not one of the colony's great merchants—but a respectable member of the community.[14]

The three men of Steendam's wedding poems had the same basic career trajectories and social status. Steendam and Marius both appear, for example, in the tax lists of 1655, and both owed roughly the same amount. With the colonists' payments ranging from ƒ 6 on the low end to ƒ 150 for the well-to-do, Steendam was assessed just ƒ 25 and Marius ƒ 20.[15] Marius, Bedlo, and Sabyn also worked as petty merchants and landlords, transporting for others or trading their own livestock, tobacco, wine, and other goods. Like Steendam, they never held powerful positions in the West India Company or civic government, but the courts did sometimes appoint them as arbiters.[16] The key difference between Steendam's career and theirs was that he left the colony and they did not, which gave them the time (after it became English) to attain the offices they never held in the Dutch period: Pieter Jacobs Marius eventually became a deacon in the Dutch Reformed Church, which continued to function as normal after the English conquest, and Isaac Bedlo became alderman and militia captain. Bedlo also happened to be the first European owner of present-day Liberty Island, home to the Statue of Liberty.[17]

Steendam's message in the Bedlo/De Potter marriage poem was somewhat bland and predictable, as far as love poems go. He wrote about the strength and durability of love in surviving the coldest winters and the hottest summer suns, the worst droughts and even the destruction of war. Love, he said, was a gloriously steadfast virtue in an ugly, volatile world. And he cast a subtle aspersion on those who, contrary to "Godly council," choose not to marry. With each of these dangers, Steendam may have had specific local and global phenomena in mind, including New Netherland's cold winters, its occasional droughts, and the First Anglo-Dutch War, which was just beginning its second year. But he did not draw those connections clearly in the poem itself.[18]

Steendam reflected more on the social benefits of marriage in the other two poems, both written in November 1655.[19] For Pieter Jacobs Marius and Maria Pieters he called marriage a good, necessary, and "priceless" institution. For Lucas Andries Sabyn and Eva Louwerens van der Wel he wrote even more dramatically that "All human affairs / depend

---

14. Many property transactions appear in Land Papers. See, for example, NYCM HH, part 1:9. For "defense," "tax," and "arbiter," see Fernow, *Records*, 1:67, 142, and 372; Charles Gehring, trans., *Council Minutes, 1652–1654* (Baltimore, MD: Genealogical Publishing, 1983), 80–81.

15. Fernow, *Records*, 1:370, 372. The symbols ƒ and fl. signify "guilder" (the florin/florijn guilder).

16. See, for example, ibid., 1:236; 3:39, 196, 220, 349, 405; 4:3, 9, 191; and 6:330, where it becomes clear that Marius and Sabyn sometimes worked/traded together.

17. For their offices, see ibid., 5:202; 6:261, 357. For Bedlo and Liberty Island, see "Spell It with a 'W,'" *New York Times*, August 14, 1886.

18. Steendam, *Zeede-sangen*, 86–88.

19. Steendam got the dates wrong in two of the three poems, probably because they were published so long after the fact. In both the Marius and Sabyn poems he was off by one month, citing December instead of November.

on Matrimony."[20] As he had before in his Africa poems, Steendam went on to draw connections between marriage and families, then families and communities and kingdoms:

> Herefrom come communities
> of hamlet, and village, and city,
> whose strength, as adornment,
> is contained in unanimity.
> Herefrom comes the free coronation
> that men grant a king:
> who for the honor, for a reward,
> his people,
> so united,
> so diminished,
> must protect.

"Do you hinder marriage?" Steendam continued. If so, you "destroy all the power" of the state or kingdom. But Sabyn had decided, for the benefit of this particular land, to marry Eva Louwerens van der Wel. In the final stanza Steendam played with van der Wel's given name ("Eve" in English) to draw a link between the world's first union—that of Adam and Eve, according to the Bible—and this union in New Netherland.[21]

In the Marius and Pieters marriage poem Steendam also offered a glimpse of the culture and humanity that can sometimes get lost in the cold analysis of these distant events. In New Netherland and the Dutch world generally, weddings were times of festivity and revelry, with beer and edible refreshments provided by the newlyweds and their families. Friends might also use the occasion to show off their writing talents, and they could and often did set the words to popular tunes and read or sing them before the gathered guests.[22] Accordingly, Steendam always listed at the start of his poems—not just his wedding poems—the tunes to which they were supposed to be sung. For Marius and Pieters he used "Lately as I Went out Hunting" (*Lestmaal als ik ging uyt jagen*).[23] In the first stanzas he reflected on the ubiquity and use of marriage, then turned his attention to the music and merriment:

> Let us now sing lustily
> for the honor of this pair:
> for they require (above all things)

20. Steendam, *Zeede-sangen*, 89, 91.
21. Ibid., 92–93. For the Bible story, see Genesis 2.
22. Jacobs, *The Colony*, 228–30. Jacobs writes about these traditions especially in connection with Rev. Henricus Selyns's poem for the Luyck/Isendoorn marriage (1663). The poem is available in Dutch and English in Murphy, *Anthology*, 132–47.
23. Steendam, *Zeede-sangen*, 89 (italics in the original). I couldn't find an exact match at the Nederlandse Liederenbank, but two possibilities are "Lestmael in 't krieken van den dag" and "Het ging een Ruyter uyt Jagen." See www.liederenbank.nl; accessed October 31, 2018.

the gaiety of the throng,

but especially the youth.

Keeping in mind that Steendam—and perhaps others—sang the poem, and that he and Marius both lived on Pearl Street, one can almost see and hear the festivities of November 13, 1655. "Girls, are you not happy?" he asked in one stanza. "What more do you have to fear?" In place of fear they should "raise a Song," wish happiness to bride and groom, and "flood the PEARL STREET with chatter."[24]

Nowhere in any of these three poems did Steendam explicitly connect marriage, families, and colonialism at any significant length. But the setting and subject, with his many reflections on marriage and general civic strength, allow us to read that message between the lines, especially because of Steendam's other New Netherland writings. At the very least, the marriage poems were a step toward "Complaint of New Amsterdam" (1659), "Praise of New Netherland" (1661), "Spurring Verses" (1662), and their positive depiction of the colony as a place of bounty and potential Dutch growth and Dutch community: an "Eternal possession," as Steendam declared in "Praise of New Netherland."[25] Read together, the marriage poems and the more famous propaganda poems, written to attract settlers, offer a united, consistent vision of colonial possibilities: Strong families make strong communities, and America was a good setting for both. Less specifically about women than marriage generally, Steendam's work is nevertheless relevant to understanding "gender frontiers" and the role that women played in staking land claims and fostering global interests, even in the so-called seaborne, commercial empire of the seventeenth-century Dutch.[26]

Whether they intended to strengthen New Netherland or not, four of the six newlyweds in Steendam's poems certainly did their part to grow the colonial population. Pieter Jacobs Marius and Maria Pieters appear nowhere in the baptismal records, suggesting that they had no children, but the other two couples did their best to make up the difference. Between the 1650s and the 1680s, Isaac Bedlo and Elisabeth de Potter had at least five children, while Lucas Andries Sabyn and Eva Louwerens van der Wel had fifteen.[27] Jacob and Sara Steendam stood witness to several baptisms during their years in New Netherland,

---

24. Steendam, *Zeede-sangen*, 90 (capitalization in the original). For Steendam, Marius, and Pieters living on Pearl Street—or at least owning property and homes there—see NYCM HH, part 1:42; Fernow, *Records*, 5:223.

25. Murphy, *Anthology*, 66. Murphy translated the same phrase ("Eeuwig-eygendom") as "inheritance fore'er."

26. Romney, "With & alongside his housewife." For "gender frontiers," see also Kathleen M. Brown, "The Anglo-Algonquian Gender Frontier," in *Negotiators of Change: Historical Perspectives on Native American Women*, ed. Nancy Shoemaker (New York: Routledge, 1995), 26–48. For the Dutch commercial empire and the Dutch as an "alongshore folk," see Donna Merwick, *The Shame and the Sorrow: Dutch-Amerindian Encounters in New Netherland* (Philadelphia: University of Pennsylvania Press, 2006), 3, 264, 267; Patricia Seed, *Ceremonies of Possession in Europe's Conquest of the New World, 1492–1640* (New York: Cambridge University Press, 1995), chap. 5. See also Donna Merwick, *Possessing Albany, 1630–1710: The Dutch and English Experience* (New York: Cambridge University Press, 1990).

27. The above-mentioned couples appear in various places in Thomas Grier Evans, ed., *Collections of the New York Genealogical and Biographical Society, Vol. 2: Baptisms from 1639 to 1730 in the Reformed Dutch Church, New York* (New York: Printed for the Society, 1901), 43–156.

and they had eight children of their own. Yet the man who contributed his writing talents so often for the growth of the colony did not contribute his offspring. Five of his eight children were born in Amsterdam or the East Indies, and of course he and Sara decided to leave America at the very time he was most actively encouraging others to settle there.[28]

The occasion of Steendam's fourth and last forgotten New Netherland poem was his daughter Vredegund's fourteenth birthday, which fell on April 1, 1669—long after he had concluded his American affairs, spent a few years in Amsterdam, and moved to the East Indies. But he used the poem to review Vredegund's life until then, dedicating five stanzas to the New Netherland period and, in the process, revealing previously unknown details about the family's experience in America and their decision to leave. The rest of the poem is also valuable for the advice Steendam gave his daughter at a critical juncture of her life, as she transitioned from child to adult and from "virgin" or "maiden" (*maagd*) to woman. If in his earlier poems he recognized the importance of women in the general sense that strong families created strong states and communities, for his daughter he described the type of adult and type of woman he had probably always had in mind.[29]

Set to the tune "Young Women Full of Joy," the Vredegund poem begins with Steendam's general reflections on birthdays, the passage of time, and the significance of the number seven in the Christian scriptures. Steendam noted that the number was doubly relevant on that particular day because Vredegund was "Two times seven, in [her] years."[30] He finally turned to her birth and American sojourn in the tenth stanza:

> The Morning sun of your birth
> I witnessed in New Netherland:
> and you, as a young plant,
> of the most pleasant sort:
> with a sweet laugh,
> promised me fruit, on that day.

But Steendam quickly pivoted from this cheerful scene to a darker one by reminding Vredegund in the next stanza that "Fate" had bound her to his nomadic, global lifestyle. To do so he employed the imagery and vocabulary of the weaver, as if the threads of their lives were unalterably entwined. Fate, he wrote, "wove your time as one / with the weft of unrest: / through the warp of my inclination."[31]

The poet then sought to prove this "assertion," as he put it, by recounting the family's

---

28. For "witness," see ibid., 33, 37, 38, 42. Evidence of the Steendam's eight children is scattered throughout archives stretching from Amsterdam to America and the East Indies. Their first child, Jacob, was born in Amsterdam in 1650 and the last, Aurora, in Batavia in 1666. See SAA 5001, 8:289; and Arsip Nasional Republik Indonesia (hereafter ANRI), Retroacta Burgerlijke Stand, inv. nr. 1 (October 21, 1666).
29. "Maagd" or "Maagden" comes from Steendam, *Zeede-sangen*, 20. The longest of the four poems in question, the Vredegund poem, runs 15–24 (35 stanzas).
30. Ibid., 15.
31. Ibid., 17. The warp and weft are the perpendicular, interwoven threads that constitute fabric.

many travels in the first years of Vredegund's life. Apparently those travels began even before they left America, for she moved "first through the terrible Hell Gate: / through the sound, and to New Haven."[32] By "Hell Gate" Steendam was referring to the East River, which is not really a river at all, but a strait separating the eastern shore of Manhattan from the western shore of Long Island and the mainland. Discovered and named by explorer Adriaen Block in 1614, Hell Gate was indeed "terrible" (*vreeslijk*), as Steendam wrote. Any pilot attempting to guide a vessel from one end to the other had to worry about its many small islands, rocks, strange currents, and at least one whirlpool. As recently as 1643 a small English ship had foundered there, and seven of the crew drowned.[33]

From Hell Gate, Steendam's vessel passed safely into Long Island Sound (he just called it "the sound") and to the English colony of New Haven. This is the most curious part of the poem because it's unclear what he was doing there. It's easy to assume that he, as a merchant, was just trading, but why bring Vredegund, as he clearly said he did? Three other sources confirm that the whole Steendam family moved briefly to New Haven in late 1656 or early 1657 and that their life there was at least partly agricultural. Perhaps because of the impending move, they sold two pieces of property on Manhattan Island in August and September 1656, which was the last time for more than a year that they would appear in person in any Dutch record.[34] The clearest evidence of their New Haven abode comes from a November 1657 court case in that colony. The Englishman Edward Perkins came to the court to complain that "Mr. Stendams" hogs had broken through a shabby fence and destroyed six bushels of peas. Perkins could not get any payment from Steendam because Steendam had hired some men to repair the fence, and they had done a lousy job. *They* should have to pay for the peas, Steendam complained. Different neighbors testified to the origin of the hogs and the amount of damage, adding that they had warned Steendam more than once that something like this might happen. They had not brought him to court before now, they added, because he was "a stranger."[35]

The Dutch stranger lost the case and was back among his own people in New Amsterdam just two weeks later, November 18, 1657. On that day he and Sara were both present for the baptism of their newborn son, Samuel, meaning that Sara had either remained in New Amsterdam to oversee the family business, returned from New Haven before Jacob, or traveled with him in early November, passing through Hell Gate a second time at the very

---

32. Ibid., 18.
33. Michael Nichols, *Hell Gate: A Nexus of New York City's East River* (Albany: SUNY Press, 2018), intro. and chap. 1.
34. New York City Municipal Archives, Records of New Amsterdam, Burgomasters and Schepens, 1:102, 108. The Steendams were in New Haven at least by May 1657, because in that month "Harmen Schuinman" (aka Harmen Smeeman) mortgaged his New Amsterdam home to pay a large debt to Steendam, "at present living at New Haven." See Theodore M. Banta, *Dutch Records in the City Clerk's Office New York* (New York: Knickerbocker Press, 1900), 1:55.
35. Franklin Bowditch Dexter, ed., *Ancient Town Records, Vol. 1: New Haven Town Records, 1649–1662* (New Haven, CT: New Haven Colony Historical Society, 1917), 327–28.

end of her pregnancy. All three possibilities are consistent with what we know about seventeenth-century Dutch women and their comparatively liberal economic and legal opportunities.[36] Sara appears far less often than Jacob in the historical record, but she was, at the very least, a gutsy, outspoken individual. Just eight weeks after the baptism, for instance, she got into some legal trouble of her own by taunting the New Amsterdam fire wardens, whose job it was to inspect her home for possible fire hazards. She must have thought them too slow, because she "railed at the Fire Wardens as Buck-sweeps," according to one account. According to another, "she said with a laughing mouth, Be you now keeping holiday amongst you, Chimney Sweeps?" She meant it as a joke, claimed her husband, but they took offense, and she refused to appear in court to defend herself. When the sheriff came to fetch her, she predicted her probable loss and probable fine, explaining, "whether I come or not, I shall give as much."[37]

Jacob Steendam did not explain in the Vredegund poem why they decided to leave New Haven, but he did mention the return to New Netherland "with our family." And he did hint at their reasons for leaving America altogether a few years later: fear of a new conflict with Native Americans and the dangers it posed. He wrote:

Chance appeared to play along
and drove from there (for the danger
of the war) your mother:
and chose to charge to me alone
the supervision of your tenderness:
led by your childish passions.

Given the timing, "the war" could have only been the Esopus Wars, which began in the fall of 1659 over questions of land and European settlement in the Hudson River Valley, about halfway between New Amsterdam and present-day Albany, New York. The Steendam family had already experienced one war with Native Americans—the Peach War—and they apparently did not want to experience another. And for good reason: During the Peach War, an alliance of different tribes had attacked colonists west and south of New Amsterdam, destroying at least twenty-eight farms, slaughtering and stealing hundreds of cattle, killing more than fifty colonists, and taking roughly one hundred captives. With the bulk of Dutch soldiers on the Delaware River at the time, the attackers had even ransacked homes in the

---

36. Adriana E. van Zwieten, "'[O]n her woman's troth': Tolerance, Custom, and the Women of New Netherland," *De Halve Maen* 72, no. 1 (1999): 3–14. For the increased presence and activity of women in western European labor markets, which contributed to the economic transformations of the Dutch Golden Age, see Tine de Moor and Jan Luiten van Zanden, "Girl Power: The European Marriage Pattern and Labour Markets in the North Sea Region in the Late Medieval and Early Modern Period," *Economic History Review* 63, no. 1 (2010): 1–33 (esp. pp. 4, 12, 29); Jan de Vries, "The Industrial Revolution and the Industrious Revolution," *Journal of Economic History* 54, no. 2 (1994): 249–70.

37. Fernow, *Records*, 2:297. Taken together, these statements by Sara Steendam belie Jacob's claim that she didn't come to court because "she is a woman," and as such, she was "timorous."

capital, including probably some of the Steendam properties, then withdrew to the west side of the Hudson River for a tense, months-long standoff and negotiation over the captives.[38]

The heart of the new wars, the Esopus Wars, was farther to the north, but the Steendams could not know that the bloodshed would never reach New Amsterdam. That fear was clearly on Jacob's mind, because he wrote the darkest of his three propaganda poems, "Complaint of New Amsterdam," in the same period. Less about enticing new colonists than the other two poems, it was still "propaganda" because, according to Frans Blom and Henk Looijesteijn, the author's main goal was to convince the regents of Amsterdam to continue supporting New Netherland at a time when they were considering selling their investment back to the West India Company.[39] "Complaint" was the only one of the three to acknowledge things like danger, mourning, and conflict, tracking the growth of the colony from its birth through 1659. New Amsterdam had spent a long time "in the loins of warlike Mars," Steendam wrote in one stanza.[40]

"Complaint of New Amsterdam" was published in old Amsterdam in 1659, yet Jacob Steendam remained in America for at least one more year, which raises the strong possibility that Sara carried the poem with her and oversaw its publication. Jacob did say in the later Vredegund poem that Sara was driven from America by the war, implying, perhaps unintentionally, that the main fear and main voice behind the decision to return to the Netherlands was Sara's. Jacob related yet another human moment—this time a sad moment—when mother and child had to say good-bye: "You wished to depart yourself," he reminded Vredegund, "when she tried to board the ship / for the grey ocean."[41] If Sara was in fact going ahead of her family to publish the poem and prepare a home for their later arrival, it would not have been the first arrangement of its kind in the colony's history, for Machtelt Willemsen, the wife of Reverend Johannes Megapolensis, had done something similar. By 1659, Willemsen and her husband had long since decided to remain in New Netherland. But they had briefly considered alternatives, and in that interlude she had traveled to Amsterdam with a manuscript, written by her husband, for a new catechism. She had it published over the objections of the local Reformed Church, then met with West India Company directors in "many tiresome conferences," as the directors put it, until they convinced her that America was the best place for her and her family.[42] There is no record that they

38. Allen W. Trelease, *Indian Affairs in Colonial New York: The Seventeenth Century* (Ithaca, NY: Cornell University Press, 1960), chap. 6; Merwick, *The Shame and the Sorrow*, 219–27.
39. Blom and Looijesteijn, "Land of Milk and Honey," 51.
40. Murphy, *Anthology*, 37. I'm using Murphy's translation in this case.
41. Steendam, *Zeede-sangen*, 18. If Romney is correct ("With & alongside his housewife," 215) that "sovereignty followed families," and that Dutch conflicts with Native Americans in New Netherland were about *which* families (native or Dutch) would ultimately inherit the land, then the Steendam departure was a small victory for Native Americans. And the Steendams certainly weren't the only colonists who returned to Europe because of violence or the threat of violence.
42. E. T. Corwin, ed., *Ecclesiastical Records of the State of New York* (Albany, NY: J. B. Lyon, 1901–16), 1:244–45, 248–49. See also D. L. Noorlander, "The Reformed Church and the Regulation of Religious Literature in the Early Dutch Atlantic World," *Itinerario* 42, no. 3 (2018): 389–90.

tried to do the same with Sara Steendam, nor did they have much motive, because Jacob was not filling any vital position in the church or company at the time.

The rest of the Vredegund poem is not about New Netherland per se. Steendam described the family's short-lived happiness in Amsterdam and how they were driven from there to the "strange land" of Batavia, giving Vredegund experience in "all four parts of the World . . . before [she] was twelve years old."[43] What he didn't mention was that, during the Amsterdam years, he continued to promote immigration to New Netherland. He was at that time affiliated with the Jan Zoet circle of poets, participating in a literary club that met regularly in Zoet's inn in Amsterdam, the *Zoete Rust* (Sweet Rest).[44] There they discussed and debated the major social issues of the day, and from their frequent references to each other in their publications we get a glimpse of their favorite topics, including religion, vice, and family relationships. Steendam tended to reveal a rather low opinion of women, blaming them for the downfall of countless great men and depicting them as angry, quarrelsome beings who, if they hoped to be saved in the kingdom of God, needed a steady man to lead them. In general, Steendam came down on the orthodox, Calvinist side in the Zoet debates, in opposition to polygamy and other forms of religious radicalism.[45] That he would do so isn't surprising, given his long church service. Yet it does raise questions about why, despite these sentiments, he would have allowed his "Spurring Verses" to appear in a pamphlet for a Collegiant settlement on the Delaware River. Because he wrote nothing about religion in "Spurring Verses," but focused only vaguely on "the colony" (*volck-planting*) and the rich resources of New Netherland, the likely answer is that the poem was a simple favor for Karel Verloove, a friend from the Zoet circle who also happened to be affiliated with the Delaware endeavor.[46]

Whatever Steendam's purpose with "Spurring Verses," the continuity of his views on religion and marriage is evident in the Vredegund poem and his other Batavian work. Now that his daughter was fourteen, he advised her to abandon childish pursuits and adopt a "virginal" or "chaste demeanor" (*maagdelijk bewind*). The last eighteen stanzas contain his explanation and understanding—and, it's probably safe to say, the Calvinistic-Dutch understanding—of how women cultivated that particular demeanor. "Ladies must be virtuous," he wrote. They should fear God, accept God's law, obey their parents, pray regularly,

43. Steendam, *Zeede-sangen*, 18–19.

44. Van Boheemen, "Dutch-American Poets," 128. See also Rudolph Cordes, "Jan Zoet, Amsterdammer: Leven en werk van een kleurrijk schrijver" (Ph.D. diss., Vrije Universiteit, 2008).

45. The poems from the Zoet circle, including some from Jacob Steendam, appear in Jan Zoet, *Parnassus aan 't Y* (Amsterdam, 1663). For Steendam's ideas on women, see 10–11, 27–28, 43–44, 72. See also P. Rixtels, *Mengel-Rymen* (Haarlem, 1669) and *De uitsteekenste digtkunstige werken door Jan Zoet* (1719).

46. For "Spurring Verses," see Murphy, *Anthology*, 68–75. For the Collegiant/Delaware settlement, see Leland Harder, "Plockhoy and His Settlement at Zwaanendael, 1663," *Mennonite Quarterly Review* 23 (July 1949): 186–99. Frans Blom and Henk Looijesteijn also believe that Steendam demonstrated in "Spurring Verses" a concern for the common people. See their essay, "Ordinary People in the New World: The City of Amsterdam, Colonial Policy, and Initiatives from Below, 1656-1664," in *In Praise of Ordinary People: Early Modern Britain and the Dutch Republic*, ed. Margaret C. Jacob and Catherine Secretan (New York: Palgrave Macmillan, 2014), 203–235.

learn to use the power of reason to navigate right and wrong, embrace the former, and shun the latter. Studying religion would teach her, Steendam continued, what God required of her, and in that way she would be "born again" and obtain "the crown of life." On the other hand, wickedness and sin were "the seed of Women," meaning that Eve was the first to succumb to the Devil's temptations in the Garden of Eden, and women everywhere still bore the shame and consequences of that failure. He warned Vredegund that the Devil would seek to seduce her with lust, sexual freedom, and the pleasures of the flesh. She would have a better chance of resisting and avoiding sin if she learned to "hate the haters who hate God."[47]

We cannot know what Vredegund thought of this advice because she left no surviving correspondence or diary. We do know that she would have heard lots of similar advice because of the home in which she was raised, and because the East India Company appointed Jacob and Sara as "father and mother" of the local orphanage soon after their arrival in Batavia.[48] In that position they were responsible for the education and upbringing, not just of the orphans, but the children of company employees who couldn't afford the costs of maintaining a household or didn't have the time, ability, or interest to parent their offspring on their own. The orphanage filled critical social and economic functions in the East Indies by Christianizing the children of European fathers and non-European mothers, supplying the company and others with apprentices and servants, and preparing marriagable young women for Christian suitors, be they Asian or European suitors. Sara's main duty as mother of the orphanage was not so different from her duty as Vredegund's mother: She was supposed to teach her biological *and* non-biological daughters the expectations and useful skills of seventeenth-century women, including, for example, sewing and making lace, which took up much of the girls' time and provided the orphanage with extra income. In general, the orphanage contributed to Dutch strength and long-term security by cooperating with the churches and schools of Batavia to build a loyal Christian community.[49]

Vredegund must have at least maintained a good reputation, because she married in the Dutch Reformed Church at the age of eighteen, and the church selected her and her

---

47. Steendam, *Zeede-sangen*, 19–24. For the standard Calvinist interpretation of Eve's sin, see John Calvin's teachings on the matter in John King, trans., *Commentaries on the First Book of Moses, Called Genesis, by John Calvin* (Grand Rapids, MI: Eerdmans, 1948), 1:172. Calvin wrote that Eve's two punishments were (1) the pain of childbirth and (2) subjection to Adam: "Thus the woman, who had perversely exceeded her proper bounds, is forced back to her own position. She had, indeed, previously been subject to her husband, but that was a liberal and gentle subjection; now, however, she is cast into servitude."
48. ANRI, Hoge Regering, inv. nr. 879 (General Resolutions), f. 172. Prior to the appointment, Steendam had been working in the same position as he had in West Africa before: lay preacher/*ziekentrooster*. Thus he blended his poetry and teaching responsiblities from the beginning of his career in Africa (teaching soldiers) to the end of his career in Batavia (teaching orphans). The title of *Zeede-sangen* translates as "Moral Songs for the Batavian Youth."
49. For the orphanage, see Hendrik E. Niemeijer, *Batavia: Een Koloniale Samenleving in de 17de Eeuw* (Amsterdam, Neth.: Uitgeverij Balans, 2005), 316–29; Ulbe Bosma and Remco Raben, *Being "Dutch" in the Indies: A History of Creolisation and Empire, 1500-1920*, trans. Wendie Shaffer (Athens: Ohio University Press, 2008), 32–33, 50–51.

husband to take her parents' place in the orphanage after they died: Jacob in late 1671 or early 1672, Sara just before Vredegund's wedding in October 1673. Neither Jacob nor his son-in-law, Cornelis Wadde, could have attained their position at the orphanage without their wives, because it was a job for one man and one woman, with the nuclear family and its relationships and hierarchies serving as model for the orphanage. Unfortunately, however, the Steendam administration didn't last long, even with Vredegund replacing her parents, because she soon followed them to the grave, dying in 1677 at twenty-two years old. Given her age, her recent marriage, and the usual physical and medical dangers of the seventeenth century, she might have died in childbirth or from complications afterward.[50]

For all the potential challenges they pose to historians, poems can sometimes augment and enrich baptismal records, court records, and other standard resources. The four poems examined in this case—just a few of Steendam's hundreds of poems—add to our knowledge of his life in America and the culture in which he participated. The topics of marriage and family were especially prominent in his work, in part because, in his endless travels, he encountered so many other cultures and so many versions of marriage and family, some of which he dismissed as something else entirely. He also wrote about them because of the heightened necessity and fragility of Christian families in young, undeveloped, contested colonial settings. If a colony was to survive and acquire all the features of Dutch civiliza-tion, he knew it required *people*, and not just individual people, but the fathers, mothers, and children who, as family units, made the small building blocks of that larger civilization. The different meanings of "father and mother" in his life (and Sara's life) is actually a good metaphor for the challenges of social planting and growth on other continents: Steendam women did not always conform to the subdued, obedient, ideal type that he described in his poems, and his "family" in Batavia, containing many orphans, was different and more diverse than the standard Dutch family. Nor were the Steendams particularly healthy and long-lived, it seems. But fathers and mothers and children in general were no less import-ant for establishing and maintaining a right over new lands in the nascent Dutch Empire.

---

50. For Vredegund's marriage, see ANRI, Retroacta Burgerlijke Stand, inv. nr. 84, f. 220. For her appointment, her mother's death, and her death, see ANRI, Hoge Regering, inv. nr. 885, f. 281, and inv. nr. 889, f. 221. Jacob's death is harder to pinpoint. He wrote his last known poem on October 8, 1671 (*Zeede-sangen*, first poem in the book; no page number), and he stops appearing in the orphanage records in January 1672. Sara ran the orphanage by herself for a time after he died, probably with Vredegund's and Cornelis's assistance. The latter had been working there as schoolmaster before his appointment as orphan father. See ANRI, Kerken van Batavia, inv. nr. 349 (January 1672).

A Model Tenement in "The City of Homes"
George Eastman and the Challenge
of Housing Reform in Rochester, New York

Nancy J. Rosenbloom

Two contrasting headlines tell the story of Rochester, which was popularly known as "the city of homes," in the first decade of the twentieth century. Rochester's business elite especially liked the tagline that originated at the chamber of commerce: "Rochester Made Means Quality."[1] But the pictures that accompanied an article aptly called "The Submerged Tenth" that appeared in local community reform magazine *The Common-Good of Civic and Social Rochester* evoked a tale of a different city.[2] Like a blast of frigid air across the shores of Lake Ontario, the story forced Rochester leaders to confront a common problem of the era: How could their beloved city maintain its image, attract industry and manufacturing, and sustain and satisfy a rising working class if poverty threatened progress? As the third-largest city in New York, Rochester had a legacy of reform, and the memory of Frederick Douglass and the recent death of Susan B. Anthony rallied community celebration. Rochester had produced a new roster of reform-minded activists for the twentieth century, including Walter Rauschenbusch, Charles Mulford Robinson, and Lillian Wald, each of whom would reach national prominence by focusing their attention on improving specifically urban problems. In this context housing emerged as a key issue.

As city leaders, community activists, and individual citizens addressed the problem of housing, many believed they could maintain a standard of quality and lift up the so-called submerged. As in other places, there were many approaches undertaken in Rochester. If

I want to thank Susan Goodier, Larry E. Jones, and the anonymous reviewers for *New York History* for their thoughtful comments on the manuscript. I also want to thank Jesse Peers, legacy collection archivist at the George Eastman Museum, for suggesting the topic and helping locate sources, and the archival staff at the Rare Books and Manuscript Division at the Rush Rhees Library at the University of Rochester and at the Local History Division of the Rochester Public Library. Finally, I am grateful to the sabbatical program at Canisius College in Buffalo, New York, for support of this project.
1. Blake McKelvey, "The First Four Decades of the Chamber of Commerce," *Rochester History* 24, no. 4 (1962): 15.
2. Samuel Hopkins Adams, "Guardians of the Public Health," *McClure's Magazine*, July 1908, 250.

the advocacy of the poor by the city's public health officer George Goler represented one point on the spectrum of progressivism, the city council's inclination to protect the political establishment and serve municipal needs created another. This essay explores how George Eastman, Rochester's premier businessman and in subsequent decades the city's most influential benefactor, began to address the problem of housing at a dynamic moment in the city's growth. To that end, Eastman experimented with the possibility of building what he called a "model tenement." While Eastman failed to convince others that his model tenement offered a viable solution, arguably his efforts demonstrate just how fluid the possibilities for the urban landscape were during this period of growth in the decade before World War I. In its own imperfect way, the model tenement was part of a larger discussion about the best ways to build quality housing, albeit in multifamily buildings, for upwardly mobile workers in neighborhoods more downtown than uptown. The inclination to consider European models might have resulted in more compact urban designs with a balance between cost efficiencies, modern engineering, aesthetic consideration, and community that sustained the personal relationships between friends and neighbors.

The model tenement championed by Eastman in 1911 and 1912 elicited strong opposition, most notably from Dr. Goler but also from the reformers writing for *The Common-Good*. City councilmen who controlled practical aspects of multifamily dwellings such as fire ordinances also objected.[3] There are three important themes that this study illuminates. First, by asking what Eastman hoped to accomplish with his plan and why opposition rallied against it, this essay explores the nature of civic reform in the Progressive Era. Second, it presents a critical perspective on how Eastman, a businessman par excellence, engaged in the debate on housing reform, an issue of local, state, national, and international significance. Lastly, it broadens the understanding of the range of possible choices that citizens in midsized cities considered as they balanced competing interests. At the beginning and in the end, all agreed that for a city to grow and prosper the availability of adequate and affordable housing demanded community resources—whether from private or public investment—in water, sewage, road paving, or other public services. Exactly what shape affordable housing would take or where it might be located resulted from debates within the community and included the failure to adopt the "model tenement."

While many feared that poverty necessarily accompanied progress, Rochester boosters sought to create an alternative picture of their hometown using dynamic imagery rather than a single snapshot. A clever advertisement published by the Rochester Chamber of

---

3. The parameters of this story are established in Blake McKelvey's classic history of Rochester, published in 1956. For a summary of both the housing crisis in Rochester and the positions initially staked out by Dr. George Goler, writers for *The Common-Good*, the Chamber of Commerce Committee, and George Eastman, see Blake McKelvey, *Rochester: The Quest for Quality, 1890–1925* (Cambridge, MA: Harvard University Press, 1956), 163–67.

Commerce in 1911 placed the city at the eye of concentric circles mapping urban development in both the United States and Canada. Only New York City loomed as large in this distorted vision where Rochester became the sun around which all other cities orbited. In the same vein, the chamber members discussed in the most sanguine language all the possibilities of growth for Rochester as "the city of varied industries," a city that in 1911 seemingly had unparalleled opportunity for economic development. Draw a circle with a radius of 85 miles, they wrote, and Rochester "embraces a population of 1,900,000." If one were to extend the circle to a radius of 750 miles, Rochester lay at the heart of about 65,000,000 people, roughly 70 percent of the total population of the United States.[4]

By 1911, Rochester had experienced sustained population growth for at least twenty years, and especially after the turn of the century. The federal census of 1910 put Rochester's population at 218,149 and that of surrounding Monroe County at 283,212. Compared to the state census figures of 1892, the number of people claiming Rochester as home in 1910 had increased significantly, with nearly half again as many people within the city limits. According to figures reported in the 1912 city directory, the population of Rochester and Monroe County grew rapidly between 1892 and 1910. Rochester had a population of 144,834 in 1892, 162,608 in 1900, 181,666 in 1905, and 218,149 in 1910. By comparison, Monroe County increased from 200,056 in 1892, to 217,854 in 1900, to 239,434 in 1905, and then leaped to 283,212 in 1910. To accommodate this growth, the city added six new wards, the Seventeenth through the Twenty-Second. Monroe County also experienced growth, but not at the same rate. In 1910, Rochester claimed over three-quarters of the county population but only a fraction of the area, which included several fast-growing towns.[5] According to the chamber of commerce, Rochester was located "in the richest agricultural county in New York State and the second richest in the United States in point of productiveness."[6] But on the basis of figures alone, the county's growth came from Rochester, and Rochester's dynamism came from diversified manufacturing that included men's clothing, optics, and photographic supplies. Multiple rail lines, including the New York Central, the Buffalo, Rochester and Pittsburgh, the Erie Railroad, the Pennsylvania Railroad, and the Lehigh Valley, shipped goods and transported people in and out of Rochester and connected the city to the broader developments across the nation.[7] In 1910, Rochester ranked as the twenty-fifth-largest city in the United States.[8]

---

4. Rochester Chamber of Commerce, *Rochester, N.Y.: The City of Varied Industries* (Rochester: Drew Allis Co., 1912), Special Collections, Rochester Public Library; *Rochester City Directory for the Year Beginning July 15, 1912* (Rochester: Drew Allis Co., 1912).

5. Bureau of Municipal Research New York, New York, *Government of the City of Rochester, New York* (Albany, NY: J. B. Lyon, 1915), 10. For the population of Rochester and Monroe County, see *Rochester City Directory for the Year Beginning July 15, 1912*. For more context, see McKelvey, *The Quest for Quality*, 331–32.

6. *Rochester N.Y.: The City of Varied Industries*, 5.

7. The author thanks Matthew Rosenbloom-Jones for clarifying which railroads were most significant to Rochester's growing economy. Additionally, there were a number of smaller railroads including electric railroads.

8. Campbell Gibson, "Population of the 100 Largest Cities and Other Urban Places in the United States, 1790 to 1990," Population Division Working Paper no. 27, Population Division, U.S. Bureau of the Census, Washington, DC (June 1998) census.gov, accessed January 14, 2015. All figures in this paragraph come from this site.

Based on its population, Rochester held the status of a second-class city according to a schemata set out in the 1894 New York State Constitutional Convention, where some delegates hoped to create some sort of uniformity in urban problem-solving.[9] Rochester seems to have been in a "Goldilocks" position: it was significantly smaller than New York City (even its individual boroughs with the exception of Richmond), only half the size of Buffalo, yet much bigger than the other second-class cities in the state.[10] Numbers alone tell only a fraction of its story, however, because of the particulars of Rochester's population growth that resulted from the spike in migration from Eastern and southern Europe. Exactly when the immigrants alighting from trains in downtown Rochester forever changed the sounds of the city streets is hard to pinpoint, but between 1900 and 1910 the foreign-born and their children accounting for much of the city's growth spoke Polish, Yiddish, Russian, Italian, or perhaps other less-familiar Slavic languages as their first language rather than English or German.[11]

Such rapid growth did not go unnoticed in promotional literature published by the chamber of commerce. As late as 1911, the chamber described a largely native-born population that included about fifty thousand of German "extraction" and twenty-five thousand of other nationalities, mostly Italian. In determining the ethnic composition of their community, the chamber focused on two important demographic facts: growth came from native-born children of the first generation and often naturalized Americans, and even while the median age in the city was moving upward the numbers of adolescents increased significantly.[12] Many stayed in school, and while their accommodation posed a challenge to the education system, few employers were blind to the potential of a skilled workforce in the not-too-distant future. Among those most forward-looking, housing loomed as not only an immediate problem but also an issue to be solved for the long term. To attract entrepreneurs and industrialists to bring new business, the chamber emphasized in its literature that Rochester remained "essentially an American city, with the best of the traditions and customs of the German added, making a most satisfactory result."[13] At the same time that this promotional literature described the character of the city's population as native-born, it also highlighted that in Rochester 65 percent of the workmen owned their homes and, most importantly, that the city "has no slums."[14]

---

9. "City Government," in *The Encyclopedia of New York State*, ed. Peter Eisenstadt (Syracuse, NY: Syracuse University Press, 2005), 330–32.

10. For comparison, the fourth-largest city in New York in 1910, Syracuse, and the fifth-largest, Albany, had populations of 137,248 and 100,253, respectively (U.S. Bureau of the Census, "Population of the 100 Largest Urban Places, 1910," https://www.census.gov/population/www/documentation/twps0027/tab14.txt).

11. For an interesting discussion of Rochester's immigrant populations see McKelvey, *The Quest for Quality*, 146–58. He clarifies that Rochester had always attracted immigrants but that previous waves of migration from Germany, Great Britain, and Canada had been largely absorbed.

12. McKelvey, *The Quest for Quality*, 158–61.

13. *Rochester, N.Y.: The City of Varied Industries*, 11.

14. Ibid.

Overcrowded, inadequate, and insufficient housing had become an identifying if not unifying characteristic of U.S. cities by 1910.[15] Ways to address the problems surfaced along parallel but not always intersecting tracts that gave voice to both the needs of progress and the growing concern for poverty. In studying the problem of workmen's housing, the Rochester chamber focused on skilled labor at Eastman Kodak and Bausch and Lomb, as well as in the city's rapidly expanding clothing factories that attracted many immigrants from the Russian Pale of Settlement. For this upwardly mobile population the chamber struggled to determine how to encourage the private construction of both small houses to buy and flats to rent.[16] Meanwhile, Rochester's activist citizens, including members of the Women's Educational Industrial Union and those affiliated with the umbrella group publishing in *The Common-Good*, drew far more attention to the deterioration of the older housing stock and the lack of access to sanitary conditions for those forced to live in lodging houses or overcrowded spaces. These strata included those who had arrived so recently to the area that they struggled with poverty, and, even more alarmingly, those unskilled and migrant workers whose low-paying day labor and seasonal work made affording rent difficult. In Rochester, as elsewhere across the Northeast, a substantial immigrant population swelled the ranks of those who struggled most. The impoverished families in the Fourth Ward became the public face of Rochester's housing problem.[17]

In broad strokes, the situation in Rochester by 1910 mirrored a heightened national awareness that the time had arrived to build new housing of one sort or another. The Rochester chamber and reform-minded citizens prioritized different aspects of the problem, but both had a good grasp of local conditions. Nevertheless, divisions that characterized housing reform agendas among progressives generally reverberated in Rochester. Historian Maureen Flanagan describes the gendered nature of this debate as it unfolded at the National Conference on City Planning in 1909 and within a group that splintered from it scarcely two years later, the National Housing Association. A difference in priorities emerged between Mary Simkhovitch and others who stressed the housing needs of people—with women and family needs front and center—and male contemporaries such

15. There is extensive primary literature on housing in a variety of urban areas, including New York and Chicago as well as smaller cities such as Pittsburgh and St. Louis. For further context on the problems of housing reform in the Progressive Era, see Roy Lubove, *The Progressives and the Slums: Tenement Reform in New York City, 1890–1917* (Pittsburgh: University of Pittsburgh Press, 1962); John F. Bauman, "Community Building versus Housing Reform: Roy Lubove and the History of Housing Reform in the United States," *Pennsylvania History: A Journal of Mid-Atlantic Studies* 68 (Summer 2001): 293–313; Howard Gillette, *Civitas by Design: Building Better Communities from the Garden City to the New Urbanism* (Philadelphia: University of Pennsylvania Press, 2010); and Maureen A. Flanagan, *America Reformed, Progressives and Progressivisms, 1890s–1920s* (New York: Oxford University Press, 2007).
16. McKelvey, *The Quest for Quality*, 165. For a more detailed discussion of changes to the near northeast, see Blake McKelvey, "Rochester's Near Northeast," *Rochester History* 29, no. 2 (1967): 1–12.
17. See the interesting compilation of articles in *The Common-Good of Civic and Social Rochester* (Rochester, NY: E. A. Rumball, 1910–14). These volumes include several articles from the Fourth Ward Survey and images of housing, children, model tenements, and more.

as John Nolen who focused more on policies—baseline economics—that emphasized planning streets, traffic, and infrastructure.[18]

In response to the crisis in Rochester, the Chamber of Commerce commissioned a study of housing that focused specifically on what they called the "high rental problem." Headed by John McCurdy, who also served on the board of trustees of Rochester Theological Seminary, the committee sought ideas from other cities facing comparable problems, including New York, Cleveland, and Baltimore.[19] Reportedly, the committee went so far as to hire a Boston architect to plan affordable rental houses along so-called model lines.[20] Their efforts built on studies done by earlier committees over the past five years, including a report that suggested that a nonprofit corporation build cottages for working men and their families.[21] After the chamber hired Sidney R. Clarke as its executive, more studies of housing followed. Clarke had arrived in Rochester following a stint at of the San Jose Chamber of Commerce. Attempting to move the questions forward and draw interest from the private sector, Clarke suggested a contest requesting architectural plans for modest homes for workers. [22] As was typical elsewhere, few real improvements had been made to address the problems of insufficient and inadequate housing by the end of the decade.[23]

With a looming urban crisis and lacking clout on many chambers of commerce and city councils, activist women sought alternative ways to address the situation. Some reformers, including Jane Addams, Florence Kelley, and Sophonisba Breckinridge, investigated conditions, demonstrated need, and looked to municipal government to do something first and foremost to improve living conditions.[24] To that end, the Rochester chapter of the Women's Educational and Industrial Union sought to investigate the local crisis, and in 1910 they invited Caroline Bartlett Crane to conduct a survey of housing problems in Rochester. Crane had many overlapping interests with the broader Rochester community. Crane was a Unitarian minister and woman suffrage activist, and her agenda articulated many of the issues of the social gospel movement popularized by Rochester's native son Walter Rauschenbusch. The work she did in Rochester most likely helped her focus a much broader agenda and realize that housing reform was essential and perhaps key to all other social improvements in an increasingly democratic society.[25] When Crane came to

---

18. Flanagan, *America Reformed*, 93.
19. McKelvey, "A History of City Planning in Rochester," *Rochester History*, October 1944, 8.
20. Ibid.
21. McKelvey, "The First Four Decades," 14. McKelvey identifies Clarke as having come from a New York City settlement house, but if he had worked in New York immediately before arriving in Rochester he had spent the previous three or four years at the chamber of commerce in San Jose, California, and had left following the earthquake. For a brief biography of Clark, see *Editor and Publisher*, April 16, 1921, 42.
22. McKelvey, "The First Four Decades," 12–15.
23. Flanagan, *America Reformed*, 93.
24. Ibid. See also Ellen F. Fitzpatrick, *Endless Crusade: Women Social Scientists and Progressive Reform* (New York: Oxford University Press, 1994).
25. See the biographical notes on Caroline Bartlett Crane that accompany the digital version of her Everyman's House, https://www.library.wmich.edu/digidb/everyman/biography.php and further biographical notes by David M. Rubinstein Rare Books and Manuscript Library at Duke University, https://blogs.library.duke.edu

Rochester, she was already well known among contemporaries as "America's housekeeper" for her work on urban sanitation.[26] As expected, she conducted a thorough survey of all housing and indoor plumbing available across the city. *A Sanitation Survey* followed the pattern of other sociological surveys of its day, and Crane used social scientific methods in her highly technical analysis of the city's sanitation and in her recommendations. At the same time, she provided a political and economic context in which to analyze the strengths and weaknesses of potential and current housing in Rochester.[27] Most importantly, her report attended specifically to conditions for contract laborers employed by the city's many clothing manufacturers. Crane concluded that up to the present Rochester had in large part escaped the "housing evils" experienced by other cities and rightfully rejoiced in "civic pride" at being called "a city of homes." However, she warned that the city's new tenement code and the tendencies of clothing manufacture to sweated work "is opulent in invitation to tenements of the worst type."[28]

Tenements of the "worst type," and especially those serving sweated work, posed a significant threat in 1911 to businessmen and workers, politicians and reformers, socialists and progressives. The shock of the Triangle Fire in New York City in March of that year was still fresh. Investigations led by Senator Robert F. Wagner were ongoing with public hearings later that year at the Rochester City Courthouse.[29] A second round of local hearings produced a series of articles in *The Common-Good*. For laborers living and working in tenements, *A Sanitation Survey* told them little they did not already know. Rochester's clothing industry was characterized by ongoing struggles over organizing trade unions and maintaining the open shop that further complicated setting priorities to attain a better quality of life. In contrast, Crane kept her attention focused on what could be achieved and improved through increased regulation, legislation, and education.

To be effective, Crane organized her findings on two levels, one political and the other practical. She believed that Rochester had some advantages in its water and sewer system largely because the city's topography allowed for natural drainage. However, Crane also pointed to the lack of progressive laws regulating housing. In the winter of 1910–11, Rochester had adopted a building code modeled directly on the New York City building code, which included regulations that many reformers rejected as inadequate. To make matters worse, Rochester politicians had asked for and received permission from the New York State Legislature that exempted the city from tenement house laws required in cities

/rubenstein/2017/07/14/new-acquisitions-rev-caroline-bartlett-crane-pamphlets/, both accessed January 23, 2019. It is important to remember that the struggle over woman suffrage in New York state remained contentious, with a state referendum failing in 1915.

26. See Rubinstein, https://blogs.library.duke.edu/rubenstein/2017/07/14/new-acquisitions-rev-caroline-bartlett-crane-pamphlets/..

27. Adams, "Guardians of the Public Health," 250.

28. Caroline Crane, *A Sanitary Survey of Rochester, New York* (Rochester, NY: Women's Educational and Industrial Union, 1911), 63.

29. McKelvey, *The Quest for Quality*, 276–77.

deemed as first class. For this reason, tenement house laws in Rochester controlled only two-story and attic houses with five or more families. Crane criticized this aspect of the Rochester code, noting especially that the Rochester law did not measure up to the New York City code and that the New York City code was itself a dismal failure at regulating housing. Crane further argued that Rochester compared unfavorably to other cities of similar size, using Columbus, Ohio, as her example. Finally, she demonstrated that Rochester codes setting optimal room size, cubic feet of air, building height, and fireproofing lagged behind those in other cities. In brief, Crane concluded that nothing good could come from the present code. [30]

Crane's analysis of Rochester's building code demonstrated a significant understanding of engineering, and her reporting was most effective in the very readable summaries of sanitary conditions in the neighborhoods she visited. Accumulations of garbage, inadequate fire protection, and over-crowded boardinghouses angered Crane as much as they provoked others interested in municipal housekeeping aspects of reform. Crane recommended a series of practical solutions; most importantly, she argued that workingmen should not be paying 26 percent of their income for rent in unwholesome conditions. Ideally, she proposed, they should have access to "model cottages" such as those on Zimbrich Street. She explained that these freestanding houses had the advantage of being near a streetcar line and were affordable, selling for $2,275. Families built equity with a $150 down payment and weekly payments of $5.00. Pragmatic but insistent on not losing the whole picture in its details, Crane explained that even the best individual model meant little without a comprehensive plan.

By reminding her audience of the need for a comprehensive plan, Crane located Rochester's problems squarely in the debate between social reformers such as Florence Kelley and Mary Simkhovitch and planners such as John Nolen.[31] Crane did not choose sides, but tried to incorporate the best of what each had to offer to improve urban life and specifically housing. Read carefully, *A Sanitary Survey* offered more than statistics; it provided specific guidance for moving forward. Taking heed of generalized advice coming from prominent civic advocates, Crane applauded Charles Robinson's attention to the width and arrangement of streets to create cheaper "minor residential districts" not "standardized for traffic" but "suited in width to the needs of residents," and she echoed Lawrence Veiller's top ten of "dont's [sic] in Housing Reform." It began with "Don't let your city become a city of tenements. Keep it a city of homes" and concluded with "Don't allow the enforcement of housing law to be nullified by politicians"[32]

Almost from the beginning, *A Sanitary Survey* ran into controversy with its target audience, the local chapter of the Women's Educational and Industrial Union. Some members

30. Crane, *A Sanitary Survey*, 87.
31. Flanagan, *America Reformed*, 94.
32. Ibid., 94. See also McKelvey, *The Quest for Quality*, 166.

were annoyed that an outsider had brought increased public attention to the realities of slum conditions; others greeted the exposure more enthusiastically as a tool to further advance the cause. Among those seizing the moment, the Reverend Edwin Rumball, editor of the popular community reform magazine *The Common-Good,* challenged city leaders to embrace housing reform.[33] Rumball had arrived in Rochester in 1908, beginning his tenure as minister at the Unitarian Church and later assuming the role of editor of *The Bulletin,* a monthly mailing from the Rochester Social Settlement on Baden Street. He nurtured the publication, transforming it into the longer and more sophisticated *The Common-Good of Civic and Social Rochester.* The magazine published articles from different perspectives and enjoyed financial support of regular advertisers across the business community, including Bausch and Lomb Optical, Michael's Stern Company, Sibley, Lindsay and Curr Co., Scrantom Wetmore Company, and Rochester Railway and Light Company, among others. Arguably, it enjoyed its greatest influence due in no small measure to the extensive discussion of the social center idea, a strategy to use public schools as community centers, and other timely issues of interest to progressives across the state and nation.[34] That nationally known investigative journalist Roy Stannard Baker had spotlighted the success of the social center movement in an article in *American Magazine* in 1910 did little to mitigate strained relations among reformers or between them and the city politicians who saw the social center movement as alternatively socialistic or a threat to a Christian cultural code that preserved Sunday for rest and not school dances.[35]

Setting to one side the host of other social issues in which he was embroiled, Rumball protested recent changes to the city's building code, fearing that any easing of rules could dramatically exacerbate current problems with rental housing. In this endeavor, Rumball turned away from politics and toward businessmen to promote a movement to build workers' housing on the outskirts of the city. To that end, he sought the goodwill and support of George Eastman, seemingly unaware that Eastman had already devised a plan—what he called a scheme—to build affordable housing in the same part of the city where some of the very worst housing deterioration had occurred. Before any correspondence with Rumball, Eastman had initiated plans for a "model tenement" located a few blocks from the Eastman Company office building and factory on State Street.

Eastman's interest in the tenement project dovetailed with his focus on ways to ameliorate conditions for his workers, a commitment that most famously produced the wage-dividend program. In June 1911, Eastman explained to Colonel Henry Strong—his mentor, partner, and the retired president of Eastman Kodak—that at the company's annual meeting he wanted a resolution that would set aside $500,000 in a "benefit, accident, and pension

33. See *The Common-Good of Civic and Social Rochester.* For more on Rumball, see the Unitarian Church, Rochester, New York Collection, Series 3: Edwin Alfred Rumball (1908–15) at the University of Rochester.
34. Kevin Mattson, *Creating a Democratic Republic: The Struggle for Urban Participatory Democracy during the Progressive Era* (University Park: Pennsylvania State Press, 1998).
35. See McKelvey, *The Quest for Quality,* 105–7.

fund for the employees."[36] Motivated to do something for "men who have grown old in our service," Eastman notably chose a payment based upon dividends declared on common stock at a proportional rate. He opposed a minimum wage on the grounds that greater worker efficiency through education, management, and technology was the preferred avenue to a higher working wage and upward mobility.[37] Affordable quality housing, like the wage dividend, offered tangible rewards to a labor force that would be secure and loyal.

To move forward with the model tenement project, in early July 1911 Eastman contacted Elgin R. L. Gould of the City and Suburban Homes Company, with offices at 15 West Thirty-Eighth Street in New York City, for advice on the suitability of several different properties in Rochester. The first, at the corner of Driving Park and Lake Avenues, would complete a parcel he already owned and represented what he called the cheapest available land in Rochester, at eight cents a square foot. The second, located between State and Frank Streets, was "about 400 feet deep and with an alley in between" and was far more expensive, at nearly one dollar a square foot, because, as Eastman told Gould, it already had substantial buildings on it.[38] A block from his offices and in the heart of the city's so-called Italian district—subsequently referred to as the "Italian site"—this lot became the preferred location for Eastman's model tenement design.

Exactly why Eastman favored the Italian site remains unclear. This property was expensive compared to other options, including the parcel on Driving Park Avenue that he purchased at the same time. Presumably, Eastman hoped to raze the buildings and move its current population, but there is no written evidence to confirm that the ethnic composition of the neighborhood rather than the distressed state of the housing motivated him. To the extent that it was widely held that a clean environment had a salubrious effect on personal habits, Eastman seems to have been more motivated by the objective conditions of the site rather than by its Italian character. Eastman did make clear two of his positions regarding this plot. First, he saw the model tenement as a viable alternative to home ownership. While he went on record that home ownership was preferable, he acknowledged that given the practical situation it was not always possible. Second, he expressed concern for those people—identified as Italian—who wanted to stay in the center of the city. He supported the option for people to live near center city and in quality housing but presumably not in his backyard.[39]

In hiring Gould, it was evident that Eastman had been attracted to the Potter building in New York City that Gould had designed, and he used this structure as a reference point.

36. Carl Ackerman, *George Eastman* (Boston: Houghton Mifflin, 1930), 234.
37. Ibid., 246.
38. George Eastman to E.L.R. Gould, July 8, 1911, Correspondence File, City and Suburban Homes Company, Eastman Manuscript Collection, George Eastman Legacy Collection, George Eastman Museum, Rochester, New York. Hereafter this collection is cited as Eastman Manuscript Collection.
39. McKelvey takes the position that Eastman saw the model tenement as slum clearance and that above all else he was interested in building cheap flats. See McKelvey, *The Quest for Quality*, 165.

The building memorialized Gould's friend and fellow social reformer, Episcopal bishop of the Diocese of New York, Henry Codman Potter. It boasted 212½ feet of frontage on the 500-block of East Seventy-Ninth Street and provided some two hundred apartments. Both the design and the cost intrigued Eastman, who commented on its cost effectiveness measured as the proportion of physical structure to its lot size.[40]

Busy with other matters during the summer of 1911, Eastman waited until the fall to finalize the purchase of the Italian site. Extended correspondence with Gould reassured him that the plan would be cost effective, and following the purchase of the site Eastman extended a contract to Gould and the City and Suburban Homes Company. The company agreed to hire an on-site expert to supervise the project in all details for compensation at 5 percent of the cost of the completed buildings, excluding the land on which they were built.[41] Unwilling to be identified publicly with the purchase of the land and the building, Eastman asked his trusted adviser Frank Lovejoy to serve as the public face for the project. At least for the moment, they agreed to use the name Frank Babbott in records pertaining to any permits required from the city as well as the real estate deeds.[42] Despite Eastman's wish to hide his connection, he nevertheless took a hands-on approach in technical aspects of building, including excavating test pits to calculate cellar depth and measuring street curbs in compliance with municipal permits, as well as attending to the design of the tenement itself. But his interest rose above the nitty-gritty of engineering and counting pennies. He seemed genuinely interested in both urban design and workers' housing. On a business trip to London, Eastman found an opportunity to talk with the architect of his new factory about housing projects for workers in Great Britain. Eastman seemed eager to incorporate a suggestion made by the architect to have courts open onto the street as they did in Glasgow, the architect's hometown.[43]

Eastman delegated supervision of the model tenement to others. Within months of completing the purchase of the Italian site, a crisis was brewing. Although Eastman, Lovejoy, Gould, and Ohm, his architect on-site, carefully researched technical matters pertaining to building the tenement, either they had not carefully read the city's building code or had assumed it could be amended with little difficulty. But Gould's assumption that Rochester's laws complied with state law, and that in the event of a discrepancy state tenement law would prevail, proved to be misguided. Since revisions allowed home rule under certain circumstances in cities the size of Rochester, it was constitutional for the local

40. Eastman to Gould, July 8, 1911, Correspondence File, City and Suburban Homes Company, Eastman Manuscript Collection.

41. Eastman to Gould December 6, 1911, Eastman Letters, Eastman Manuscript Collection.

42. Lovejoy to Gould, December 9, 1911, Correspondence File, City and Suburban Homes Company, Eastman Manuscript Collection.

43. Eastman to Gould, December 19, 1911, Eastman Letters, Eastman Manuscript Collection.. Eastman is an interesting executive because of his curiosity about worker housing for his expanding English plant. See Daniel T. Rodgers, *Atlantic Crossings: Social Politics in a Progressive Age* (Cambridge, MA: Harvard University Press, 1998) for more context on the possibilities of cross fertilization of idea.

building codes to vary from state codes. When such variations occurred, local building codes prevailed if there were conflicting standards pertaining to fire safety. For this reason, the first direct conflict between Eastman and Gould on one side and reform activists under the direction of Rumball on the other centered on whether the model tenement could be exempted from the city's fire code. Eastman's representatives insisted that the model tenement met safety standards at least as stringent as those in the current code, but Rumball disagreed. Played out in the public square, what might have been a tempest in a teapot quickly became a firestorm.

In March 1912 an announcement in the local press intimated that Eastman was building a model family tenement. With Eastman's name now in attached to the project, Rumball wrote directly to him, expressing his personal disappointment in both the tenement and in Eastman's efforts to build this type of multifamily structure. Rumball lectured Eastman on his moral responsibility to "educate this city in the question of the proper housing of the workers," ostensibly in single-family homes or small cottages. He then further antagonized Eastman by preaching that tenements bring absolute and serious social evils into a community. Rumball tried to persuade Eastman that he should support the Garden City model that had become popular in England instead of a model tenement. Writing as if the industrialist was unfamiliar with efficiencies and costs, Rumball stated, "I do not think that conservatively approached such an effort would cost any more than the erection of this tenement; it would certainly be a tremendous advertisement for the Kodak and Rochester and its indirect education of the Landlords of this city would go beyond measure."[44]

Rumball feared that a so-called model tenement presented an opening wedge to others who would build the worst rather than the best of tenements in Rochester. Catching himself, Rumball apologized to Eastman for his preachy tone but then excused his breach of etiquette by suggesting that perhaps Eastman had not thoroughly researched the housing situation. On this point Rumball could not have been more mistaken, because there seems to have been little that Eastman did not research before investing his resources or name. Eastman quickly responded with an outline of points under the rubric "in re Rochester model apt for working class."[45]

Eastman challenged Rumball on three separate issues, stressing the significance of each. First, he clarified that the population he intended to serve consisted of the small-wage earners. However, he also argued that the "model tenement" created an alternative to the "hovels unfit for human habitation" where fifty thousand Italians were living in Rochester. In this way, Eastman vindicated the idea of a so-called model tenement as an attempt to

44. Rumball to Eastman, March 24, 1912, Correspondence File, City and Suburban Homes Company, Eastman Manuscript Collection.

45. Suggestions for reply to Edwin A. Rumball's March 24, 1912, letter to Mr. George Eastman in re Rochester model apt for working class, typescript, Correspondence File, City and Suburban Homes Company, Eastman Manuscript Collection.

improve housing opportunities for both the poorer classes and the wage earners. Second, he advocated for this model because "its fireproof features, modern sanitary appliances—steam heat—hot water—public baths and showers—laundry and steam clothes dryers—garbage incinerators with light and ventilation . . . first class janitor service and the roof designed for the use of the tenant . . . offered to wage earner at a rental within his means."[46] For Eastman, access to modern appliances had the potential to alleviate suffering more effectively than simply reducing the population density in a given building. Lastly, Eastman explained that Rochester's existing housing stock included many poorly constructed and primitive tenement buildings without modern sanitation and fire escapes. The model-building he supported was consistent with the new tenement codes. Moreover, he jettisoned the assumption that this model precluded cottages suitable to other city locations.[47]

If Rumball wanted to engage public opinion, Eastman had plenty of ideas about how to gain the upper hand. As a master businessman, Eastman sought ways to sell his ideas to the local community. He showed imagination in marketing the model tenement to local citizens, suggesting a way to stage the living space to make it attractive and to invite the public to see the apartments. To that end, he wrote Gould, it would be "a good thing to leave temporary door openings between a whole series of apartments" so that the public could go "up one stairway, through a whole series of apartments on each floor and down another stairway." To make the model building even more attractive, Eastman added, local department stores could furnish the apartments simply and inexpensively, "marking each article plainly with the price."[48]

Eastman held a low opinion of reformers like Rumball who wrote letters and had "discussions about the common good" but in Eastman's estimation accomplished little of measurable significance, at least in economic terms. As a strategic decision, though, Eastman sought to engage Rumball and sent him a letter setting parameters for a productive conversation. Eastman suggested limiting criticism of housing to the specific topic at hand, which according to him revolved primarily around whether there existed conditions among the poorer classes in need of "remedying" in "the central portion of the city." Assuming that Rumball agreed, he proceeded to ask a question with two very direct and seemingly mutually exclusive responses: Is it better to remedy the conditions where they exist, he asked, or to remove the people? Relentless in his approach, Eastman exhorted Rumball to carry one or the other possibility to its logical conclusion. He then asked that Rumball either suggest ways to remedy conditions where they were or offer a plan to remove people from their homes.[49]

By engaging Gould's company for the Rochester work, Eastman had turned to one

46. Ibid.
47. Ibid.
48. Eastman to Gould, March 26, 1912, Correspondence File, City and Suburban Homes Company, Eastman Manuscript Collection.
49. Eastman to Rumball, April 1, 1912, Eastman Correspondence Files, Eastman Manuscript Collection.

of several of New York's leading housing reformers. Whether intentionally or not, Eastman stepped into a developing conflict between Gould and Lawrence Veiller, who had
lobbied for the New York Tenement House Law in 1901. [50] Gould and his company sought
to promote business and make a good investment while also serving philanthropic ends.[51]
Alternatively, Veiller focused his energy forcing housing to meet the standards set in modern codes.[52] By 1912, Eastman must have been aware that Veiller and Gould represented
different positions on housing reform, though all three men shared a keen awareness that
new stock had to be built to accommodate the urban poor. Now immersed in confronting
opposition to the "model tenement," Eastman followed up his letters to Rumball and Gould
with another to Veiller, at the time secretary and director of the National Housing Association.[53] Seeking his candid opinion, Eastman asked Veiller about the impact of tenements
on a city like Rochester. Predictably, Veiller called tenements "a curse to a city" and argued
that "if the city has not already become irreclaimably a tenement city, those who wish it
well should do all in their power to make and keep it a city of small houses."[54] Declaring
that only New York and perhaps Boston were "irreclaimably lost," Veiller optimistically told
Eastman that even Chicago might still become "in the main a small house city."[55] Veiller
admitted the potential and the inevitable adaptation into housing of some buildings on
downtown business streets or other buildings that had space above ground-level stores.
These adaptations, which were classified as "technically tenements" only affirmed Veiller's
core belief that small houses created better living standards than tenements in American
cities. Additionally, Veiller pointed out to Eastman that the English model that was enjoying increasing popularity started with the premise that spread-out towns and individual
houses opened new ways of thinking about cities. He wrote that this model had broad
European appeal and said the idea had prevailed at the recent Vienna International Congress, where even Germans aspired to replace their tenements with "the English home, the
cottage, the individual house." Finally, Veiller quoted Alfred T. White, a highly respected
housing reformer who sat on the board of directors of Gould's City and Suburban Homes
Company. Although in *Sun-Lighted Tenements* White had lauded the model tenements in
Manhattan and Brooklyn, Veiller explained that White also maintained that it was only the

---

50. See John F. Bauman, "Community Building versus Housing Reform,". 296, for an important distinction
between Veiller and Gould that had emerged before Eastman began his model tenement project. In addition
to the rich literature on differences among middle-class reformers, see Flanagan, *America Reformed*, 86, for the
gendered nature of some of these different emphases among housing reformers who shared an abhorrence of
inadequate conditions.
51. Bauman, "Community Building versus Housing Reform." See Gould's papers in Special Collections, Milton
S. Eisenhower Library, Johns Hopkins University.
52. Bauman, "Community Building versus Housing Reform," 298.
53. For the proceedings of the meeting see National Housing Association, Proceedings of the First National
Housing Conference Held in New York, June 3, 5, and 7, 1911, *Proceedings of the Academy of Political Science in
the City of New York*, vol. 2, April 1912 (Academy of Political Science, Columbia University, New York 1912).
54. Veiller to Eastman, April 3, 1912, Correspondence File, George Goler, Eastman Manuscript Collection.
55. Ibid.

shape of Manhattan Island that forced tenement housing and that White believed even the best tenement "leaves much to be desired."[56]

In advising Eastman against building a model tenement, Veiller objected on two separate criteria: the social effect and the health effect. With regard to the first, Veiller decried the impact of tenements on any sort on family life and quoted Charles Eliot, president emeritus of Harvard, who attributed to tenements what he considered a decline in family life for "all our urban population." Veiller also lamented the shift in recreation from private areas within the home and its gardens to public venues such as the streets, theaters, and saloons.[57] Perhaps the irony was not lost on Eastman, whose film stock served the Motion Picture Patents Company and accounted for the lion-size share of American-made pictures currently showing in the theaters across the nation's cities currently swept up in nickel madness.

On the second point, that of the impact of any tenement on health, Veiller was even more adamant in his opposition. He also was corresponding directly with Dr. George Goler, Rochester's health officer whom both Veiller and Eastman respected. Goler and Veiller exchanged a number of letters between April and June 1912 and worked together as comrades in arms while keeping their connection personal and private. Without Eastman's knowledge, Veiller asked Goler to intervene with Eastman and convince him not to build a model tenement. Eastman enjoyed a good relationship with Goler and defended him to Gould, explaining: "Goler is a perfectly honest man and has a great reputation for the way in which he has controlled our milk supply."[58] Trained in pediatrics, Goler expressed special concern for children's health and welfare.[59] For this reason, Eastman first believed that Goler objected most strenuously to the tenements because they offered inadequate space for children to play. To remedy that, he suggested paving the roofs of the model tenement for a playground.

As the discussion between Veiller and Eastman developed, it became increasingly important to Veiller to pursue private channels as a means of influencing the direction of Rochester housing reform. Above all, he feared that the model tenement could be successful and that its very success might stimulate others to build tenements. At stake was the possibility that Rochester would become a "tenement house city instead of what it is now, a city of homes."[60] For that reason, he asked Goler to encourage Eastman toward "small houses" as "model buildings for the working man."[61] After another meeting between the

---

56. Ibid.
57. Ibid.
58. Eastman to Gould, March 30, 1912, Correspondence File, City and Suburban Homes Company, Eastman Manuscript Collection.
59. Theodore Brown and Elizabeth Fee, "George Washington Goler: The Biggest Crank and the Best Health Officer in the United States," American Journal of Public Health, February 2010, ,237, a, https://ajph.apha publications.org/doi/10.2105/AJPH.2009.184010
60. Veiller to Goler, April 2, 1912, Correspondence File, George Goler, Eastman Manuscript Collection.
61. Veiller to Goler, April 15, 1912, Correspondence File, George Goler, Eastman Manuscript Collection.

two men, Eastman agreed that single-family and cottage-style housing might be prefer-able, but he held to his pragmatic viewpoint that the best option was not available to all those who lived in the city and, most importantly, was not necessarily their own choice. Pointing out that some people wished to remain closer to the city center where single-family homes were either unavailable or not affordable, Eastman held the position that the model tenement could serve that population better than other existing options. On this point he reaffirmed that "something had to be done for people who could not live on the outskirts."[62]

Even as Eastman encouraged Gould to respond to the lack of outdoor playgrounds, he also concluded that the building code, specifically the requirement for fire escapes, stood squarely in the way of his plans for housing. At first, Gould and Eastman decided to ask the city council for an exception to the rule that tenements had to include fire escapes. Because Eastman had investigated building materials and concluded that fireproof staircases served the same end as fire escapes, he was confident such staircases would work. Still, he thought it politically prudent to wait until April 9 in order to allow members of the city council time to discuss the proposed change. City law required two weeks' notice before asking for an amendment to the building code, but it would in fact be four weeks until the amendment arrived before the city council.[63] Eastman was out of town when the request for an amend-ment reached the floor, and his assistant Frank Lovejoy wrote to Ohm, Gould's on-site supervisor, and informed him that serious questions had arisen in the city council's law committee. Rather than amending the law to allow fireproof staircases as an alternative to fire escapes in the model tenement, the city council decided to delay the vote to the next meeting. Lovejoy requested that Gould send an expert from the company to testify before a joint public hearing of the public safety committee and the law committee as to whether fireproof staircases offered sufficient protection.[64]

Even though Eastman was adamant that disagreement over the technical aspects of fireproofing the tenement could be fully resolved, he was sensitive to his standing in the community, and especially to the impact of public opinion on members of the city council. For this reason, Eastman and Gould focused attention on the larger issues of improved housing for workers' families, and together they planned a campaign in the local press to illustrate the decrepit conditions in which some people lived. Gould suggested using the photographer from the *Rochester Herald* to take pictures of existing tenement conditions in

---

62. Eastman to Gould, April 5, 1912, Correspondence File, City and Suburban Homes Company, Eastman Manuscript Collection.
63. Eastman to Gould, March 29, 1912, Correspondence File, City and Suburban Homes Company Eastman Manuscript Collection. There is nothing in the minutes of the Common Council in April or May to reflect their discussion. There is a brief affirmation of a discussion of the building code and fire hazards in the Law Committee to the Common Council in Minutes, May 14, 1912, *Proceedings of the Common Council for 1912* (Rochester, NY: Rochester Herald Press, 1913), 270.
64. Lovejoy to Gentleman of the City and Suburban Homes Company, Attention Mr. Ohm, April 25, 1912, Correspondence File, City and Suburban Homes Company, Eastman Manuscript Collection.

ROSENBLOOM A MODEL TENEMENT IN "THE CITY OF HOMES" 105

the "Hebrew district" of Rochester and specifically to capture "overcrowding and poor sanitation . . . as well as lack of fire protection."[65] As an outsider, Gould took the position that "many people in Rochester do not yet realize that any objectionable tenement conditions exist there" and believe that "their city is so much better off than others."[66]

At this point, Eastman was unwilling to challenge local sentiment, and he suggested to Gould that they delay building the model tenement until the initial firestorm of public opinion against it had subsided. Nevertheless, Gould advised plowing ahead with the project; ignoring what he regarded as stubborn and wrongheaded opinion, he pressed forward to find a way around impediments that resulted from the existing laws regarding fire protection.[67] He seemed to believe that what lay at the heart of the issue was compliance with provisions in the New York State tenement house law, specifically a cubic air ordinance and fireproofing. For this reason he took the position that it would be sufficient to fireproof the first floor, place fireproof walls around staircase halls that extended above the roof, equip hallways with fireproof self-closing doors, and require fire escapes for buildings with four or more stories. Gould believed fire escapes were unnecessary, but he was willing to comply with the general code and continue the project.[68]

Similarly, when the Rochester city fire chief raised concerns about dumbwaiters that connected to the cellar and might carry smoke to the stairwells, Gould reassured Eastman that the self-closing door worked to contain the smoke. After all, Gould wrote, he had seen that happen himself. Still, to avert any potential problem, Gould suggested prohibiting the storage of wood in the cellar and creating an alternative system for tenants to store valuables within a fireproof section of the cellar. Dealing with these details struck Gould as minor, and he remained confident that with the support of the press, specifically the *Herald*, his model would prevail. Gould predicted both a "long waiting list" and a "battered" [building code] commission.[69]

While Gould worked out the details of fire protection, Goler and Veiller orchestrated a behind-the-scenes campaign to rouse public opinion against the model tenement. Veiller recruited to their campaign Charles Robinson, one of Rochester's favorite sons, who was nationally recognized among the most influential city beautiful planners of his day.[70] Goler patiently and persistently discussed all these concerns with Eastman. By June 17, Gould and Veiller each seemed to think he had convinced Eastman. Adding to the drama, both men

65. Gould to Eastman, May 23, 1912, Correspondence File, City and Suburban Homes Company, Eastman Manuscript Collection.
66. Ibid.
67. Gould to Eastman, June 1 and 8, 1912, Correspondence File, City and Suburban Homes Company, Eastman Manuscript Collection.
68. Gould to Eastman, June 12, 1912, Correspondence File, City and Suburban Homes Company, Eastman Manuscript Collection.
69. Gould to Eastman, June 13, 1912, Correspondence File, George Goler, Eastman Manuscript Collection.
70. For further information on Charles Robinson, the City Beautiful Movement, and an interpretation of the context of housing reform in Rochester see Blake McKelvey, "A History of City Planning in Rochester."

were actively engaged in the National Housing Association, a group that Veiller headed but that was not without its own inner conflicts.[71]

By the end of June 1912, the model tenement project had reached a standstill. In addition to Goler's persuasive arguments, Eastman had concluded that the political situation in Rochester created distinctly unfavorable conditions for experimenting with a building that carried the stigma of slum tenements. He refused to enter directly into political negotiations with the aldermen, thus ending the possibility of a compromise. At the same time, he made clear that he would not fight the city council or the tenement commission, even though he still clearly believed that his proposed "model" tenement offered superior fire-safety protection. Even some months later when Gould tried to resurrect the project by proposing a six rather than a four-story structure that included fire escapes, Eastman rejected the plan. He believed that the question of fire escapes was actually a subterfuge and that if the city council committee could not sink the model tenement on that basis it would find another way to prevent it.

The city council refused to allow Eastman to proceed on the Italian site for reasons they never clarified. Eastman's reluctance to push the matter aggressively, however, suggests an understanding of local conditions and a respect for existing power relationships. He did not back off his position that the model was viable; to the contrary, he wrote convincingly that his model provided better security than the current code mandated. He confirmed to Veiller that "I can just as emphatically state that, because I believe it would be a fire trap, I would not build a building in accordance with the present law, which provides for fire escapes in lieu of all fireproofing of stairways and ground floor."[72] In the argument over fire hazards and egress, technical questions completely overtook the social aspects of how best to satisfy housing needs at the Italian site. While in the short-term the rejection of a model tenement in Rochester's downtown deterred Eastman from immediately razing a neighborhood block that most critics agreed offered meager, and in many cases substandard, shelter to its residents, no one offered any ideas about how to address the slum conditions in which the most vulnerable continued to live.[73]

Refusing to accept that the tenement structure was in and of itself an evil form, Eastman had posed for local consideration the possibility of a model tenement as a viable alternative for workingmen's families. The long-term consequences of the failure of a so-called model tenement confirmed the importance of the ideal of home ownership as emblematic of the heart and, insofar as possible, the soul of Rochester. Veiller's unwavering belief that small cottages at a distance from the downtown would best serve the interests of workingmen's families prevailed, and its popularity with Eastman's workers helped define the

71. Flanagan, *America Reformed*, 93. While Flanagan sees gender as a distinguishing feature in approaches to housing reform and urban planning, that dichotomy does not offer a satisfying explanation of divisions among those interested in housing reform in Rochester.

72. Eastman to Veiller, June 27, 1912, Correspondence File, George Goler, Eastman Manuscript Collection.

73. McKelvey, *The Quest for Quality*, 331.

suburban expansion of greater Rochester. It does not appear that Veiller had come in person to Rochester nor seen firsthand the conditions, geography, or topography of the city. From his own perch in the city, Rumball also refused to consider the possibility that a model tenement might be innovative in improving housing in the overcrowded cities. He adamantly insisted that very idea was an oxymoron and compared a model tenement to a model disease, arguing that the lack of home privacy, congestion, and social evils for boys and girls outweighed any potential good that might come from building family tenements.[74]

The failure of the model tenement scheme offers critical perspectives on George Eastman, the possibilities of housing reform, and the nature of progressivism more broadly. There is no direct evidence that Eastman was heavily invested in the scheme or tremendously disappointed at its outcome. Nevertheless, the incident demonstrates that Eastman was scarcely as apolitical in this period of his life as the literature might suggest.[75] The choices he made reflect a sophisticated understanding of local conditions and the power of vested interests, including local and state politicians.[76] Moreover, Eastman was pragmatic and aspired with plans like the successful shared-dividend program to find ways for his company to benefit society and the city of Rochester even as he enriched himself. The failure to experiment with building a model tenement downtown as a means of expanding housing for the rising working classes helps to contextualize the subsequent development of suburban tracts with affordable freestanding homes. There is no evidence to suggest that the failure of the model tenement upset Eastman. To the contrary, he became more involved in urban development and helped lay the groundwork for a bureau of municipal research, which would have a profound impact on the city and the manner in which it would address not only housing but other issues pertinent to civic well-being. When the Rochester Bureau of Municipal Research was incorporated on April 20, 1915, with Eastman as it first chairman, it made a powerful statement of purpose: "To get things done for the community through *cooperation with persons who are in office*, by increasing efficiency and eliminating waste" and "To serve as an independent non-partisan agency for *keeping citizens informed about the city's business*."[77] Its leaders sought both intelligent planning and enlightened public cooperation to transform Rochester, they wrote, from a city with "good city government" to the "most progressive and serviceable government in the United States."[78]

---

74. Letter from Rumball, *Common Good*, July 24, 1912.
75. For example, see Elizabeth Brayer, *George Eastman: A Biography* (Baltimore: Johns Hopkins University Press, 1996).
76. Ibid., 376.
77. Rochester Bureau of Municipal Research, *The Purposes and Organization of the Rochester Bureau of Municipal Research, Inc.* (Rochester, NY: Democrat and Chronicle Print), 3. http://babel.hathitrust.org/, accessed July 13, 2015.
78. Ibid., 4.

Whether the direction in which the bureau took Rochester was progressive is moot, since few could agree (then as now) on the nature of progressivism. Exploring the nature of housing reform and housing shortages at the end of the first decade of the twentieth century in Rochester, a city experiencing booming population growth, reveals two distinct trends. On the one hand, shortages for the upwardly mobile could be attended to in a variety of ways and by private construction. On the other, no one effectively addressed the conditions of those who were caught in the worst housing and had few options. The composition of the distressed population changed over time even as housing shortages, dwellings without indoor plumbing, outdoor water closets, and fire disasters remained endemic in some city wards throughout the coming decade. What happened in Rochester was consistent with progress elsewhere in urban America, where beautification and planning took precedence over other projects. The national conversation on housing reform had a significant impact on George Eastman and set local parameters for the development of housing in the city of Rochester.

Consumption in the Adirondacks
Print Culture and the Curative Climate

Mark Sturges

Nearing the end of his life, Edward Livingston Trudeau, the most famous tuberculosis doctor in America, penned a medical memoir that tells the story of his own diagnosis with tuberculosis, his miraculous recovery after retreating into the Adirondack Mountains of northern New York, his formation of the Adirondack Cottage Sanitarium, and his scientific research in the emerging field of bacteriology. While chronicling his professional accomplishments, Trudeau also devotes a great deal of attention to his leisure pursuits, recalling memorable hunting trips, paying tribute to his favorite Adirondack guides, and delivering a larger-than-life character sketch of Adirondack hotel proprietor Paul Smith. Thus, *An Autobiography* (1915) depicts Trudeau as *both* nineteenth-century sportsman and turn-of-the-century scientist—Gilded Age alter egos that he adopted at pivotal moments in his struggle against tuberculosis.

To visually reinforce this dual identity, some early printings of the book include two portraits of Trudeau in the attire of his twin passions. The first photograph, dating from roughly 1873, when Trudeau spent his first summer in the Adirondacks in pursuit of health, features a genteel sportsman dressed in fashionable hunting clothes, sitting on a stump, cap on the ground, trusty rifle resting between his legs. The second photograph, taken for promotional purposes in the Saranac Laboratory circa 1894, pictures a modern medical doctor wearing a white lab coat, standing at a workbench before an array of test tubes and beakers, performing his latest scientific experiment. These two portraits embody different (but related) cultural responses to tuberculosis in the late nineteenth century, illustrating in snapshot form the popular belief in the health benefits of a change in climate and the expanding medical knowledge of the disease based on the germ theory of bacterial infection.[1]

Published on the eve of U.S. involvement in World War I, Trudeau's *Autobiography* is

---

I wish to thank Philip Terrie, Mary Hotaling, Sarah Gates, and two anonymous readers for their helpful feedback on earlier drafts of this article, and Michele Tucker at the Saranac Lake Free Library for her assistance during my time there. I am also grateful to St. Lawrence University for providing the sabbatical leave and grant funding that has supported my research on Adirondack literature and history.
1. The first edition of *An Autobiography* was published by Trudeau's close friend Charles M. Lea, a summer visitor to the Adirondacks and the owner of a distinguished publishing firm devoted to medical materials (Edward

"Dr. Trudeau, The Huntsman (1873), Three Months after Arrival at Paul Smith's." Edward
Livingston Trudeau, *An Autobiography* (Garden City, NY: Doubleday, Page, 1916), plate 3.
(COURTESY OF THE ADIRONDACK COLLECTION, SARANAC LAKE FREE LIBRARY)

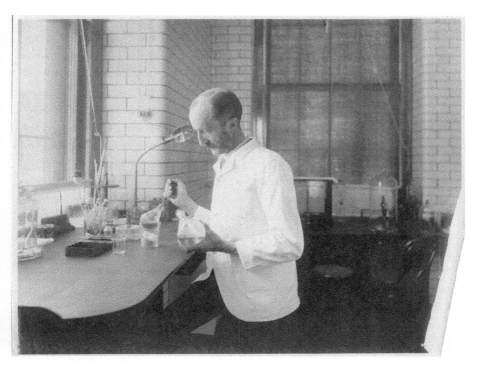

"Dr. Trudeau, The Investigator (1894)." Edward Livingston Trudeau, *An Autobiography* (Garden City, NY: Doubleday, Page, 1916), plate 9. (COURTESY OF THE ADIRONDACK COLLECTION, SARANAC LAKE FREE LIBRARY).

noteworthy, not only because it captures overlapping attitudes toward human health and the environment in the post–Civil War era, but also because it displays how a culture of outdoor recreation influenced the nation's medical treatment of tuberculosis. In the second half of the nineteenth century, tuberculosis patients flocked to remote corners of the United States, seeking refuge from the oppressive air of industrial cities and hoping for the health benefits of a curative climate. From the arid deserts of New Mexico to the boreal forests of northern New York, from the Rocky Mountains of Colorado to the White Mountains of New Hampshire, a cure industry emerged, profited for a half-century, and left lasting impacts on the cultural landscapes of those regions.[2] During this era, print culture, especially

---

Livingston Trudeau, *An Autobiography* [Philadelphia: Lea and Febiger, 1915]). Because copies of this edition are rare, I quote from a more widely available edition published for the National Tuberculosis Association in 1934. For a biography of Trudeau, see Mary B. Hotaling, *A Rare Romance in Medicine: The Life and Legacy of Edward Livingston Trudeau* (Saranac Lake, NY: Historic Saranac Lake, 2016).

2. On the social history of tuberculosis, see Billy Jones, *Health Seekers in the Southwest, 1817–1900* (Norman: University of Oklahoma Press, 1967); Mark Caldwell, *The Last Crusade: The War on Consumption, 1862–1954* (New York: Atheneum, 1988); Barbara Bates, *Bargaining for Life: A Social History of Tuberculosis, 1876–1938* (Philadelphia: University of Pennsylvania Press, 1992); Sheila M. Rothman, *Living in the Shadow of Death: Tuberculosis and the Social Experience of Illness in American History* (New York: Basic Books, 1994); Georgina D.

sportsman's literature, played a persuasive role in debates about the curative potential of America's wilderness regions. Taking the Adirondack Mountains of New York as a case study and Trudeau's life story as a touchstone, this article examines a few popular works of regional literature and reconstructs the conversation that unfolded across the span of Trudeau's influential career.

In the two decades following the Civil War, popular authors like William H. H. Murray, Marc Cook, and George Washington Sears, in collaboration with medical experts like Dr. Alfred Loomis and Dr. Joseph Stickler, fashioned a narrative of the Adirondacks as a curative climate, constructing a cultural myth that fueled the development of a tourist economy and facilitated the transformation of the region into a health-seeking destination. Not only did these writers influence environmental attitudes underlying the belief in a wilderness cure, effectively training male readers to seek an outdoor experience that would renew their health and, simultaneously, their masculinity, but they also commodified the Adirondack climate in a fashion that enabled the rise of a cure industry. The standard narrative of tuberculosis history holds that Robert Koch's discovery of the tubercle bacillus in 1882 advanced a medical revolution that entailed a shift in cultural perceptions of the disease, leading away from a climate-oriented pursuit of health and toward a hygiene-oriented public-health campaign and sanatorium treatment system. The two photographs of Trudeau, dated 1873 and 1894, reflect this narrative, but the Adirondack print archive also reveals that a popular belief in the curative climate persisted into the twentieth century. Rather than a sudden epistemic shift, the late nineteenth century featured an epistemic overlap in which theories of medical geography maintained a degree of influence alongside the new germ theory of disease.[3]

Trudeau's career evolved in the midst of this epistemic overlap. Ever inquisitive, Trudeau absorbed prevailing theories of medical geography, climatology, and bacteriology, tested them in his own scientific research, and put them to work at the Adirondack Cottage Sanitarium, which opened its doors in 1885, the same year that New York State established the forest preserve. In fact, the growth of Trudeau's sanatorium and the increasing prevalence of cure cottages in the Saranac Lake area coincided with the conservation movement that led to the creation of the Adirondack Park in 1892 and the "forever wild" provision in the state constitution in 1894. The standard narrative of Adirondack environmental history suggests that a culture of outdoor recreation, the romantic aesthetics of regional art and literature, increasing anxiety about destructive logging practices, and a utilitarian argument

---

Feldberg, *Disease and Class: Tuberculosis and the Shaping of Modern North American Society* (New Brunswick, NJ: Rutgers University Press, 1995); and Nancy Tomes, *The Gospel of Germs: Men, Women, and the Microbe in American Life* (Cambridge, MA: Harvard University Press, 1998).

3. For the standard narrative of the bacteriological revolution, see Bates, *Bargaining for Life*, 25–41; Rothman, *Living in the Shadow of Death*, 179–210; Feldberg, *Disease and Class*, 36–80; Tomes, *The Gospel of Germs*, 21–154; and Michael Worboys, *Spreading Germs: Disease Theories and Medical Practice in Britain, 1865–1900* (Cambridge: Cambridge University Press, 2000).

for watershed protection came together in the last two decades of the nineteenth century to influence the regional wilderness preservation movement. Only in passing do tuberculosis health seekers enter the historiography of environmentalism in the Adirondacks, yet they played a key role in regional cultural mythology, helped to transform Saranac Lake into a health resort, and reinforced environmental values that supported wilderness preservation.[4]

In *The Birth of American Tourism*, Richard Gassan describes how a tourist economy developed in New York's Hudson Valley in the early nineteenth century (circa 1820s) and later spread to other parts of the Northeast. To be sure, the Adirondack tourist industry followed this earlier model, and in doing so it combined three components that Gassan regards as essential to the growth of regional tourism: "a compelling destination with homelike accommodations, a comfortable travel infrastructure, and a cultural infrastructure that gives the tourist a model of thinking about what he or she is experiencing."[5] While the extension of transportation networks (i.e., steamboat, stagecoach, and railroad lines) and the construction of new hotels and "great camps" were the primary factors supporting Adirondack tourism in the post–Civil War era, one ought not underestimate the power of the print culture networks that guided visitors into the region and became a signature part of their experience. Without denying the influence of a physical travel infrastructure in shaping an Adirondack culture of tourism and health-seeking, this article highlights the "cultural infrastructure"—the stories, tropes, and texts—that invested the region with the romance of outdoor recreation and a mythology of the curative climate.[6]

By focusing on a region with a rich documentary archive and teasing apart a complex fabric of sportsman's literature, tuberculosis narratives, national print culture, and nineteenth-century climate science, this study may be of interest to scholars seeking to understand the intersections between human health, medical history, and regional environmental

---

4. For the standard narrative of Adirondack environmental history, see Philip G. Terrie, *Forever Wild: Environmental Aesthetics and the Adirondack Forest Preserve* (Philadelphia: Temple University Press, 1985); Frank Graham Jr., *The Adirondack Park: A Political History* (New York: Knopf, 1978); and Paul Schneider, *The Adirondacks: A History of America's First Wilderness* (New York: Henry Holt, 1997). Terrie's more recent history of the region revisits this standard narrative with the aim of uncovering social tensions between wealthy outsiders and working-class residents, but because this admirable project demands broad brush strokes, he devotes only a few words to tuberculosis health seekers. See Philip G. Terrie, *Contested Terrain: A New History of Nature and People in the Adirondacks*, 2nd ed. (Syracuse, NY: Syracuse University Press, 2008), 64–65.

5. Richard H. Gassan, *The Birth of American Tourism: New York, the Hudson Valley, and American Culture, 1790–1835* (Amherst: University of Massachusetts Press, 2008), 5. On the growth of tourism in nineteenth-century America, see also John F. Sears, *Sacred Spaces: American Tourist Attractions in the Nineteenth Century* (Amherst: University of Massachusetts Press, 1989); Cindy S. Aron, *Working at Play: A History of Vacations in the United States* (New York: Oxford University Press, 1999); and Marguerite S. Shaffer, *See America First: Tourism and National Identity, 1880–1940* (Washington, DC: Smithsonian Institution Press, 2001).

6. On the role of transportation networks and tourist accommodations in the Adirondacks, see Terrie, *Contested Terrain*, 66–74, and Schneider, *The Adirondacks*, 183–85, 241–76. For more on the great camp era, see Harvey H. Kaiser, *Great Camps in the Adirondacks* (Boston: Godine, 1982). Harold K. Hochschild's studies of the region also chronicle the role of railroads and great camps. See, for example, *Adirondack Railroads, Real and Phantom* (Blue Mountain Lake, NY: Adirondack Museum, 1961) and *Doctor Durant and His Iron Horse* (Blue Mountain Lake, NY: Adirondack Museum, 1961).

histories.[7] Additionally, the story of Adirondack health seekers invites renewed attention in light of the growing interest in climate history. In recent years, environmental historians have recovered the historical agency of the climate by examining how global climate trends and regional weather events have influenced political systems, economic relations, settlement patterns, and colonial encounters, and in turn they have evaluated the impact of human behavior on the climate itself, especially in relation to anthropogenic climate change. Most scholarship has tended to focus on the hot topics of the Little Ice Age and the Anthropocene, and the critical trend is toward broad, sweeping studies of long-term climate patterns and their effect on the fate of civilizations. A grounded focus on Adirondack health seekers in the years following the Civil War, however, demonstrates that cultural perceptions of climate also determined the shape of regional identity, and tracing the Adirondack climate debate from the 1860s through the 1880s illuminates how a particular climate narrative was popularized and disseminated through the various channels of nineteenth-century print culture. Textual history, in other words, sheds light on climate history.[8]

As climate historians have shown, neither physical climates nor cultural perceptions of those climates have remained stable across time; indeed, the nineteenth-century study of "climate science"—a term that did not exist in cultural parlance but which serves as a convenient shorthand for a set of ideas then coalescing—entailed a different set of theories and practices than it does today. Whereas twenty-first-century climatologists regard Earth's atmosphere as a dynamic system subject to change in response to natural forces and

---

7. More than a decade ago, Gregg Mitman challenged environmental historians to engage in this kind of investigation, but much work remains to be done. See Mitman, "In Search of Health: Landscape and Disease in American Environmental History," *Environmental History* 10, no. 2 (2005): 184–210. Mitman's study of nineteenth-century hay-fever health seekers in New Hampshire's White Mountains also provides a model for understanding how health seekers shaped the place history of the Adirondacks. See Mitman, "Hay Fever Holiday: Health, Leisure, and Place in Gilded-Age America," *Bulletin of the History of Medicine* 77, no. 3 (2003): 600–635.

8. On recent trends in climate history, particularly within the field of early American environmental history, see Joyce Chaplin, "Ogres and Omnivores: Early American Historians and Climate History," *William and Mary Quarterly* 72, no. 1 (2015): 25–32; and Katherine Grandjean, "It's the Climate, Stupid" [Review of *Climate Change and the Course of Global History: A Rough Journey*, by John L. Brooke, and *Global Crisis: War, Climate Change and Catastrophe in the Seventeenth Century*, by Geoffrey Parker], *William and Mary Quarterly* 72, no. 1 (2015): 159–67. In the same issue of the *William and Mary Quarterly*, Thomas Wickman observes that the Little Ice Age varied in effect and intensity depending on the region, season, and time period, and thus the impact of climate on early American history "can only be fully understood through 'grounded histories.'" Wickman, "'Winters Embittered with Hardships': Severe Cold, Wabanaki Power, and English Adjustments, 1690–1710," *William and Mary Quarterly* 72, no. 1 (2015): 59. For a fascinating "grounded history" of New England with a focus on its winter ecologies and colonial power relations, see Thomas M. Wickman, *Snowshoe Country: An Environmental and Cultural History of Winter in the Early American Northeast* (Cambridge: Cambridge University Press, 2018). In highlighting cultural perceptions of climate rather than its material agency, I follow an approach adopted by Karen Ordahl Kupperman in "Fear of Hot Climates in the Anglo-American Colonial Experience," *William and Mary Quarterly* 41, no. 2 (1984): 213–40; and "Climate and Mastery of the Wilderness in Seventeenth-Century New England," *Seventeenth-Century New England*, ed. David D. Hall and David Grayson Allen (Boston: Colonial Society of Massachusetts, 1984), 3–37. This emphasis on cultural perception also characterizes the more recent study by Anya Zilberstein, *A Temperate Climate: Making Climate Change in Early America* (New York: Oxford University Press, 2016).

human interventions, nineteenth-century practitioners of climate science considered the atmosphere to be relatively unchanging and instead emphasized the effect of weather and climate on human bodies.[9] Thus, they practiced what some historians refer to as "medical geography," an expansive field with roots in the ancient world that has for centuries examined the relationship between human health and the environment. In the late nineteenth century, medical geographers sought to explain the connection between tuberculosis and climate by compiling data on the weather and topography of particular regions, and as their work gained credibility in the scientific community it led to the creation of the American Climatological Association in 1883. Only when taking into account these historical differences can one fully appreciate the climate debate that influenced cultural attitudes toward the Adirondacks in the final decades of the nineteenth century.[10]

Three rhetorical features recur in both sportsman's literature and tuberculosis narratives written in the Adirondacks in the postwar years, and these features also defined Trudeau's influential career. First, sportsmen and health seekers constructed a pilgrimage pattern in which an individual retreats into the forest and undergoes a personal transformation. Invoking the parlance of popular romanticism, these narratives depicted the Adirondacks as a sacred space imbued with miraculous qualities and capable of renewing both body and spirit. Second, these works fashioned a frontier ethos that involved the performance of masculinity and rugged self-reliance in a wilderness landscape, typically through participation in field sports (hunting and fishing) or outdoor recreation (camping and canoeing), both of which increased in popularity in the late nineteenth century. This dimension of sporting culture and tuberculosis treatment signaled a cultural anxiety about the loss of masculine vigor and, in turn, prescribed outdoor recreation as a means of reinvigorating the health of the body politic and reinforcing national identity. Finally, proponents of the wilderness cure made an appeal to the emerging authority of climate science, either by cribbing sources from the medical press or by recording their own pseudoscientific observations about climate, weather, topography, and air quality. In doing so, they participated in a late-nineteenth-century climate discourse that professionalized *and* popularized the study of climatology.

These three rhetorical features—pilgrimage pattern, frontier ethos, and climate science—fired the public imagination and worked together to commodify the Adirondack climate and market it for mass consumption by an audience of outdoor enthusiasts and tuberculosis health seekers. Ultimately, then, late-nineteenth-century perceptions of the

9. Some environmental thinkers of the late nineteenth century did, however, recognize that deforestation and industrialization could alter regional climate patterns. See, for example, George Perkins Marsh, *Man and Nature; or, Physical Geography as Modified by Human Action* (New York: Scribner, 1864).

10. On the history of medical geography, see Gregg Mitman and Ronald L. Numbers, "From Miasma to Asthma: The Changing Fortunes of Medical Geography in America," *History and Philosophy of the Life Sciences* 25, no. 3 (2003): 391–412; and Nicolaas A. Rupke, ed., *Medical Geography in Historical Perspective* (*Medical History,* supplement no. 20) (London: Wellcome Trust Centre for the History of Medicine, 2000).

curative climate cannot be separated from the consumer culture of outdoor recreation, the expanding tourist economy, and the persuasive appeal of mass-market print media.

The Adirondack Pilgrimage

After being diagnosed with tuberculosis in 1872, Trudeau acted on the advice of his physician and traveled to South Carolina, but there his health further deteriorated. Returning to New York, he continued to suffer daily fevers and weight loss, so in the spring of 1873, after waiting for the birth of his second child and ensuring his family's health, he decided reluctantly to accompany his friend Lou Livingston to the Adirondacks. From Plattsburgh the two undertook a strenuous overland journey by horse-drawn wagon to the St. Regis House, a fashionable hotel popular among sportsmen and known colloquially as Paul Smith's. As Trudeau later recalled the scene in *An Autobiography*, he arrived at Paul Smith's rattled from the long trip, nearly too weak to stand, and immediately requested that a guide carry him to his room. "Why, Doctor," said the guide, in a rustic refrain often repeated in accounts of Trudeau's Adirondack legend, "you don't weigh no more than a dried lamb-skin!" Facing exhaustion and emaciation, Trudeau put his faith in the health-inducing qualities of the wilderness and experienced a rising sense of hope: "Under the magic influence of the surroundings . . . I felt convinced I was going to recover." The following morning, another guide prepared a boat "with balsam boughs and blankets" and invited Trudeau to join him for a float. "My hunting blood responded at once," Trudeau remembered. As the guide rowed him down the river, he spotted two deer; recumbent in the boat, the invalid rested his rifle on the gunwale, took aim, and killed a buck.[11] The symbolism is artless and obvious, yet it reveals a core belief of sportsman's culture: by taking the life of a wild animal, Trudeau began to renew his own health and vigor.

In recounting this scene, Trudeau cast himself as a paradigm of illness and recovery, reinforced a popular myth of retreat and redemption in the wilderness, and crafted a script for other tuberculosis health seekers to follow. But Trudeau did not originate this script, and in fact, he reenacted a pilgrimage pattern established in the antebellum era by such writers as Charles Fenno Hoffman and Joel T. Headley and later extended by William H. H. Murray, author of the rollicking *Adventures in the Wilderness; or, Camp-Life in the Adirondacks* (1869), a book that popularized recreational camping in the years following the Civil War.[12] In addition to celebrating the romantic scenery and sporting opportunities of the Adirondacks, Murray insisted that the regional climate exhibited unique health-inducing

---

11. Edward Livingston Trudeau, *An Autobiography* (Garden City, NY: Doubleday, Page, 1934), 80.
12. Charles Fenno Hoffman, *Wild Scenes in the Forest and Prairie* (New York: Colyer, 1843); Joel T. Headley, *The Adirondack; or, Life in the Woods* (New York: Baker and Scribner, 1849); William H. H. Murray, *Adventures in the Wilderness; or, Camp-Life in the Adirondacks* (Boston: Fields, Osgood, 1869). In 1858, Ralph Waldo Emerson and fellow luminaries from the Boston area also participated in this pilgrimage pattern by traveling into the Adirondacks in the company of William James Stillman and setting up the famed Philosophers' Camp. See James Schlett, *A Not Too Greatly Changed Eden: The Story of the Philosophers' Camp in the Adirondacks* (Ithaca, NY: Cornell University Press, 2015).

qualities. "Another reason why I visit the Adirondacks, and urge others to do so," he wrote, "is because I deem the excursion eminently adapted to restore impaired health."

> To such as are afflicted with that dire parent of ills, dyspepsia, or have lurking in their system consumptive tendencies, I most earnestly recommend a month's experience among the pines. . . . The spruce, hemlock, balsam, and pine, which largely compose this wilderness, yield upon the air, and especially at night, all their curative qualities. . . . Not a few, far advanced in that dread disease, consumption, have found in this wilderness renewal of life and health.[13]

To support these claims, Murray related the story of a young man who suffered from an acute case of tuberculosis and retreated into the Adirondacks. Approaching death and unable to walk, the invalid hired a guide who covered the bottom of a boat with cedar, pine, and balsam boughs and rowed his ailing client into the wilderness, where the "healing properties" of the evergreens worked their magic.[14] Five months later, the young man returned home a picture of good health, living proof of the region's curative climate.

Following the didactic content of chapter 1, the remaining chapters of *Adventures in the Wilderness* function primarily as vignettes of outdoor sport and recreation. Murray narrates his triumphant trout-fishing exploits, a whitewater paddling adventure, a mishap while crossing a carry (i.e., portage), a day on the lakes shooting loons, and a foggy night jacklighting for deer; he describes a country dance, tells a regional ghost story, and delivers a romantic sermon about the spiritual qualities of the wilderness. Whether mocking his own anti-dancing diatribe, casting himself as a hapless wilderness traveler, or drawing attention to his own narrative unreliability, Murray displays a robust sense of humor, and even those chapters that depict him as a heroic sportsman echo the tall-tale tradition of nineteenth-century frontier sketches popularized by such periodicals as William T. Porter's *The Spirit of the Times*. The tall-tale style of these later chapters may have prompted Murray's more astute readers to revise their interpretation of his earlier anecdote about the young man's miraculous recovery from consumption. Beyond their comic effect, tall tales of this variety also serve a psychological function: by exaggerating the extremes of climate and weather, they allow listeners to assuage their fears and anxieties about hostile, indifferent, or mysterious natural forces. So one ought to resist the smug temptation to dismiss Murray's tale of a recovering invalid as mere mockery; he captured a deeply ingrained cultural myth guiding social behavior in the postbellum era, and in an ironic historical punch line, his joke would soon be cleansed of humor and recast as medical wisdom.[15]

---

13. William H. H. Murray, *Adventures in the Wilderness*, ed. William K. Verner (Syracuse, NY: Syracuse University Press, 1989), 11–12.

14. Ibid., 13.

15. Founded in New York City in 1831, *The Spirit of the Times* was a popular sporting newspaper that ran humorous stories about hunting and frontier life in the Southwest. The paper underwent various editorial changes during the 1850s and 1860s but was still in print when Murray published *Adventures*. See Norris

Following its publication in the spring of 1869, *Adventures in the Wilderness* became an immediate bestseller and inspired a well-documented wave of tourism in the Adirondacks, a so-called Murray Rush that earned the author a nickname—"Adirondack" Murray—and invited the ire of disappointed readers who found the climate, accommodations, or sporting opportunities less idyllic than his depiction. Murray caused a stir, in part, because of his forceful, self-assured style and his bold claims of authenticity. Readers gullible enough to accept at face value his hyperbolic depictions of hunting and fishing, or his rose-colored assertions about the bugless ease of backcountry travel, were occasionally dubbed "Murray's Fools." Yet those who recognized the book's sense of humor—and therefore did not take his claims so literally—found amusement in his ironic exaggerations. From both fronts, *Adventures in the Wilderness* received numerous reviews, and whether the critics defended or debunked its claims, checked its facts, or qualified its enthusiasm, they all enlarged Murray's reputation.[16]

Adventures reached a wide audience thanks to its publication by the influential Boston firm Fields, Osgood, and Company. The successor of Ticknor and Fields and precursor to the twentieth-century publishing powerhouse Houghton Mifflin Company, this syndicate set the standards of nineteenth-century American literary taste by advancing the careers of Hawthorne, Longfellow, Thoreau, and Stowe, among others, and it shaped the public imagination by printing the *Atlantic Monthly* and *North American Review*. Benefiting from the financial support and publicity infrastructure of this publishing house, Murray achieved widespread notoriety, and estimates suggest that consumers purchased tens of thousands of copies of *Adventures in the Wilderness*: the book went through at least ten printings in the first four months, and Murray later boasted that it sold at the rate of five hundred copies per week. Aware of the book's participation in multiple forms of consumerism, the publishers soon brought out a Tourist's Edition that featured a water-resistant waxed cover, a foreword by a railroad agent, a detailed train schedule, and a foldout map of the Adirondacks. Murray's fame, therefore, was very much the product of a post–Civil War mass-market print industry.[17]

W. Yates, *William T. Porter and the Spirit of the Times: A Study of the Big Bear School of Humor* (Baton Rouge: University of Louisiana Press, 1957). On the genre of the tall tale, see Carolyn S. Brown, *The Tall Tale in American Literature and Folklore* (Knoxville: University of Tennessee Press, 1987).

16. On the impact of Murray's book, see Terrie, *Forever Wild*, 68–76; Warder H. Cadbury, Introduction, *Adventures in the Wilderness*, by William H. H. Murray, ed. William K. Verner (Syracuse, NY: Syracuse University Press, 1989), 11–75; Terence Young, *Heading Out: A History of American Camping* (Ithaca, NY: Cornell University Press, 2017), 21–48; David Strauss, "Toward a Consumer Culture: 'Adirondack Murray' and the Wilderness Vacation," *American Quarterly* 39, no. 2 (1987): 270–86; and Alisa Marko Iannucci, "Summer of '69: Adirondack Murray and the American Wilderness Vacation," *ISLE* 16, no. 1 (2009): 119–35.

17. On the history of Ticknor and Fields, see Michael Winship, *American Literary Publishing in the Mid-Nineteenth Century: The Business of Ticknor and Fields* (Cambridge: Cambridge University Press, 1995), 9–23; Joel Myerson, "Ticknor and Fields," *American Literary Publishing Houses, 1638–1899*, vol. 49, pt. 2, ed. Peter Dzwonkoski, *Dictionary of Literary Biography* (Detroit: Gale, 1986), 461–66; and Lynne P. Shackelford, "Fields, Osgood and Company," *American Literary Publishing Houses, 1638–1899*, vol. 49, ed. Peter Dzwonkoski, *Dictionary of Literary Biography* (Detroit: Gale: 1986), 163. For sales estimates of Murray's book, see Cadbury, Introduction, 40; and Young, *Heading Out*, 28.

Adventures also elicited a strong reaction because it appeared at a pivotal moment in postwar social history. The two decades preceding its publication entailed a population boom that accelerated the pace of urbanization in states in the Northeast and Mid-Atlantic. Rapid industrialization and economic growth expanded the professional classes, and many residents of large metropolitan areas began to suffer from new nervous disorders triggered by overwork and exhaustion. In response, they seized opportunities to escape the stifling conditions of American cities, and catering to this demand, the tourist industry fostered a growing enthusiasm for outdoor recreation and wilderness vacations. Facing anxieties about their health and masculinity, some American men put their faith in "muscular Christianity," a Victorian ideology that advocated physical exercise as a means to restore one's body, revive one's spirit, and reinvigorate one's masculinity. Under these influences, the hard-edged Protestant work ethic and theology of the antebellum era softened into a postwar culture of middle-class consumerism oriented toward the accumulation of both material goods and spiritual experiences. These factors created the ideal conditions for *Adventures* to succeed. A Congregationalist minister by training, Murray became a mass-market evangelist who commodified the Adirondacks and marketed the region to urban professionals seeking a sporting adventure, a summer vacation, or a wilderness cure.[18]

As evidence of its cultural appeal, *Adventures* even inspired a kind of nineteenth-century meme, the Murray satire. In 1870, *Harper's New Monthly Magazine* printed a parody by Charles Hallock, an elite sportswriter and subsequent founder of *Forest and Stream*. Hallock's main characters, a group of incompetent sportsmen, form an amateur club under the supervision of a professorial expert; he then promptly disappears, leaving the club with a copy of Murray's book to serve as their guide. They travel to the Adirondacks in the summer of 1869, encounter a throng of tourists, many of them ill, and eventually arrive at Paul Smith's, where they hunt and fish and hire a guide to take them on a tour of the lakes. On their journey into the wilderness, the club members meet "a consumptive-looking Yankee," who inquires of them, "Is it healthy in there? Because, you see, I'm kinder ailing. . . . They say the mountain air is good for invalid folks."[19] Later, the travelers discover the same man camping on Raquette Lake (Murray's favorite locale), where he has experienced a remarkable recovery, which *Harper's* illustrated with a satirical before-and-after sketch alluding to Murray's anecdote while also forecasting Trudeau's experience three years later.

Writing retrospectively in *An Autobiography*, Trudeau insisted that, when he first sought his health at Paul Smith's in 1873, he had no preconceptions about the curative

---

18. For a general overview of these historical trends, see Charles W. Calhoun, ed., *The Gilded Age: Perspectives on the Origins of Modern America*, 2nd ed. (Lanham, MD: Rowman and Littlefield, 2007). For a history of nervous disorders in the nineteenth century, see George Frederick Drinka, *The Birth of Neurosis: Myth, Malady, and the Victorians* (New York: Simon and Schuster, 1984). For a definition of "muscular Christianity," see Donald Hall, ed., *Muscular Christianity: Embodying the Victorian Age* (New York: Cambridge University Press, 1994), 7–8. Strauss discusses Murray's connection to this movement in "Toward a Consumer Culture," 270–86.
19. Charles Hallock, "The Raquette Club," *Harper's New Monthly Magazine*, August 1870, 326.

BEFORE GOING TO THE ADIRONDACKS.

AFTER GOING TO THE ADIRONDACKS.

Charles Hallock, two illustrations from
"The Raquette Club," in *Harper's New Monthly
Magazine*, August 1870, 334–35.

potential of the Adirondack climate. "I was influenced in my choice of the Adirondacks," he wrote, "only by my love for the great forest and the wild life, and not at all because I thought the climate would be beneficial in any way, for the Adirondacks were then visited only by hunters and fishermen and it was looked upon as a rough, inaccessible region and considered a most inclement and trying climate."[20] Trudeau may have intended to distance himself from Murray's legacy because the medical community regarded Murray as a huckster and associated him with the quacks who peddled homeopathic remedies to the desperately ill. Yet Trudeau is rumored to have met and defeated Murray in a shooting competition at Paul Smith's in 1867—the good doctor could handle a gun!—and preceding his legendary 1873 trip to the Adirondacks he took an earlier hunting vacation to Paul Smith's in 1870.[21] At the time, Trudeau had been working as a physician in New York City, where Murray's book

---

20. Trudeau, *An Autobiography*, 77–78.
21. Reports of Trudeau's encounters with Murray and Paul Smith appear in a special issue of the *Journal of Outdoor Life* (June 1910) devoted to Trudeau's legacy. See especially Charles C. Trembley, "Dr. Trudeau as a Woodsman," *Journal of Outdoor Life* 7, no. 6 (1910): 173–75.

was popular, and socializing with a crowd of sporting enthusiasts. Given these contexts, it is fair to assume that, at some point in time, Trudeau learned of Murray's book; even if he had no awareness of its existence, which is hard to believe, he unwittingly participated in the Murray Rush. Regardless of his initial reasons for visiting the Adirondacks, by the time Trudeau wrote *An Autobiography* in 1915 he had so fully absorbed Murray's pilgrimage pattern as to have made it a part of his personal legend.

The Climate Cure

In the early 1880s, Trudeau contributed to a second wave of the Murray Rush when his personal testimony appeared in the writings of Marc Cook, a New York City newspaper-man and recently diagnosed consumptive who had read Dr. Alfred Loomis's 1879 medical treatise promoting the Adirondack curative climate and promptly packed his bags for a year in the North Woods. After spending a summer camping at Paul Smith's and a winter lodging in nearby Bloomingdale, Cook reported on his experiences in the essay "Camp Lou," published in *Harper's New Monthly Magazine* in May 1881, and later expanded his account into a health seekers' guidebook, *The Wilderness Cure*, printed later that year. In both texts, Cook described his extreme illness, his retreat into the Adirondacks, and his restoration of health, thus replicating the scene in Murray's book, which he had purchased and read on his way into the wilderness. Although he was not a sportsman, Cook neverthe-less sought his health at Paul Smith's, the regional hub of sporting culture, and his writings persistently employed sporting tropes, referring to his endeavor, for instance, as "the great health hunt."[22] *Harper's New Monthly Magazine*, which had printed Hallock's parody of Murray a decade earlier, also coded "Camp Lou" as a work of sportsman's literature by illustrating it with images evocative of outdoor recreation.

Implying that the wilderness cure required the performance of a frontier ethos, Cook advised his fellow invalids to embrace the rigors of camp life and remain in the Adiron-dacks through the winter, and he included detailed instructions for setting up camp, pre-paring food, and hiring guides. He laid particular stress on the benefits of tent life, describ-ing in detail how to erect and outfit a semipermanent canvas tent similar to the one that Trudeau occupied during later summers at Paul Smith's. To convince his urban readers that camp life did not require abandoning all comforts, Cook cataloged the household goods that one might cram into such a rustic structure: a bed, bookshelf, easy chair, and writing table; a woodstove; a trunk and an ottoman; a clock and a mirror; a chessboard, cribbage board, field glasses, books, newspapers, manuscripts, and writing materials; a pipe and cigars to exacerbate one's consumptive lungs. In short, Cook's camping regimen domesti-cated the wilderness by fully incorporating the material abundance of a middle-class con-sumer culture. Furthermore, while presenting his recipe for recovery, Cook also accounted

---

22. Marc Cook, "Camp Lou," *Harper's New Monthly Magazine,* May 1881, 869.

"PAUL" SMITH'S HOTEL.

A CARRY.

Marc Cook, three illustrations (above and previous page) from "Camp Lou," in *Harper's New Monthly Magazine*, May 1881, 868, 876, 878.

for the economics of an Adirondack vacation. *The Wilderness Cure*, for example, included a chapter calculating the costs of a full year in the region, estimating a range of expenses for working-, middle-, and upper-class health seekers.[23] Likewise, "Camp Lou" maintained that a season in the wilderness was affordable for a hypothetical "clerk" and boasted facetiously that "the wilderness is poverty's paradise."[24]

Contributing to the post-Civil War tourism boom in the Adirondacks, Cook tailored his writings as the invalid's alternative to such regional guidebooks as E. R. Wallace's *Descriptive Guide to the Adirondacks* and Seneca Ray Stoddard's *The Adirondacks: Illustrated*, both of which began appearing as annual publications in the 1870s but lacked practical information for health seekers. To provide such information, Cook adopted a rhetorical style—characterized by journalistic integrity, technical detail, didactic advice, and the narrative authority of firsthand experience—that emulated the recreational camping guides then coming into vogue, such as George Washington Sears's *Woodcraft*, published by Forest and Stream in 1884. By framing his tuberculosis narrative as an instructional guide, Cook marketed the leisure activities of camping and outdoor recreation to an audience

23. Marc Cook, *The Wilderness Cure* (New York: William Wood, 1881), 136–47.
24. Cook, "Camp Lou," 877–78.

of (mainly middle-class) tuberculosis health seekers, and his curing regimen anticipated some of the core principles of the sanatorium system, especially its emphasis on patient commitment, individual forbearance, and open-air treatment. When he declared that "the first duty of the patient should be to live out-of-doors as much of the time as is practicable," he echoed the medical advice that Trudeau and Loomis were beginning to dispense to their patients. Likewise, he accurately predicted that the Adirondacks would soon become a health resort: "Here, within reach of thousands who could never hope to journey to far-away places, nature provides a sanitarium, destined, in the Reporter's belief, to become the future Mecca for consumptive patients."[25]

Like Murray, Cook promoted the Adirondacks in a print venue that reached a wide range of American readers, but unlike Murray, who capitalized on the book trade, Cook owed his brief popularity to periodical culture. Initially published in *Harper's New Monthly Magazine*, Cook's tuberculosis narrative received "a flood of inquiries" from readers demanding more information, and this reception inspired him to expand the essay into a book.[26] Although it is unclear how well *The Wilderness Cure* sold, "Camp Lou" appeared in one of the most popular nineteenth-century magazines, enabling Cook to inject his faith in the curative climate into the very mainstream of American culture. Founded in 1850 as a promotional tool for the Harper Brothers' book trade, *Harper's Magazine* fashioned itself as a national literary periodical aimed at a variety of middle-class and affluent readers. In order to please the largest majority of readers, the editors adopted a policy that avoided political controversy and social criticism, preferring to reinforce, rather than challenge, conventional values. Insofar as it attracted and maintained readers, this policy worked well, for subscriptions surpassed one hundred thousand by 1860, and despite losing many Southern readers during the Civil War, the magazine weathered the sectional crisis and continued as one of the most influential periodicals throughout the Gilded Age. Conservative in approach, the editors favored a sentimental literary style that avoided rigorous analysis of social problems and instead emphasized the emotional response of those who endured personal hardships.[27]

---

25. Ibid., 875, 878.

26. Cook, *The Wilderness Cure*, author's note.

27. For this history of *Harper's Magazine*, I draw on Howard Horsford, "Harper and Brothers," *American Literary Publishing Houses, 1638–1899, Dictionary of Literary Biography*, vol. 49, part 1, ed. Peter Dzwonkoski (Detroit: Gale, 1986), 192–98; Barbara Perkins, "Harper's Monthly Magazine," *American Literary Magazines: The Eighteenth and Nineteenth Centuries*, ed. Edward E. Chielens (Westport, CT: Greenwood Press, 1986), 166–71; Sheila Post-Lauria, "Magazine Practices and Melville's *Israel Potter*," in *Periodical Culture in Nineteenth-Century America*, ed. Kenneth M. Price and Susan Belasco Smith (Charlottesville: University Press of Virginia, 1995), 115–32; and Thomas Lilly, "The National Archive: *Harper's New Monthly Magazine* and the Civic Responsibilities of a Commercial Literary Periodical, 1850–1853," *American Periodicals* 15, no. 2 (2005): 142–62. Admittedly, this characterization may oversimplify the great variety of materials that Harper and Brothers published in the nineteenth century. In contrast to *Harper's New Monthly Magazine*, for example, *Harper's Weekly* (launched in 1857) maintained a more politically minded editorial policy, printed Thomas Nast's political cartoons, and helped to expose the Crédit Mobilier scandal. But even in that venue, Nast's satirical attacks on public figures eventually met with the disfavor of editor William George Curtis, who sought to protect the genteel decorum of the magazine. See Fiona Deans Halloran, *Thomas Nast: The Father of Modern Political Cartoons* (Chapel Hill: University of North Carolina Press, 2012), 221–44.

Cook's tuberculosis narrative straddled the line between two literary styles contending for priority at *Harper's* during the 1880s. For the most part, "Camp Lou" fit the pattern of the sentimental romance. It was not a work of investigative journalism exposing the social problem of tuberculosis or the lack of suitable treatment options; instead, it told the personal story of a young consumptive whose professional career was interrupted due to illness and who bravely sought his cure in the wilderness, persevered through the winter, and triumphed because of his individual fortitude. Cook distanced himself from narrative events by adopting a third-person perspective, a common technique in nineteenth-century sentimental literature, which often featured omniscient narrators or detached spectators who observed the plight of the poor, sick, or downtrodden and guided the audience through a proper emotional response. A few years after "Camp Lou" appeared in *Harper's*, William Dean Howells published his now-famous series of editorials lambasting sentimental romance and advocating a literature of realism. Cook also embraced some aspects of this emerging literary movement: a newspaper reporter by trade, he aimed for a degree of factual detail that created the illusion of realism; he supported his claims by citing medical sources; and he crafted a sketch of full-time Adirondack residents in the style of local color regionalism, an aesthetic that Howells championed in his editorial columns.[28]

In both essay and book form, Cook's writings popularized a conversation about climate science then under way in the medical press. An earnest publicist for the Adirondacks as a health resort, Cook made a case for the "magical results of the climate" and asserted his "faith in the cold-weather theory" that advised overwintering in the region.[29] He also credited Dr. Alfred Loomis with inspiring his own retreat into the wilderness: "Camp Lou" provided a long synopsis of Loomis's 1879 address to the New York State Medical Society, "The Adirondack Region as a Therapeutical Agent in the Treatment of Pulmonary Phthisis," and *The Wilderness Cure* reprinted Loomis's paper in its entirety. In fact, Cook's book was published by the same company that printed *The Medical Record*, a weekly journal in which Loomis's address first appeared, indicating that the medical press enabled this particular climate narrative to reach both scientific and general audiences.

A New York City physician who suffered from consumption, Loomis had discovered that vacationing in the Adirondacks benefited his health. While summering at Paul Smith's, he befriended Trudeau and supported the young consumptive's decision to overwinter in the Adirondacks in 1874. Later in the 1880s, he assisted in the formation of the Adirondack Cottage Sanitarium by referring patients to Trudeau's care and publicizing the institution in New York City. Loomis also served as first president of the American Climatological Association, an organization founded by a group of physicians in 1883 for the purposes of advancing the study of medical geography. In subsequent years, Loomis and his colleague Dr.

---

28. On Howells's promotion of realism, see Amy Kaplan, *The Social Construction of American Realism* (Chicago: University of Chicago Press, 1992), 15–43. Cook's portrait of "year-round inhabitants" appears in *The Wilderness Cure*, 86–95, and in "Camp Lou," 875–77.
29. Cook, *The Wilderness Cure*, 73–74, and "Camp Lou," 84, respectively.

Joseph Stickler, editor of *The Adirondacks as a Health Resort* (1886), engaged in a climate rivalry with physicians from other parts of the country, especially Charles Denison, whose *Rocky Mountain Health Resorts* (1880) promoted the Colorado cure industry by insisting on the benefits of an arid climate.[30]

Although Loomis was slow to embrace the germ theory of tuberculosis, he was an early and influential advocate for climatic treatment. In his 1879 address he stated emphatically in language approximating Murray's that the Adirondacks possessed unique health-inducing qualities: "It is not surprising that in such a region the tired worker and worn-out invalid find the rest and quiet which is so powerful a restorer of health."[31] Hitherto the region had been regarded as unhealthful because of its cold, wet weather, but Loomis and Trudeau argued that temperature and rainfall were less important than the purity of the air and drainage of the soil. Collaborating to shift medical opinion, the two doctors advised "camping out" as the best treatment option and asserted that "tent-life, and a return to the invigorating, out-of-door existence of the savage is Nature's antidote for a disease which is almost an outgrowth of civilization and its enervating influences."[32] Thus did an ideology of primitivism, inherited from Romanticism, underlie the medical response to tuberculosis in the late nineteenth century, but physicians found support for such deeply held cultural myths in the facts of scientific empiricism. Loomis and Trudeau, for instance, collected twenty case studies of consumptives curing in the Adirondacks, and Loomis closed his address by presenting this data as proof of the curative climate.

Marc Cook died in 1882, just a year after his tuberculosis narrative appeared in the popular press. The same year, two serendipitous encounters changed the course of Trudeau's career: first, he learned of Robert Koch's discovery of the tubercle bacillus and initiated his own effort to replicate Koch's experiments; second, he read about the German sanatorium system and hatched plans for his Adirondack Cottage Sanitarium based on the open-air treatment developed by Hermann Brehmer and Peter Dettweiler. In subsequent years, Trudeau went on to conduct more advanced studies in bacteriology, growing cultures of tubercle bacillus, testing the effects of environmental conditions on the health of infected animals, and experimenting with vaccines and germicides. Despite these evolving scientific investigations, he never entirely abandoned his earlier faith in the curative potential of climate and outdoor life. In fact, his first scientific studies contributed to the field of medical geography, and in 1886 he became a member of the American Climatological Association, a group that provided a venue for his earliest research.

While residing at Paul Smith's in the summer of 1886, Trudeau captured fifteen rabbits

---

30. On Loomis and his relationship to Trudeau, see John Conway, *Loomis: The Man, The Sanitarium, and the Search for the Cure* (Fleischmanns, NY: Purple Mountain Press, 2006); and Hotaling, *A Rare Romance in Medicine*, 39–41. On the American Climatological Association, see Mitman and Numbers, "From Miasma to Asthma," 391–412.

31. Alfred L. Loomis, "The Adirondack Region as a Therapeutical Agent in the Treatment of Pulmonary Phthisis," *The Medical Record: A Weekly Journal of Medicine and Surgery* 15, no. 17 (1879): 386.

32. Ibid., 387.

and divided them into three groups. He inoculated the first group with the tubercle bacillus, enclosed the rabbits in a box, and confined them in a dark basement; he left the second group uninfected but also enclosed in a box, which he placed outdoors at the bottom of a deep hole in the ground; he inoculated the third group and released the rabbits on Spitfire Island in a setting that resembled Marc Cook's camp at nearby Osgood Pond. After a few months, the first group had suffered the most: four of five rabbits had died, and the fifth was severely ill. Every rabbit in the second group had survived, but they were malnourished and mangy. In the third group, one rabbit perished early in the experiment, but at the end of four months, enjoying an outdoor life and nutritious diet, the others were thriving and healthy. For Trudeau, the experiment proved that the essential elements of tuberculosis treatment were "hygiene, climate, and feeding—in other words a favorable environment."[33] To benefit from environmental conditions, the patient must comply with doctor's orders by following a regimen of rest and open-air therapy; theoretically, this treatment could occur anywhere, but on an emotional, intuitive level, Trudeau believed in the geographic exceptionalism of the Adirondacks, perhaps because the region offered invalids an opportunity to take the cure in a beautiful setting and, if they enjoyed field sports, to engage in the performance of a frontier ethos by hunting, fishing, or camping in the wilderness.

The Canoe and the Cough

Another regional writer who adopted a frontier ethos and forged a link between physical health and outdoor recreation was George Washington Sears, a former shoemaker and newspaper editor from Wellsboro, Pennsylvania, who paddled a lightweight cedar canoe through the Adirondacks on three occasions in the early 1880s. Writing under the pen name "Nessmuk," Sears described his canoe trips in a series of eighteen letters published in *Forest and Stream*, the premier American sporting journal of the late nineteenth century. Advocating a "go light" philosophy, these letters popularized solo canoeing and camping while providing free publicity for Sears's boat builder, J. Henry Rushton, whose northern New York boat shop became a site of innovative canoe design and production in the late nineteenth century. Nessmuk played a key role in Adirondack history because he contributed to a democratic expansion of outdoor recreation by modeling a type of wilderness vacation for those Americans who could not afford to hire guides or lodge at a hotel. In the process, he also documented a culture of health-seeking in the region, yet this dimension of his legacy has received less critical attention than it deserves.[34]

---

33. E. L. Trudeau, M.D., "Environment in Its Relation to the Progress of Bacterial Invasion in Tuberculosis," *Transactions of the American Climatological Association* 4 (1887): 136.

34. On Nessmuk's legacy and Rushton's canoes, see George Washington Sears, *Canoeing the Adirondacks with Nessmuk: The Adirondack Letters of George Washington Sears*, ed. Dan Brenan (Syracuse, NY: Syracuse University Press, 1993), 3–32; Christine Jerome, *An Adirondack Passage: The Cruise of the Canoe* Sairy Gamp (Halcottsville, NY: Breakaway Books, 2013); and Atwood Manley, *Rushton and His Times in American Canoeing* (Syracuse, NY: Syracuse University Press, 1968).

Although Sears did not identify his illness in print, the evidence suggests that he suffered from tuberculosis: during the Civil War, he was discharged from the Union army after repeated asthma attacks; his writings complain frequently of pulmonary troubles; while traveling in the Adirondacks, he exhibited the tell-tale symptoms of tuberculosis ("I coughed almost incessantly and had sweating spells every night"); and his obituary hinted at his "consumptive tendencies."[35] Like many tuberculosis victims who feared being branded as outcasts, Sears may have preferred to keep his condition a secret, or perhaps he never received a formal diagnosis; either way, his writings abounded with overt and covert references that signaled consumption to his readers. Given his health history, Sears may have selected the Adirondacks as a paddling destination, in part, because he hoped to restore his own health—indeed, his first letter praised "the benefit of open air" found in the Adirondacks—and in that sense he reenacted the pilgrimage pattern made popular by Murray and Cook.[36] But unlike these previous writers, whose testimonials rang with exuberant optimism, Sears brought a newsman's shrewd cynicism to the North Woods and used it to evaluate the veracity of the wilderness cure.

Immediately upon entering the Adirondacks, Sears began gathering reports of invalids who had come to the region in pursuit of health. In the summer of 1880, he interviewed a camp owner named Albert Jones and framed his story as a parable of the wilderness cure. Suffering "a general physical breakdown" due to overwork and financial anxiety, Jones retreated into the Adirondacks, expecting to die there. He embraced "an open-air, carefree life," enjoyed a rapid recovery, and then returned home to manage his business but soon experienced a relapse. Jones repeated this retreat-recovery-relapse pattern a second and third time before finally abandoning his business life and settling permanently in the Adirondacks, where he opened a boardinghouse. "He has regained health and spirits," reported Nessmuk, "and would, on the whole, make an excellent subject for 'Adirondack' Murray." Conflicting accounts, however, led Sears to qualify his initial optimism. On Fourth Lake he passed the former camp of a young man "afflicted with incipient consumption" who had made a "fair trial" of the wilderness cure in a "healthful location" but nevertheless died. "Not all invalids improve by coming here," Nessmuk concluded, giving the region a mixed review: "Scores come here for health who will tell you frankly that they might as well have stayed at home. Very many receive decided and permanent benefit. Some bad cases of asthma and consumption in its first stages are apparently cured. One thing is certain: you pay your money, you do not always take your choice."[37]

Nessmuk's skepticism intensified during his second trip to the Adirondacks. Paddling the Fulton Chain Lakes in July 1881, two months after Marc Cook's "Camp Lou"

---

35. Sears, *Canoeing the Adirondacks with Nessmuk*, 117. "The Death of 'Nessmuk,'" *Forest and Stream*, May 8, 1890, 305–6.

36. Sears, *Canoeing the Adirondacks with Nessmuk*, 36.

37. Ibid., 50–52.

was published, Sears witnessed several "invalids of the Lung Disorder type, who did not seem very favorably affected by the damp, chilly weather," and he blamed Cook's essay for inspiring a "brigade of consumptives" who came to the region seeking a miracle cure but found only disappointment, betrayal, and bad weather.[38] In response to this apparent Cook Rush, Nessmuk reported the rumor that "a dozen consumptives had already died on the Saranac Waters" and cited a regional authority to discredit Cook's claims: "Paul Smith had said he would, by five hundred dollars, rather the article 'Camp Lou' had never been written."[39] In contrast to Loomis and Trudeau, Nessmuk argued that the cold, wet climate exacerbated pulmonary conditions, and despite his lack of medical expertise he recommended the headwaters of the Delaware and Susquehanna Rivers as more promising destinations. Although he conceded that some invalids had recovered in the Adirondacks, on the whole his second round of letters rejected the popular belief in the region's curative climate.

Such skepticism may have resulted from Sears's own failed quest for health. During his 1881 excursion he endured a nagging cough, experimented with multiple cough remedies, and found only temporary relief in homemade balsam tea. The rainy weather that summer especially aggravated him, prompting a snarky portrait of the health seekers with whom he spent a night on Third Lake. Much to his chagrin, however, Sears began to experience symptoms resembling consumption, and to an observer he may have blended into the Cook Rush: "I had joined in the little band of coughers, coughing oftener and louder than any of them."[40] Indeed, if the canoe was the dominant image in Nessmuk's letters, the cough was his chorus, a sensory detail signifying the frustrated hope of the health seeker, as evident in the following weather report:

July 16th. Gale with heavy rain. Frequent showers; wind mainly from the north.

17th. Heavy wind and cold rain from the north, everyone shivering with cold. Five people in the house with hard, chronic coughs. Bark, bark, all night.

18th. Rain, rain; blow, blow, from the north, as usual. Cough, cough. Five of us keep it up. Two will most likely never be better.

19th. Like the 18th, cold and rainy. Rained all night.

20th. Put on a gum coat, took my little hatchet, and went for the woods. Made a fire that would roast an ox, and got nearly dry—for once. Still raining. Rains nearly all the time. 'Tisn't the most favorable weather for lung diseases; not the healthiest region, I should say. Parties who come for health are every day going out, disgusted and sick.[41]

---

38. Ibid., 95.
39. Ibid., 112.
40. Ibid., 97.
41. Ibid., 99.

Most enervating of all, poor health prevented the performance of masculinity so essential to Nessmuk's frontier ethos, and thus his final letter of 1881 concluded on a sour note of defeat: "I had sought the wilderness for health. I had lost instead of gaining."[42]

Despite this setback, Sears intended to return to the Adirondacks the following summer, but illness forced him to postpone this third trip until 1883. When he finally made the excursion, he "gained in health with every day's exercise and sport" and promptly reversed his position on the wilderness cure. "In spite of the exceptionally cold, wet summer," he wrote, "sportsmen and healthseekers are enjoying the woods most satisfactorily. With at least five out of every six who come to this region for health, the improvement is decided and speedy. I have personal knowledge of some cases that seem almost marvelous."[43] The next year, perhaps hoping to capitalize on the success of his letters, Forest and Stream published Sears's *Woodcraft* (1884), a popular guide to recreational camping that further reinforced the connection between physical health and outdoor sport by opening with a general argument about the need for recreation in a nation that works itself to exhaustion.[44] Thus, rather than refuting the myth of the wilderness cure, Sears's later writings evolved toward a tentative acceptance of its occasional possibility.

The publication context of Sears's writings may have further influenced his wavering attitude. While Cook aimed his advice at consumptives and Trudeau presented his research to the medical community, Sears wrote for an audience of sportsmen, many of whom had a proprietary stake in protecting their hunting and fishing grounds and therefore bemoaned the transformation of the Adirondacks into a health resort. Founded in 1873 by Charles Hallock, *Forest and Stream* devoted its pages to a range of outdoor topics, including, of course, hunting and fishing, but also natural history, fish culture, dog breeding, and boating. When George Bird Grinnell took over the paper in 1879–80, he transformed it into a propaganda tool for his conservationist agenda, and for the next thirty years his editorials advocated new game laws, forest conservation policies, and rigorous protection for public lands, most notably in Yellowstone and the Adirondacks. Though Sears came from a lower social class than Hallock and Grinnell—as a boy, he worked in a cotton mill; as a young man he went to sea on a whaling ship; and upon his return he trained as a shoemaker—he shared their knowledge of the newspaper trade, having edited the *Tioga County Agitator* in northern Pennsylvania. Thus, when he penned his letters to *Forest and Stream* in the early 1880s, he wielded a nuanced understanding of periodical culture and adopted a persona that enabled him to become one of the paper's most popular contributors.[45]

Nessmuk's letters resonated with readers of *Forest and Stream* because he embraced

---

42. Ibid., 135.
43. Ibid., 141.
44. George Washington Sears, *Woodcraft; by "Nessmuk"* (New York: Forest and Stream Publishing, 1884), 1–2.
45. For this background on *Forest and Stream*, I draw on John F. Reiger, *American Sportsmen and the Origins of Conservation* (New York: Winchester Press, 1975), 21–49.

a like-minded sportsman's code and conservationist agenda. He recorded the quantity of fish and game and ridiculed Adirondack Murray for his recreational shooting of loons. More acerbically, he railed against dam-building projects and criticized Verplanck Colvin's utilitarian approach, which he considered hypocritical because it endorsed forest conservation while inviting the commercial exploitation of the Adirondacks.[46] Beyond their content, Nessmuk's letters also appealed to readers because of their direct, chummy language and humorous, self-deprecating style. As part of "the woodland fraternity," he assumed the voice of a club member speaking frankly to fellow sportsmen in the know.[47] To amuse this audience, he affected a manly frontier ethos and then undercut this heroic stance by poking fun at his own age, physical frailty, and self-inflicted mishaps. Likewise, when he joined the crowd of health seekers coughing through the night, he staged the failure of the wilderness cure in a way that opened a space for his more sophisticated, skeptical readers to mock the enthusiasm of the masses. Elsewhere, Sears slipped into a newspaper editor's wry persona to play a game of good-natured myth-busting, and readers came to trust his credibility because he presented his opinion as an empirical, level-headed assessment gained from direct experience.

While entertaining readers with his nimble wit, sardonic sense of humor, and self-effacing irony, Nessmuk identified two primary factors—outdoor recreation and tuberculosis health-seeking—that guided visitors into the Adirondacks in the late nineteenth century, and he represented these cultural agents with two vivid symbols: the canoe and the cough. In the final decades of the nineteenth century, these two motive forces merged into a cultural movement that commodified the Adirondack climate, shaped the course of regional history, and influenced the conservation efforts leading to the creation of the Adirondack Park.

Although tuberculosis health seekers do not loom large in the Adirondack conservation movement, they did play a supporting role. In 1890, Alfred Loomis joined with other prominent physicians to form the Adirondack Park Association, a group that lobbied for the acquisition of public lands, and Trudeau served on this organization's executive committee.[48] Meanwhile, the New York State Forest Commission issued multiple annual reports praising the Adirondack Cottage Sanitarium and enumerating the region's "climatic advantages." "The sanitary value of our forests cannot be over-estimated," the forest commission testified, citing as evidence a paper by Loomis about the health benefits of evergreen forests

---

46. Appointed by the State of New York in 1872 to complete a survey of the Adirondacks, Colvin authored numerous government reports and tirelessly advocated for forest conservation through the final decades of the nineteenth century. Sears, however, questioned Colvin's simultaneous promotion of economic development schemes, especially dam-building projects. For a collection of Colvin's writings, see *Adirondack Explorations: Nature Writings of Verplanck Colvin*, ed. Paul Schaefer (Syracuse, NY: Syracuse University Press, 1997).
47. Sears, *Canoeing the Adirondacks with Nessmuk*, 156.
48. On the Adirondack Park Association, see New York State Forest Commission, *Annual Report . . . for the Year 1894* (Albany, NY: J. B. Lyon, 1895), 111–12; and Graham, *The Adirondack Park*, 122–23.

and a testimonial by Trudeau about the social benefits of the Saranac Lake cure industry. "As a sanitarium for the State and city of New York alone," Trudeau wrote, "the value of this region is inestimable, and many professional men will be at a loss where to send their suffering patients . . . unless some steps be immediately taken to save the State this heritage that should be preserved for the people."[49] By no means an ardent environmental activist, Trudeau applied a utilitarian mindset to conservation issues, and in later years, recognizing the view from his sanatorium as a crucial asset, he called upon state administrators to preserve nearby forest lands.[50] Thus, the combined motive forces of the canoe and the cough prepared the public to accept new arguments for wilderness preservation, and any complete picture of Adirondack environmental history must account for this connection between outdoor recreation and tuberculosis treatment.

Historians of the Adirondacks have devoted much attention to the 1894 New York State Constitutional Convention, during which the celebrated "forever wild" provision was passed.[51] In doing so they have emphasized how several delegates delivered speeches that bemoaned the negative effects of deforestation and promoted the preservation of forest lands (especially in the Adirondacks) for the sake of watershed protection and outdoor recreation. But a close reading of the floor debate also reveals that a recognition of the region's health-inducing qualities went hand in hand with this watershed argument. In the longest speech on the topic, David McClure, the chairman of the committee that proposed the amendment, called the Adirondacks "priceless as a place for seeking, finding, and preserving health." Echoing Murray, Cook, and company, he continued, "Any of you . . . who have had relatives or friends whose lives have been prolonged in those mountains by the balmy air and soft breezes which fill the place, know how invaluable these woods are for such purpose."[52] Likewise, William Goodelle insisted that "the Adirondacks furnish a vast sanitarium, not only for the people of this State, but from all over the country. They go there by the thousands to have their health restored and to have their vigor renewed and to have their constitutions built up."[53] Another delegate, Charles Mereness began his remarks by stating, "I have an exalted opinion as to the vast importance of our forest preserve as a health resort."[54] And praising the Adirondacks for its varied greatness ("this great water

---

49. New York State Forest Commission, *Annual Report . . . for the Year Ending December 31, 1891* (Albany, NY: J. B. Lyon, 1892), 129–31. The forest commission began to recognize the region's value as a health-seeking destination as early as its 1888 report, and the commissioners specifically mentioned the Adirondack Cottage Sanitarium in their 1891 and 1893 reports. These reports quote from Loomis's "Evergreen Forests as a Therapeutic Agent in Pulmonary Phthisis," *Transactions of the American Climatological Association* 4 (1887): 109–20.
50. On Trudeau's later conservation efforts, see Hotaling, *A Rare Romance in Medicine*, 173.
51. See, for example, Alfred L. Donaldson, *A History of the Adirondacks* (Harrison, NY: Harbor Hill Books, 1977), 2:187–96; Graham, *The Adirondack Park*, 126–32; and Terrie, *Forever Wild*, 104–8.
52. *Revised Record of the Constitutional Convention of the State of New York, May 8, 1894, to September 29, 1894* (Albany: Argus, 1900), 4:132.
53. Ibid., 143.
54. Ibid., 147

supply, this great sanitarium, this great health resort"), Edward Brown reminded his listeners of "the great number of pleasure seekers, the great number of invalids that annually
visit that territory, not only in summer, but also in winter."[55] In a remarkable moment preceding the final vote on the amendment, one delegate (Nicoll Floyd) even proposed adding
a clause that would allow the forest commission to lease lands to health seekers in the
Adirondacks, justifying his position on the grounds of health-care access: "It has been for
years a well-known resort for persons afflicted with pulmonary diseases, and has proved
to them a great blessing. If we prevent any leasing we shut out from the North Woods that
class of frequenters. . . . It is in the interests of this class of people, to whom we ought not
deny this health-giving, life-giving region of the North Woods."[56] As this evidence suggests,
by the final decade of the nineteenth century the myth of the curative climate had become
so ingrained in cultural perceptions of the Adirondacks that it figured into the most significant political debates in New York State and had a direct impact on both public health and
public policy.

Adirondack Climate Narratives

In the late nineteenth century, popular authors and medical experts harnessed multiple
forms of print media to disseminate a climate narrative that figured the Adirondacks as a
curative region. Enduring into the twentieth century, this narrative commodified the climate for the twin purposes of outdoor recreation and tuberculosis recovery, and it left a
lasting mark on the Adirondacks by accelerating the growth of a tourist economy, facilitat-
ing the rise of a cure industry, and supporting the foundational environmental policies that
continue to define the region. Eventually, however, medical advancements and new drug
treatments led to the decline of tuberculosis as a public-health crisis, and as a result, the
Trudeau Sanatorium closed its doors in 1954, marking the end of an era and making way
for a new climate narrative.

Throughout the 1970s and 1980s, Adirondack environmentalists expressed an increasing anxiety about the harmful effects of acid rain, which ranked alongside new home development as a major threat to the region's freshwater and forest resources.[57] Amid such
concerns about the perils of industrial culture, journalist Bill McKibben left New York
City and relocated to the Adirondacks, where he discovered a newfound purpose in life
writing about the natural world and fighting on its behalf. In the late 1980s, McKibben
sounded an alarm about anthropogenic climate change in an environmental manifesto
published serially in *The New Yorker* and then as a book with the unhappy title *The End of
Nature* (1989), the first book about global warming written for a general audience. Although

55. Ibid., 156.
56. Ibid., 706–7.
57. Jerry Jenkins, Karen Roy, Charles Driscoll, and Christopher Buerkett, *Acid Rain in the Adirondacks: An
Environmental History* (Ithaca, NY: Cornell University Press, 2007).

he cited an abundance of scientific evidence, McKibben sought to motivate his readers with a vigorous dose of apocalyptic rhetoric. Adopting a jeremiad structure that bemoaned the broken contract between humans and the natural world, he forecast impending disasters and advised his fellow Americans to abandon their consumer lifestyles in favor of a pattern of living lightly on Earth. Despite this sweeping vision of global calamity, *The End of Nature* grounded its argument in moments of lived experience in the Adirondacks, and its most affecting passages occur when McKibben imagines how his home region may irrevocably change in the coming century.

A few years later, aware that the gloomy tone of his first book had failed to kindle a movement, McKibben turned to a more optimistic project, *Hope, Human and Wild* (1995), in which he traveled the world searching for examples of sustainable living. Even while visiting far-flung places in Brazil and India, however, he once again rooted his environmental vision in the Adirondacks, celebrating the region as a model of wilderness preservation and stewardship. While describing the destruction and regeneration of the region's forests, McKibben echoed a theme of recovery that had begun in the nineteenth century: "For conservationists imagining not simply the salvation of what remains pristine, but the restoration of what has been degraded, this is just about the most heartening spot on earth."[58] In more recent years, Adirondack scientists have reached a consensus that the next century will bring a general warming trend to the region, which will entail reduced winter snowfall and lake ice cover, more annual rainfall and frequent severe storms, and a pattern of erratic, unpredictable weather. In the context of this new Adirondack climate narrative, the conversation has shifted toward questions of adaptation: How will regional ecosystems respond to ongoing climatic changes? And how can local communities maintain their identities and economies when these changes disrupt the status quo?[59]

Despite a fringe element of climate deniers, the reality of anthropogenic climate change has become ingrained in the public consciousness, and as the next century unfolds it will play a larger geopolitical role and inspire more regional policies aimed at sustainability and

---

58. Bill McKibben, *Hope, Human and Wild: True Stories of Living Lightly on Earth* (Boston: Little, Brown, 1995), 31.
59. To follow the trajectory of climate research in the Adirondacks, which has involved significant debate about the accuracy of weather data and the legitimacy of predicting future trends, see Bill McKibben, "Future Shock: The Coming Adirondack Climate," *Adirondack Life*, April 2002, www.adirondacklifemag.com/blogs /2014/09/18/future-shock; J. Curt Stager and Michael R. Martin, "Global Climate Change and the Adirondacks," *Adirondack Journal of Environmental Studies* 9, no. 1 (2002): 6–13; J. Curt Stager, Stacy McNulty, Colin Beier, and Jeff Chiarenzelli, "Historical Patterns and Effects of Changes in Adirondack Climates since the Early 20th Century," *Adirondack Journal of Environmental Studies* 15, no. 2 (2009): 14–24; J. Curt Stager and Mary Thill, "Climate Change in the Champlain Basin: What Natural Resource Managers Can Expect and Do," report prepared for the Nature Conservancy, May 2010; Jerry Jenkins, *Climate Change in the Adirondacks: The Path to Sustainability* (Ithaca, NY: Cornell University Press, 2010); Curt Stager, "Water Proof," *Adirondack Life*, April 2013, www.adirondacklifemag.com/blogs/2013/04/15/water-proof; Mike Lynch, "Dealing with Climate Change," *Adirondack Explorer*, May 10, 2016, https://www.adirondackexplorer.org/stories/dealing-climate -change; Brandon Loomis, "Winter's Decline Expected to Alter Adirondacks," *Adirondack Explorer*, December 28, 2018, https://www.adirondackexplorer.org/stories/winters-decline-expected-to-alter-adirondacks; and Brandon Loomis, "Warming Threatens to Upend Ecology on Adirondack Lakes," *Adirondack Explorer*, April 23, 2019, https://www.adirondackexplorer.org/stories/warming-threatens-adirondack-lakes.

resilience. This is the defining environmental narrative of our age, one that raises profound questions about the fate of human civilization, and while confronting its unprecedented scale we may forget that other climate narratives once shaped human destiny. A backward glance at Adirondack history, however, serves as a reminder that climate knowledge is always culturally situated and often contested. Nineteenth-century health seekers made the best use of the information available to them. Many consumptives who traveled to the Adirondacks failed to recover, and departed in disgust; some died in the region; others got lucky, experienced a renewal of health, and became proponents of the wilderness cure. All took risks and endured a frightening degree of uncertainty, causing many to embrace a climate narrative that promised a miraculous recovery. Facing a different set of challenges but similar uncertainties, we may find little comfort in knowing that most of these health seekers perished before the medical breakthroughs of the mid-twentieth century. But following the example of their fearless leader, who was "ever possessed of a large fund of optimism," they did not all lapse into despair either.[60] Perhaps we too can take a lesson from Trudeau and ease the suffering of our fellow humans while working hopefully toward a better future.

---

60. E. L. Trudeau, "The Value of Optimism in Medicine," *American Journal of the Medical Sciences* 140 (1910): 1.

Community NY
Centering Diversity in *Stonewall: 50 Years Out*

Christine L. Ridarsky

On April 5, 2019, the Central Library of Rochester and Monroe County opened a historical exhibition titled *Stonewall: 50 Years Out*. The exhibit commemorates the fiftieth anniversary of the 1969 uprising at New York City's Stonewall Inn that sparked the gay liberation movement and explores the history of Rochester's LGBTQ+ communities. Most significantly, it does so in a way that centers the lives and experiences of people who have been marginalized within traditional narratives, both historically and in contemporary society.

The exhibition stems from a partnership that developed about three years ago between the library and the Gay Alliance of the Genesee Valley (recently renamed the Out Alliance). At that time, the alliance began transferring archive and manuscript collections from its library to the public library's Local History and Genealogy Division. The materials had been amassed by Alliance historian Evelyn Bailey during research for *Shoulders to Stand On*, a documentary film she produced in 2013. The film spurred interest in LGBTQ+ history and resulted in additional donations in the years that followed. By 2015 it had become clear that the Alliance did not have the staff, space, or appropriate storage conditions to properly house them, and Bailey approached the Central Library.

The first few acquisitions had been fully processed and described by the Central Library by late 2017, and staff began to discuss ways of promoting the collections' availability. At the same time, members of Rochester's LGBTQ+ communities were asking how they should commemorate the Stonewall anniversary in 2019. An exhibition in the Central Library would do both. In the spring of 2018, Local History and Genealogy Division manager Christine L. Ridarsky called a meeting attended by people representing a wide variety of expertise, ranging from library, archives, and museum professionals and university scholars to LGBTQ+ activists and community members. The result was a plan for a community-curated exhibit to be held in a space that was free and welcoming—the Central Library.

One challenge became immediately evident. *Shoulders to Stand On* had come to be

STONE WALL 50 YEARS OUT

Title Graphic
for Exhibition
(COURTESY OF THE
CENTRAL LIBRARY
OF ROCHESTER AND
MONROE COUNTY)

recognized within the mainstream gay and lesbian community as the official history of Rochester's LGBTQ+ community, but the film focused on the story of gay and lesbian civil rights, political activism, and institution building in the post-Stonewall era. In other words, it concentrated on the white, working- and middle-class individuals who were at the forefront of the gay liberation movement and on the organizations they established. Ridarsky wanted to challenge that narrative—or at least expand it—to be more inclusive. This meant finding ways of including people who were black and brown, people who identified as bisexual, queer, transgender, or otherwise gender nonconforming, and people with disabilities. But Ridarsky knew that as a white, straight woman, she was not the person to do that. She would need to recruit diverse people to sit on the curatorial team alongside those who represented the mainstream gay and lesbian story. This would prove challenging, and it would take many months of repeated outreach by Ridarsky and others to finally convince a few queer people of color that their voices were truly valued.

Together, the curatorial team was able to find a way to expand the "official" history presented in *Shoulders to Stand On* to incorporate African American and Latinx people and organizations into the traditional institutionally focused narrative. But they went even further. In an effort to highlight the diversity of today's LGBTQ+ communities and to center the people and stories that are traditionally overlooked, the library commissioned black queer photographer Adrian Elim to create twenty-five portraits. These fill much of the exhibit's back wall and are also scattered throughout display cases. Alongside each image is a personal story or poem provided by the subject that explains some aspect of their

"Writing is that thing that empowers and inspires me," says Lundon Knight. "When I write, I like to think about everything I've ever been through . . . then I make something creative out of it." Portrait of Lundon Knight by Adrian Elim. (COURTESY OF THE ROCHESTER PUBLIC LIBRARY.)

personality or life experience. Together, the photos and stories offer a glimpse at the humanity that resides within every person.

The exhibition was on display through July 20, 2019. For more information, visit ffrpl.org.

———————————————

Stonewall: 50 Years Out was curated by Evelyn Bailey, Tamar Carroll, Ralph Carter, Larry Champoux, Susan David, Adrian Elim, Patti Evans, Brandon Fess, Michelle Finn, Larry Francer, Christopher Goodwin, Justin Hubbell, Miranda Mims, Miss Rickey Snowden, Jamie Spiller, Jeremy Tjhung, and Lina Zigelyte, under the leadership of city historian Christine L. Ridarsky. Graphic design by Corinne Clar and Travis Johansen.

Artifact NY
Nineteenth-Century Water Main

Don Wildman

Beneath the teeming streets and sidewalks of Lower Manhattan, under some of the most densely built and *rebuilt* urban environment on the planet, lay the vestiges of hundreds of years of human habitation. Construction and utility crews have licensed archaeologists on call for the inevitable moments when excavations bring them face-to-face with New York City's buried past. In October 2004, during a routine installation of an electric service box at Coenties Slip Park near South Street Seaport, workers uncovered a length of bored-out log several feet underground. It was determined that this hollowed hemlock had served as an early nineteenth-century water main, still retaining the now-corroded metal ring that once stabilized its connection to a network of subterranean conduit throughout the city. This log pipe, along with two other sections found at the site, recalls a complex if underhanded plan to bring fresh water to a thirsty and diseased Manhattan, a scheme orchestrated by one of America's most notorious figures.

At the rise of the nineteenth century, Manhattanites faced an urgent water crisis. A disorganized system of wells, pumps, and ponds left an expanding population of twenty-two thousand residents severely undersupplied. Many sources had become dangerously contaminated by careless industry and human and animal wastes. The city's many residential privies had begun to seep into the groundwater. The whole polluted mess inevitably led to outbreaks of cholera and yellow fever, which over decades killed thousands. Like Philadelphia and Boston, New York badly needed to innovate its water system if the city was to grow and prosper, but unlike those other cities, New York would do so in its own peculiar and idiosyncratic fashion, following the dubious leadership of Aaron Burr.

Burr was a powerful and influential New Yorker with an ironclad résumé. He had commanded a regiment in the Revolutionary War, been elected to the New York State Assembly, served as New York's attorney general, and even run for president of the United States in 1800. He was a calculating player on the New York political scene, and as Manhattan faced this pressing water crisis Burr spied an opportunity not only to address the desperate need but to slake his own thirst for power and riches.

Early nineteenth-century log water mains recovered from Manhattan's Coenties Slip during park renovations in 2004. (PHOTO BY JOAN H. GEISMAR)

Burr established the Manhattan Company, a private, for-profit entity established by in 1799 to transport fresh water from the Bronx River to Lower Manhattan, eleven miles south. However, in the company's state-approved charter, Burr had inserted a clause that allowed surplus capital to be used for fiscal debt and deposit transactions. The water utility would also be a bank! In time, cost-saving decisions were made to transport water *not* from the Bronx but rather from a spring-fed source much closer to town that city dwellers back to the Dutch had used for various purposes: a small, befouled lake known as Collect Pond. Over time, the company would only ever connect four hundred paying subscribers to its network.

Burr would leave the Manhattan Company soon after, eventually going on to serve as vice-president under Thomas Jefferson. In 1808—the same year the Manhattan Company divested itself of its water operations, thus becoming solely a bank after all—Burr infamously shot and killed Alexander Hamilton in a duel. He would spend his remaining decades under a cloud of suspicion pursuing political and financial glories he would never achieve.

As for the Manhattan Company, despite drastic shortcomings its water system remained in service until 1842, when renewed efforts to address still-rampant disease finally

Water main pipe detail after conservation treatment in 2016. (COURTESY OF NEW YORK STATE MUSEUM COLLECTIONS)

resulted in a genuine solution, the Croton Aqueduct. The bank, which grew into a financial giant, eventually constructed its headquarters on Wall Street and in 1955 merged with Chase National to become Chase Manhattan Bank.

Today, the New York City water supply is managed by three different municipal agencies and is one of the largest water systems in the world, a sprawling atlas of upstate dams, reservoirs, and tunnels that efficiently deliver 1.2 billion gallons of fresh water every day to nine million NYC residents—a far cry from the days of corrupt politicians and their hollow, wooden pipes. For more information about NYC's water supply, listen to *A New York Minute in History*, episode #8, "The Story Behind New York City's Water Supply." https://wamcpodcasts.org/a-new-york-minute-in-history/

BOOK REVIEWS

The Thomas Indian School and the "Irredeemable" Children of New York

By Keith R. Burich. The Iroquois and Their Neighbors. Syracuse: Syracuse University Press, 2016. 224 pages, 3 halftones, 6" x 9." $59.95 cloth, $29.95 paperback, $29.95 ebook.

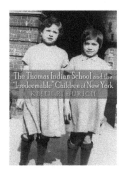

Keith Burich has produced the first scholarly book on the Thomas Indian School, which operated on the Seneca Nation of Indians Cattaraugus Reservation for a century beginning in the middle of the 1850s. This is an important project because state education programs for native peoples have received far less study from historians than the large federal boarding schools like Carlisle. Thomas lasted longer than these off-reservation boarding schools, and several decades after this approach had fallen out of favor with federal policy makers. The Thomas School looms large in the memories and experiences of Iroquois people in New York State, and no scholar has explored fully its impact on the state's native peoples and families. This is then a necessary project exploring an important subject. Burich's work, however, never quite succeeds in overcoming his inability to access the most essential primary sources and his unwillingness to look past some of his own assumptions about the boarding school experience, even when the evidence clearly shows that the reality was more complex.

Burich traces the school's origins as an asylum for orphaned and destitute Indian children. Crumbling conditions on New York's reservations provided a steady stream of students, some of whom spent their entire childhoods at the institution. By 1875 it was clear "that the asylum's facilities and staff were not adequate to handle the ever-increasing influx of children from reservations across New York" (57). The New York State Board of Charities took over and shifted the school's mission from education directed toward assimilation to institutionalization designed to isolate Native American children from what officials considered the dangerous influences offered at home.

The consequences were horrific. As "the purpose of the institution shifted from education for acculturation and assimilation . . . to isolating and insulating the children from the destructive influence on reservations," the periods of commitment increased. The school's policies and approach created in the students "a state of dependency and perpetual childhood that guaranteed the students' inability to adjust to life outside the institution" (86). They arrived at Thomas from families broken by the forces of colonialism; "the same 'pathologies' that landed them at Thomas—poverty, divorce, alcohol abuse, and domestic violence—followed them when they left, ensuring that there would be future generations of Thomas students." Burich appropriately cites the social worker Katherine Tidd, whose 1943 report found that Thomas damaged the students who enrolled and provided them with no benefits they could not have received at home with their families (116).

Burich's evidence is anecdotal and limited, necessarily so. He relies on a collection of interviews of former Thomas students published by the Seneca Nation of Indians and according to his notes, on a single interview with one Seneca woman that he conducted. Beyond that, indigenous voices remain largely mute in his study. We hear from policy makers but not pupils. The student case files for the school are closed to researchers, so Burich could not get access to one of the sources that may have provided the best evidence for the school's effect on children. Perhaps he might have followed the students through other sources: the council minutes of native nations, if he could get access to those; town and county records for those who left the reservation; the occasional newspaper article. But this is laborious work, and it is impossible to predict how much information it might have yielded without putting in the many required hours.

The evidence that Burich does provide in places suggests that he may not be attuned enough to the school's ambivalent legacy. The Mohawk Andrew Herne, disappointed by the public-school opportunities at home, hitchhiked to Thomas to enroll. Burich points out that for many of the children, "Thomas provided a far better educational opportunity than the public schools on or near their respective reservations" (89). The Seneca Arthur Nephew remembered the school as the best part of his life. "We were taken care of, we had shelter, we had food, we had medical care, we had all kinds of recreation, and all kind of trades we could learn," he wrote (91). Thus, it appears that Burich's claim that the school left children "unable to survive outside an institutional setting where every aspect of their lives was dictated and controlled by the institution" (107) is at best an oversimplification that underestimates the resilience and toughness of Iroquois families and children. His claim that the school left its students shattered in self-esteem and "unable to adjust to life after Thomas" seems inadequately supported (111). There was suffering to be sure, as Iroquois people have pointed out. But there was more to Thomas, and its students, than that.

The author relies heavily on several sources, like the well-known Meriam Report, for its criticism of the government boarding school system, but many voices were engaged in this debate in a variety of publications. It is disappointing that Burich did not tap into this longstanding debate. He makes little use of newspapers and state government documents outside of the Thomas School materials. For his discussion of Seneca communities before Thomas opened its doors, it is surprising that Burich did not make use of the rich Quaker collections housed at Haverford, Swarthmore, and other archives in Pennsylvania or of the federal agency records housed at the National Archives.

There are other problems with Burich's book. Though it is short, with about 170 pages of text exclusive of notes, tighter editing could have reduced it by a third and, at times, the text is repetitive and disorganized.

The Thomas School plays an important role in the history of Iroquois communities in New York State. In making this argument, Burich is correct. But this work is inadequately sourced, for reasons only in part beyond the author's control. The legacy of the Thomas School is complex. Reconstructing its history is a massive undertaking that remains incomplete.

Reviewed by Michael Oberg. Oberg is Distinguished professor of history, State University of New York College at Geneseo.

Blood in the Water: The Attica Prison Uprising of 1971 and Its Legacy

By Heather Ann Thompson. New York: Pantheon Books, 2016. 752 pages, illustrations, maps, 6" x 9." $35.00 cloth, $17.95 Vintage paperback, $17.95 ebook.

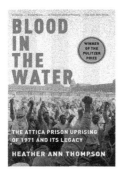

Blood in the Water by historian Heather Ann Thompson may well be the definitive book about the 1971 prisoner uprising at the maximum-security correctional facility in upstate New York. Thompson obtained primary sources that had not been available to other researchers. As she discusses in "State Secrets," her introduction to the book, she was invited to the New York State Museum by an archivist and saw the Attica documents, photos, clothing, and other artifacts that were stored there. She also was able to conduct oral history interviews with participants in the event who gave her access to documents in private collections. Other Attica documents turned up in the Erie County courthouse in Buffalo, New York. But, in spite of the Freedom of Information Act (FOIA), she was not able to obtain some documents held by state agencies. As the fiftieth anniversary of the Attica uprising approaches, the number of eyewitnesses to and participants in this event will be fewer. Future researchers on Attica will find it difficult to write a more thoroughly researched work. But Thompson asserts that her account is incomplete because government officials and law enforcement officers have worked to conceal the truth of what happened at Attica in the four days from September 9–13, 1971.

In spite of her own distrust of the efforts of agents of the state to control the historical narrative, Thompson writes about what happened at Attica using careful documentation that captures the complexities of the people and the situation in which they found themselves. Even the police and corrections officers who strip, beat, and abuse the prisoners who survive the violent retaking of the prison are first introduced as men waiting to learn the fate of relatives and friends. At the same time, Thompson highlights the racism that powered their fury and played a role in the decision-making by Governor Nelson Rockefeller and his advisers.

Thompson's book is divided into ten parts, each beginning with two or three pages from the perspective of an individual who was caught up in the turmoil of the uprising. These brief biographical perspectives include that of African-American prisoner Frank "Big Black" Smith, who is put in charge of the security force that the prisoners created to bring order to D Yard (the recreation area they had taken over). Thompson also introduces Michael Smith, a young white corrections officer, who is one of the men taken hostage. This other Smith has left college to get married and taken a job with benefits in the prison. The bios of the two men and the other individuals Thompson introduces provide both context and grounding for the reader who will have many names to remember. But these names and faces may be familiar to those who have seen the news clips and interviews done with survivors on the twenty-fifth anniversary of the uprising.

Thompson won the 2017 Pulitzer Prize for History for *Blood in the Water*. Her ability to describe what happened as a gripping narrative is one of the strengths of the book and makes it accessible to all readers. Using both primary and secondary sources, Thompson presents parallel and overlapping timelines for the uprising. This is particularly effective when negotiations to end the uprising are underway and the participants are unaware of what is happening elsewhere. During these sections of the book, Thompson is masterful in depicting the shifting moods in D Yard and among the journalists, politicians, and religious leaders whom the prisoners have requested as outside observers. She uses the tools of creative nonfiction to convey the tension as these men, enter the yard, and depart to deliver the prisoners' demands to Russell G. Oswald, the new, reform-minded commissioner of the Department of Corrections Services. Oswald then delivers their demands to Rockefeller, the governor of New York since 1959.

As Thompson reveals, the decisions by Rockefeller, a Republican with a "liberal reputation" (19), to follow President Richard Nixon's example by getting "tough on crime," and by Black Panther leader Bobby Seale to come to the prison but leave soon after he is finally allowed inside, have consequences—as does that of William Kunstler, the civil rights lawyer whose role changes from observer to defense attorney, and his ill-timed reference to the death of a corrections officer.

Thompson portrays the inhuman conditions that existed at Attica before the spontaneous takeover of D Yard by the prisoners. After four days of negotiations, heavily armed New York State Police launched an assault to retake the yard. The decision by the governor to send in the state police rather than the National Guard resulted in the deaths of thirty-nine men, prisoners, and hostages. Over a hundred others were wounded, some of the prisoners shot at point-blank range by police officers.

In her dedication, Thompson writes: "For all who were killed at the Attica Correctional Facility more than four decades ago . . . And for all who were wounded, maimed, tortured, and scarred on September 13, 1971." Her goal is to tell as much of the story of what happened at Attica as she has been able to uncover, with the hope that this will help the survivors of the uprising to move toward healing and that "a bit more justice will be done" (xvii). In the latter parts of the book she discusses the various commissions that were appointed to investigate what happened at Attica and in the aftermath as New York launched its own "War on Drugs." These parts of the book may be of less interest to the general reader, but they are important to understanding why the uprising at Attica still resonates in discussions of crime and punishment.

Thompson's book provides a companion work to law professor's Michelle Alexander's *The New Jim Crow: Mass Incarceration in the Age of Color Blindness* (New Press, 2010). Thompson writes about the tension between the self-described "political prisoners" from urban areas who are sent to Attica and the white corrections officers in upstate New York. Thompson book explores the issues raised in episode 12 of *Eyes on the Prize*, "A Nation of Law?" the award-winning documentary about the Civil Rights Movement, the second half of which is about the Attica uprising and includes the grainy black-and-white video recorded by the state police. Thompson writes about the Black Panthers, the Puerto Rican Young Lords, and the white "revolutionaries" who are at Attica. She notes the role of the FBI at Attica and the impact of rumors and misinformation. Readers who are interested in the mass media coverage of the uprising will also find Thompson's work useful.

This book is highly recommended for discussions about both the Attica uprising and mass incarceration.

Reviewed by Frankie Y. Bailey. Bailey is a professor at the School of Criminal Justice, University at Albany.

The Revolution of '28: Al Smith, American Progressivism, and the Coming of the New Deal

By Robert Chiles. Ithaca: Cornell University Press, 2018. 298 pages, 10 halftones, 1 map, 4 charts, 6" x 9." $32.95 cloth, $26.99 e-book.

Robert Chiles's examination of Al Smith, progressivism in the presidential election of 1928, and the coming of the New Deal sheds light on a previously neglected area of U.S. electoral history. Smith's campaign in 1928 resonated with millions of urban workers who abandoned their quiet acceptance of status quo (often the Republican Party too) in favor of a progressive Democratic Party, realigning the electorate in the process. Chiles peels back the historical record to expose a myriad of events and players, economics from numerous vantage points, and voting patterns. In tracing Smith's career, Chiles weaves together various stories to explain the growing chorus of advocates, voters, and government officials (Smith being the foremost) seeking progressive government programs nationally, as espoused by Smith in 1928, and finally delivered under the New Deal in the 1930s.

The first two of the book's five chapters outline Smith's growth as a progressive—an education fostered by reformers such as Mary Dreier, Frances Perkins, Lilian Wald, and others—and his program as governor of New York, where he championed a broad reform agenda. The three remaining chapters outline the campaign of 1928, the voters' reaction, and an explanation as to how the 1928 campaign spurred a revolution before the New Deal. The story is strengthened through its plentiful use of archival materials, oral histories, and newspapers, giving flesh and blood to working-class Americans as they turned toward the Democrats *because* of Smith.

Of course, Chiles also cites—and in some places challenges—the historiography of the period. Paula Eldot, who in carefully delineating Smith's governmental record, interpreted Smith's program "as an important source of the New Deal." Similarly, Matthew and Hannah Josephson, biographers of Smith based on the papers of FDR labor secretary Frances Perkins, claimed the "beginnings of the Welfare State" began with Smith. In contrast, William Leuchtenburg, who extensively researched the New Deal and FDR, found Smith more "conservative" and concluded that "the notion of a planned society" was repugnant to Smith (180-81). Similarly Arthur Schlesinger, famed researcher of the New Deal and the politics that brought it, contends Smith was more interested in "protecting the individual against the hazards of society." (180). Chiles contends it would be too simplistic to say Smith created the New Deal but, he did play a central role within the rising social welfare, progressive movement and served as a central figure in bridging the gap from state to federal stage. What makes this work worth reading is the logical, linear progression outlined by Chiles, who states that while "Smith's progressivism *did not* constitute the genesis of the New Deal," noted biographer of New Deal Senator Robert Wagner J. Joseph Huthmacher was correct in stating that "many New Deal programs were *akin* to those [Smith] had espoused in Albany" (italics original) (181–82). Limited to New York, Smith's program did not have a national theater, combat the Great Depression, or expand as liberally as the New Deal. In a sense, Smith was in the middle of the movement chronologically, but he brought a message to the national stage in 1928 that revolutionized an electorate conducive to progressivism as never before. But it was Franklin Roosevelt—four years later—who capitalized on Smith's revolution and established the New Deal.

But how did Smith do it? One key is that, in stark contrast to the other presidential elections of the 1920s, Smith's candidacy in 1928 spurred ethnic minorities, workers, fellow Catholics, "wets," and numerous other peripheral minorities (Jewish, French Canadian, Polish, Portuguese voters, to name a few) to vote Democratic—many for the first time. Smith's program struck a progressive chord in working class and ethnic enclaves. In direct contrast to Herbert Hoover, who claimed the national Republican Party had created a post—Great War economy, Smith heralded change that promised help to those not benefiting from the superficially placid economy of the 1920s. Workers whose wages were cut or who were laid off, ethnic voters tired of being taken for granted by the Republican Party, those with no health care, flocked to hear from the governor of New York about how he would address these issues in the Empire State—and nationally. Long before Smith expounded social welfare as federal purview in 1928, "cultural empowerment with social welfare appeals had been the formula of Smith's progressive governorship" (6). Governor Smith's "reform vision" targeted the same demographics nationally that he did in New York: "urban, ethnic, working-class voters who emerged as the core of the Democratic coalition during the New Deal era" (9). In 1928 "the reform proffered by Smith . . . was transformed by its sponsor into a people's initiative" (70).

Chiles offers solid evidence for progressive transformation in chapters 4 ("The People's Verdict") and 5 ("The Revolution before the New Deal"). The author's deep dive into the impact of Smith's programs on voter behavior explains Hoover's "ambiguous rout" (126). Statistical analysis shows "substantial inroads for the Democratic Party" were made "among recent-immigrant, Catholic and Jewish laborers across the Northeast and the Midwest" (126–27). While some "pockets of struggling farmers" supported Smith, it was the urban vote, particularly in factories, that portended the migration to the Democrats due to Smith (128). Voting patterns in large cities showed a tremendous spike in the votes for Smith as compared with previous Democratic tickets, thus heralding "the elevation of the great urban centers to prominence within the Democratic Party" (131). Many northeastern mill and factory cities experienced mass movements of traditionally Republican ethnics (e.g., Poles, French Canadians) to the Democrats under Smith. It was to these voters that Smith appealed, and, in return, these voters moved into the Democratic camp supporting a social welfare, labor, progressive program at the federal level. Though Smith lost in 1928, he set the stage for a receptive, energized, and growing Democratic Party to take back the presidency and enact major progressive reforms federally (as touted by Smith), a condition further aided by the Depression and by amplified calls for the federal government to act on behalf of a suffering populace.

After 1928, Smith's allies did not fade away; "all of these figures became New Deal Democrats and Roosevelt supporters" (198). Smith mysteriously became a bitter critic of the New Deal. It may have been due to Smith's affinity for his new business life, or it may have been bitterness for not having won his party's nomination in 1932. The strange change in Smith—though historical fact—detracts from the story, mainly because it was Smith who served as the penultimate step before progressive government achieved its long-awaited national emergence, and acceptance, under the New Deal.

In total, this is a very good work, one that highlights the "why" in regard to Smith's appeal nationally and his transformative contribution to the Democratic Party and the ultimate election of FDR.

Reviewed by Johnny Evers. Evers holds a PhD from the University of Albany and is director of government affairs with the Business Council of New York State. He also serves as the Albany County historian.

The Three Graces of Val-Kill: Eleanor Roosevelt, Marion Dickerman, and Nancy Cook in the Place They Made Their Own

By Emily Herring Wilson. Chapel Hill: University of North Carolina Press, 2017. 232 pages, 30 halftones, 5 ½" x 8 ½." $25.00 cloth, $19.99 ebook.

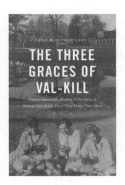

Emily Herring Wilson's *The Three Graces of Val-Kill* is impeccably researched, well written, and beautifully illustrated; it encapsulates in literary form the highly evocative sense of place created by Eleanor Roosevelt, Marion Dickerman, and Nancy Cook in the architectural embodiment of Val-Kill. While indeed scholarly, this book has a poetic tone that rolls along like the rivulets of Fall-Kill Creek and pulls the reader into the easygoing spirit of a weekend retreat with short chapters and comfortable prose.

Wilson's prologue puts us at FDR's childhood home and the nexus of Sara Delano Roosevelt's matriarchal power in the Hudson Valley, Springwood's breakfast table in the late summer of 1924. So, the story begins the day after FDR had suggested building the cottage at Val-Kill. For the reader, Wilson reveals the liberation this cottage represents for Eleanor Roosevelt and "the three Graces." The geographical distance between Springwood and Val-Kill is less than three miles, but they are worlds apart in their countenance and design. Both structures embody the women who lived there—Sara Delano Roosevelt's Springwood with its dark-wooded Victorian style and adherence to strict social protocols; Val-Kill's knotty pine and insouciant comfort where Eleanor, Marion, and Nancy would live more freely and remotely.

Eleanor Roosevelt is an iconic figure. What makes this book timely is the narrative arc that reexamines her personal and professional relationships with Marion Dickerman and Nan Cook as a couple, with all the highs, lows, and rifts that human relationships entail. Wilson's presentation of facts is admirable (see, e.g., 4), though I think she errs on the side of conservative interpretation of a same-sex relationship in this day and age. On the back cover, Wilson illustrates the monogram on one of Val-Kill's linen napkins, "EMN," each woman's first initial embroidered thereon. In a nineteenth- or early-twentieth-century household, the linen in a bridal trousseau would feature just such an embroidered monogram of conjoined initials of a heterosexual couple based on etiquette conventions. It would be interesting to know who had embroidered these "for company" napkins. My posthumous hope for Eleanor, Marion, and Nancy is that the structure of this relationship sustained them.

Other scholars have examined in more forthright terms Eleanor's friendships and relationships with women and men beyond the context of her marriage to FDR. These include William H. Chafe's 1984 "Biographical Sketch," in Hoff-Wilson and Lightman's *Without Precedent;* in a number of Blanche Wiesen Cook's books about Eleanor Roosevelt (e.g., her 2016 *Eleanor Roosevelt: The War Years and After, 1939–1962, Volume 3,* page 6); Susan Quinn's 2016 book *Eleanor and Hick: The Love Affair That Shaped a First Lady.* Susan Ware's exploration of ER's friendship with Molly Dewson (and Polly Porter) in their Democratic National Committee work in the late 1920s and Dewson's work as a New Dealer throughout the 1930s after FDR is elected president in *Partner and I: Molly Dewson, Feminism, and New Deal Politics.* It seems inordinately heterosexist to judge anyone for a relationship outside the context of a skewed marriage, never mind these women reformer/ activists whose decades of work contributed so much to social justice and humanity as a whole. I hope for their sake that they were sustained by their relationships—that just seems like a human right to me in 2019.

Wilson deftly discusses the reorganization of domestic life for Eleanor, Marion and Nan, "and the fact that friends sent gifts of china and silver showed how they embraced the women's choice to be a family" (66). Indeed, as the center of the Roosevelt universe shifted from Albany to Washington, DC, Eleanor called upon Marion and Nan to help entertain parties of political guests at Val-Kill (77). They traveled with Eleanor and some of her children to Campobello Island, the Roosevelt summer home in Canada, and to Europe. The Roosevelts as a political power couple with five children had to rely on other people's time and skills to manage the social and entertainment schedule, as well as the children, discussed at length in chapter 4, "The Family Vacation," until the younger boys aged out of traveling with three women.

Val-Kill Industries, a craft workshop to teach marketable skills to the young people in rural Dutchess County, is a fascinating study of localized production to garner job creation. Nan Cook took charge of the workshop, though it functioned better in theory than in practice from 1926 to 1936. In theory, it propped up the sagging agricultural economy by creating jobs for local people in traditional woodworking and textile craft workshops (114–19). Eleanor promoted this venture, and thereby garnered more of the publicity from it than Nan Cook, who ran the operation and was the craftsperson (118). Marion's partnership with ER in creating the Todhunter School in New York City began in the late 1920s with Eleanor teaching there a few days per week. The ongoing presidential focus of FDR's life in Washington D.C., and ER's increasing role as First Lady shifted the power dynamics of these intimate friendships, and by 1938 these partnerships were dissolved, leaving unresolved emotions and hurt feelings (151). The magic of human dynamics changed in these relationships by the late 1930s, and after 1945, when FDR died suddenly, an awkward period followed at Val-Kill that lasted until Marion and Nan moved to New Canaan, Connecticut, in 1947 (169).

Wilson follows each woman through to her death—ER and Nan in 1962 (175) and Marion in 1983 (176) —leaving us on the bridge with the creek and the birds at Val-Kill. This book adds depth and dimension to our understanding of many people in the Roosevelts' orbit, especially the women whose friendships sustained Eleanor and likely buoyed FDR's political career and Eleanor's status as First Lady to the world.

Reviewed by Sarah A. Johnson. Johnson has a PhD from the University of Brighton and is the former director of the Putnam History Museum, Cold Spring, New York.

The Suffragents: How Women Used Men to Get the Vote

By Brooke Kroeger. Albany:SUNY Press, 2017. 390 pages, illustrations, 7" x 10." $80.00 cloth, $24.95 paperback, $24.95 e-book.

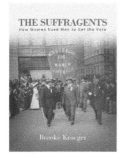

In April 1899, Susan B. Anthony took the podium at the National American Woman Suffrage Association Convention in Grand Rapids, Michigan, to read a letter from her dear friend and life-long colleague, Elizabeth Cady Stanton. Reflecting on the lack of male support for the suffrage cause after fifty years of activism, Stanton lamented, "It is pitiful to see how few men ever made our cause their own" (Susan B. Anthony and Ida Husted Harper, *History of Woman Suffrage* [Indianapolis: Hollenbeck Press, 1902], 4:338). Stanton would have been somewhat heartened had she lived into the next decade to witness the formation of the New York Men's League for Woman Suffrage. At the prompting of National American Woman Suffrage Association president Anna Howard Shaw and his mother, Fanny Garrison Villard, Oswald Garrison Villard, the editor of the *New York Post* and the *Nation*, coordinated the first formal meeting of the Men's League in the late fall of 1909. Suffrage advocate and reform rabbi Stephen Wise assisted Villard, his close friend, with the league's founding. *The Suffragents: How Women Used Men to Get the Vote*, is Brooke Kroeger's chronicle of the Men's League activities from its inception at the City Club of New York through the end of the campaign for suffrage in New York in 1917.

The rapid societal and political transformations the United States experienced during the Progressive Era provide a backdrop for the final phase of the suffrage movement that Kroeger concentrates on. From the beginning of the book to its coda she offers intriguing biographical details about the men and women who helped change the public sentiment toward suffrage. Well connected in Greenwich Village radical circles, Men's League secretary Max Eastman, a young Columbia University graduate student with a growing reputation as a writer and speaker, emerges as the central figure in the league's nascent years. Kroeger traces Eastman's activities and those of the other gentlemen suffragists—or, to use the British moniker, "Suffragents"—by drawing heavily from countless newspapers and magazines from the early decades of the twentieth century. When Eastman resigned from the League to assume the editorship of the Socialist *Masses* in 1912, investment banker James Lees Laidlaw, husband of Harriet Laidlaw, a leader of the New York State Woman Suffrage Association, stepped in to lead the organization. Not only did Laidlaw prove instrumental when it came to increasing the league's visibility and finances in the Empire State, but he and his wife traveled across the country to promote men's support of the woman suffrage movement by helping to found other men's leagues as far west as Montana.

While it is difficult to assess the full impact that men's leagues had on male politicians and, more importantly, on male voters, Kroeger does an admirable job of informing the reader about the appeal the organization had among the upper echelons of society by focusing on distinguished men listed on league membership rosters. Her images include a number of official Men's League documents, such as the league's constitution and membership lists, but unfortunately they are difficult to read. The yearbook-style portraits located across from each chapter's opening page are a bit more useful, albeit in some cases the named portrait is the only mention of that member in the entire book. The impressive variety of illustrations, including portraits, posters, cartoons, campaign publicity, and more goes a long way in giving readers a broad sampling of the suffrage propaganda that inundated the American public during the closing years of the campaign.

Driven by newspaper headlines pertaining to the New York Men's League, Kroeger's most important contribution to suffrage scholarship is in the compendium of primary source materials that she has compiled relating to the New York men's place in the state and national woman suffrage movement. She makes commendable attempts throughout the work to reference the wider reaches of the suffrage fight in Albany, and in Washington, and even provides an occasional link to the battle in Great Britain. Framed around ten chapters each covering approximately one calendar year, Kroeger interjects several provocative personal scandals into the narrative, although they seem to add little when it comes to explaining the trajectory of the suffrage movement. The lack of a sharp analysis and historiography may disappoint those seeking a historical critique of men's pro-suffrage and anti-suffrage activities. However, there is no denying that this book that will appeal to a broad audience interested in how men came to participate in an already highly organized women's movement.

Reviewed by Karen Pastorello. Pastorello chairs the Women and Gender Studies Program at Tompkins-Cortland Community College. She is coauthor, with Susan Goodier, of Women Will Vote: Winning Suffrage in New York State *(Cornell University Press, 2017).*

Activist New York: A History of People, Protest, and Politics

By Steven H. Jaffe. Foreword by Eric Foner. New York: New York University Press, 2018. 304 pages, illustrations (some color), 8" x 10." $40.00 cloth.

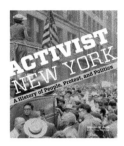

In *Activist New York: A History of People, Protest, and Politics*, Steve Jaffe makes the case for a continuous history of activism in New York City politics, starting with Quakers petitioning Peter Stuyvesant and concluding, as of now, with the four hundred thousand pussy-hatted participants in the Woman's March protesting the inauguration of the current president of the United States. *Activist New York* is a product of a permanent exhibit on display at the Museum of the City of New York's Puffin Foundation for Social Activism, though the exhibit, which opened in 2012, preceded its companion volume by six years. The volume is a thoughtful and well-illustrated account of radicals, reformers, protesters, and malcontents, arranged in sixteen chronologically arranged short chapters, with shorter inserts on other movements within the chapters. Some of the subjects covered in this book include labor militants, anarchists from Emma Goldman to Occupy Wall Street, gay and lesbian liberationists, suffragists, abolitionists, Latino militants, Communists, the New Negro in interwar Harlem, John Peter Zenger printing potentially libelous newspapers attacking colonial governor William Cosby, Orson Welles producing the radical musical *The Cradle Will Rock*, and builders of low-income housing in Brooklyn and the Bronx in the 1970s and 1980s.

Any book of this sort has to make choices on what to include within its space limitations, and *Activist New York* generally succeeds in providing a good mix of topics both expected and somewhat surprising. I particularly liked the two Latino chapters (one on José Martí and the Cuban independence movement, another on the Young Lords), and the chapter on Johnny Ray Youngblood, Louis Gigante, and housing reform. Still there were some surprising omissions. Labor activism drops out of the book after the early twentieth century. Educational reform, probably the most pervasive form of civic activism in New York City, receives little space in the book. Why a chapter on Cuban nationalism and so little on Irish nationalism or Zionism? What about temperance and other Protestant-inspired reformers like Charles Parkhurst? And though Jaffe does mention that not all activists were left of center, a chapter devoted to recent right-wing activism, such as the anti-integrationist Parents and Taxpayers organization, or anti-abortion activists, employing the street demonstration tactics of their left-of-center counterparts, could have been a useful counterpoint to the bulk of the book.

For all the topics Jaffee chose to write about, his accounts are excellent, to the point, based on the best current scholarship, lively, and illuminating. A few quibbles. The heading

"Socialist Legacies: Housing Cooperatives and the Amalgamated Bank" neglects the key role played by Jewish anarchists, especially Abraham Kazan, in the building of the Amalgamated Houses, and subsequently in the United Housing Foundation (headed by Kazan), the developer of both Rochdale Village and Co-op City. I would have liked a little more nuance in the account of anti-Communism in the 1950s, which is largely reduced to a fight between the Communist Party, USA, and various McCarthyite reactionaries, with not enough attention paid to liberal non- and anti-Communists, who often were progressive activists in their own right.

For all the accomplishments of *Activist New York*, in the end one is left wondering if the category of activism is too ambiguous and amorphous to contain all these protest movements under a single conceptual rubric. Jaffe acknowledges the slipperiness of the term and offers a definition: "Activism is what happens when ordinary people mobilize in hope of shaping their society's future through collective public action" (12). I would add that activism, as the term is currently understood, usually involves a higher level of politics, a devotion to a specific cause, rather than, say rallying for a political candidate or a labor dispute.

The term *activist* first entered the political vocabulary during World War I, referring to persons in Continental Europe of pro-German sympathies, and eventually expanded to include persons on the far left, it was usually used as a term of opprobrium. Its sense changed only in the 1950s and 1960s, when the Civil Rights Movement claimed the term for themselves. It is not surprising that activism in its modern meaning came of age in the decades when the Old Left, closely tied to unions and working-class militance, largely fell apart, to be replaced by the New Left's proliferation of causes.

Although right-wing activism is part of the story Jaffe needs to tell, it is in some ways tangential to the main theme of the book, which is the course of progressive activism in New York City. Like any good book, *Activist New York* raises many questions, some probably unanswerable. Is there a connection between the generations of activists Jaffe discusses? Do they stand on the shoulders of their predecessors? Is progressive activism cumulative or Sisyphean? Reading Jaffe's book, I wondered if a companion volume, less inspiring perhaps, *Reactionary New York*, could detail the ways in which activists and "reactivists," in perpetual reaction to the other, have together shaped the complex trajectory of the city's political history.

In the end, though, I am not sure if totaling up the successes and failures of Jaffe's activists is really that important. What the activists Jaffe profiled share is a deep discontent with the way things are and a determination to use "collective public action" to change things. One can learn from their successes and their failures, and learn as well that every important victory will have to be fought anew. If there is an underlying connection between the activists Jaffe writes about it is their determination to take on what often seemed to be futile and unwinnable causes and how their successors, in different ways, continue the struggle.

Reading *Activist New York*, I was reminded of something African-American religious thinker Howard Thurman once said: "There are two kinds of ideals. There are the ideals that are ultimate and in a very real sense always far out beyond anything that can be achieved. They are like far-off lighthouses whose glow is far away in the distance. There are also ideals that seem to be created out of the stubborn realities, in the midst of which people work and live. Always they are close at hand, a part of the immediate possibility, always being achieved but never quite fully achieved" (Thurman, Howard. *Meditations of the Heart* (Boston: Beacon Press, 1981), page 34.) The activists Jaffe studied all espoused and worked for these two types of ideals—the blurry ideals on the edge of the horizon and the short-term goals in front of their faces. Thurman hoped that as people they work toward realizing them "these two kinds of ideals will in time prove to be of one piece." One can only hope so.

Reviewed by Peter Eisenstadt. Eisenstadt is the editor in chief of The Encyclopedia of New York State *(Syracuse University Press, 2005), and the author of* Rochdale Village: Robert Moses, 6,000 Families, and New York City's Great Experiment in Integrated Housing *(Cornell University Press, 2010) and the forthcoming* Against the Hounds of Hell: A Life of Howard Thurman *(University of Virginia Press). He is an affiliate professor of history at Clemson University.*

Battle for Bed-Stuy: The Long War on Poverty in New York City

By Michael Woodsworth. Cambridge, MA: Harvard University Press, 2016. 424 pages, 24 halftones, 6 /8" x 9 ¼." $36.00 cloth, $36.00 e-book.

Groundhog Day seemed to strike whenever Mayor Robert F. Wagner appeared on Capitol Hill during the 1950s and 1960s to testify about New York City's juvenile delinquency crisis. To dramatize the situation of aimless young men, roving in gangs, stealing, fighting, stabbing, or even shooting each other, Wagner carried a bag of proof. He would take his seat before the staid senators and unpack "his usual collection of machetes, zip guns, and knives seized from the clutches of gang members" (86). No matter what types of intervention New York initiated, the problem remained, year after year. One person who regularly saw Wagner perform with this "suitcase of knives and things" soon thought that "he just left the suitcase here each year and opened it up at the hearings" (32).

Wagner and local youth organizers had seized on a formula. Highlight a moral panic. Develop programs that reformed individuals through self-help. Fund those initiatives. Tout incremental progress. Bemoan continued crisis. Repeat.

By the time John F. Kennedy became president, Wagner's routine helped convince Washington to act with boldness. The President's Committee on Juvenile Delinquency and Youth Crime (PCJD) unleashed a federal funding stream that supported local initiatives designed to attack the root causes of gangs and violence. By the early 1960s, Wagner's city had years of experience experimenting with community-based programs that brought education, social-work outreach, job training, and life-skills development to wayward young men. These comprehensive approaches, designed and implemented at the local level, defined juvenile delinquency as a cultural issue born from social needs associated with poverty. Young men formed gangs because they had no purpose or sense of belonging in life. They lacked direction because they did not have jobs. Employment evaded them because they lacked sufficient education and recreation resources. If on-the-ground intervention occurred and provided education, recreation, employment, and purpose, then gangs, youth violence, and juvenile delinquency would disappear.

But New York City's problems with juvenile delinquency, poverty, and violence during the post–World War II era, especially in its growing black and Puerto Rican communities, seemed endless. As they worsened, America declared war against poverty.

Michael Woodsworth's comprehensive and fascinating study of the "long war on poverty" shows how, from the mid-1940s through the mid-1970s, New York City emerged as a laboratory for experimenting with ways to eliminate the entrenched poverty, social alienation, and political powerlessness that festered in ghettos. Ghettos formed after decades of racial discrimination had forced black citizens into communities that experienced an outflow of taxes and investment capital through twin forms of racialized metropolitan economic development during the New Deal years. Money from government and banks flowed away from underdeveloped, "redlined" city communities, which were predominantly black, and poured into government-subsidized, owner-occupied suburbs, which were predominantly white. Unique to Brooklyn's ghetto, Bedford-Stuyvesant, the subject of Woodsworth's history, was a sizable cadre of community-minded, politically ambitious activist-homeowners. The area had block after block of stressed and suffering, but still salvageable, beautiful brownstones. Through exhaustive research (the author consulted nearly every relevant archival source, newspaper article, and oral history interview), extensive details (the author writes about every major local black leader, organizer, and organization in Brooklyn), and in prose that is, at times, delightful to read (Woodsworth describes a young Robert F. Kennedy as a "jutted-jaw anticommunist" [218] and "imposing Brooklyn housing projects where rat infested rookeries once slouched" [34]) the author reveals how "postwar Bed-Stuy served as a testing ground for a series of pioneering ideas about urban reform and community action" (13).

The blueprint for a community-based, national War on Poverty, Woodsworth argues, trickled up from the streets of central Brooklyn in the mid-1950s, to New York's City Hall during the Wagner and John V. Lindsay years (1954–73), and finally to Capitol Hill in the 1960s. Beginning in the 1950s, central Brooklyn's settlement houses, churches, and block associations set their sights on attacking juvenile delinquency by dispatching social work-ers and youth organizers, known as "detached workers," to steer young men away from gangs and violence and toward organized recreation, school, and jobs. Woodsworth dis-cusses how when the moral panic over youth violence reached city hall, grassroots activists pointed to their positive work to extract funds. The late 1950s saw a consortium of local activists and organizations called the Central Brooklyn Coordinating Council for Youth (CBCC) organize an attractive program called "Teens in Industry" to connect rebellious young men in Bedford-Stuyvesant with job training in local businesses (79–80). The fed-eral involvement in local fights against poverty that began with Kennedy's PCJD gave way to President Lyndon B. Johnson's War on Poverty and its Office of Economic Opportunity, which funded Community Action Agencies (CAA) designed to enlist the "maximum feasi-ble participation" of poor people in the elimination of their own impoverished conditions. "Nowhere were the War on Poverty's complex local realities—the limitations and possibili-ties, the deep roots and lasting legacies," writes Woodsworth, "more vividly on display than in Bedford-Stuyvesant" (12).

Overall, *The Battle for Bed-Stuy* traces how a "technocratic vision of progress replaced grassroots protests" (274). Each chapter highlights the growth of a different local, anti-pov-erty effort in Bedford-Stuyvesant. The CBCC evolved alongside the Bedford-Stuyvesant Neighborhood Council. By the early 1960s they shared the organizing stage with Brooklyn's premier CAA, Youth in Action (YIA). Chapter 5 recounts the maddening municipal pol-itics of red tape and turf wars that kept YIA from receiving federal anti-poverty funding. To cut through the bureaucracy in 1966, the junior senator from New York, Robert F. Ken-nedy, partnered with local leaders—the CBCC's Elsie Richardson and Brooklyn's reformist political leader Thomas Russell Jones, for example, as well as business and philanthropic elites—to create a new comprehensive, anti-poverty institution, the community develop-ment corporation (CDC). Chapters 6–8 narrate the rise and fall of the nation's flagship ur-ban CDC, the Bedford-Stuyvesant Restoration Corporation (BSRC). Woodsworth details all the petty squabbles, steamrolling politics, backroom deals, paternalism, and mau-mau-ing that made BSRC possible. Franklin A. Thomas, the first president of BSRC, produced tremendous successes during his ten years at the helm, Woodsworth shows, because his leadership eschewed a vision of community development that tied empowerment to activ-ism and instead fostered managerial proficiency that sought empowerment through results. BSRC secured a sizable mortgage pool to build housing, refinance mortgages, and facilitate home improvements. It sparked commercial development. It created neighborhood buy-in through the Community Home Improvement Program (CHIP), among other programs (303).

In the end, the success and shortcomings of Bedford-Stuyvesant's War on Poverty occurred because the local movement reflected most the needs, aspirations, and goals of homeowners, not the community's hard-core poor. The positive effects that the long War on Poverty had on central Brooklyn happened because "Bed-Stuy's middle class activists treated brownstones as valuable resources in the battle to halt capital flight, knit community bonds, and build black assets" (317). Woodsworth's conclusion showed how, in the words of one central Brooklyn activist, Jitu Weusi, "the great land grab" eventually came to Bedford-Stuyvesant (317). Those brownstones that black Brooklynites prized and protected so much became repositories for a reverse flood of capital back into the black ghetto. Gentrification, and a new war on the poor, ensued. For poor people in Bedford-Stuyvesant, it was Groundhog Day all over again.

Reviewed by Brian Purnell. Purnell is the Geoffrey Canada Associate Professor of Africana Studies and History at Bowdoin College and the author of Fighting Jim Crow in the County of Kings: The Congress of Racial Equality in Brooklyn *(University Press of Kentucky, 2013), winner of the NYSHA Dixon Ryan Fox Manuscript Prize.*

Radical Gotham: Anarchism in New York City from Schwab's Saloon to Occupy Wall Street

Edited by Tom Goyens. Urbana: University of Illinois Press, 2017. 270 pages, 6 halftones, 1 chart. $95.00 cloth, $28.00 paper, $19.95 e-book.

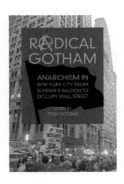

In the seven and one half years since Occupy Wall Street signaled a resurgence of the left, anarchism and socialism have vied for the interest and sometimes the allegiance of young progressives in New York and across the country. Tom Goyens, who has expanded our understanding of New York's radical past in his study *Beer and Revolution: The German Anarchist Movement in New York City, 1880–1914* (2007), here offers an anthology of essays by scholars exploring anarchism's enduring appeal to successive generations in the nation's capital of leftist agitation. *Radical Gotham* should be required reading for anyone interested in the intersection of radicalism, urban life, ethnic politics, and cultural production in the modern world, a saga in which New York has played an outsize role.

Goyens's excellent introduction underscores the book's major themes, all of them tied to "the premise that anarchism is and has been a distinct, resilient, transnational, and significant political philosophy and movement that deserves to be studied on its own turf" (2). Anarchism—both an ideology and a mode of action defined by rejection of "politics, capitalism, and any form of coercive authority" (9)—emerged out of arguments between rival nineteenth-century European socialists. Anarchism's triple emphasis on the absolute freedom of the individual, the need for a cooperative egalitarian economy, and the evils inherent in state power (whether a capitalist or socialist state) found fruitful soil in New York. The city became a refuge and hothouse for overlapping circles and generations of immigrant and native-born anarchists (characteristically, when Johann Most—arguably New York anarchism's founding father—died in 1906, mourners delivered eulogies in five languages). Because anarchists believed that their own actions should "prefigure" the ideal society they were trying to create, New York's diverse social spaces—immigrant saloons and cafés, avant-garde theaters, art installations, squatters' apartments, and public parks—have repeatedly become settings for envisioning a transformed world. Above all, Goyens argues that anarchism has enjoyed a continuous presence in New York for 150 years, its attractions discovered by succeeding generations of seekers who have reshaped it for their own uses.

Essays by Goyens, Kenyon Zimmer, Marcella Bencivenni, and Christopher J. Castañeda document the ways in which German, Italian, Spanish, Cuban, and Eastern European Jewish immigrants created anarchist cultures that were both distinct and in dialogue with each other. During the golden age of New York anarchism in the late nineteenth and early twentieth centuries, figures such as Most, Emma Goldman, Saul Yanovsky, Maria Roda, and Pedro Esteve shaped community life, journalism, literature, and labor relations in ways often minimized by earlier historians. A connecting thread between these essays is the notion that, rather than being an exotic transplant rooted in European circumstances, anarchism was fundamentally an outgrowth of experiences in New York and the United States, where events like the Haymarket bombing in Chicago (1886) and the strike by silk workers in Paterson, New Jersey (1913), galvanized and defined the commitments of radicals.

Contributions by Anne Klejment, Andrew Cornell, and Allan Antliff excavate the anarchist roots of social and cultural activism in mid-twentieth century New York. Klejment argues that Dorothy Day's Catholic Worker movement should be understood as an anarchist project, while Cornell examines the role of the little-known Why?/Resistance Group in keeping anarchism alive among pacifist intellectuals and activists during the 1940s and 1950s. Antliff demonstrates how Judith Malina and Julian Beck's Living Theatre kept the flames of artistic and experiential freedom (both venerable anarchist ideas) burning from the Cold War years to the Counterculture of the 1960s and beyond. Each of the essays shows how it was New York City—increasingly the world's crossroads—that enabled nonconformists to share and amplify anarchist-influenced ideas across disciplines, communities, and generations.

Radical Gotham's final essays trace New York anarchism from the late 1960s to the early 21st century. As Caitlin Casey reveals, the group of rebels who called themselves the Motherfuckers—"flower children with thorns" (161) in one view—exemplified an angry, defiant strain of anarchism that emerged as part of the Lower East Side "Scene" in the late 1960s, foreshadowing later resistance by neighborhood artists, tenants, and squatters against gentrifiers, police, and city officials. The combination of cultural self-expression and political dissent remained a potent hybrid, as showcased in Erin Wallace's examination of the artist-activist Gordon Matta-Clark, Alan W. Moore's reminiscence of the Lower East Side institution ABC No Rio, and Heather Gautney's consideration of Occupy Wall Street. These individuals and groups critiqued what each viewed as the corrosive onslaught of capitalism and state power in an era of urban crisis and/or in the new Gilded Age of dominant high finance that followed.

Each essay enhances an understanding of how the city both shaped and was shaped by anarchists—a recurrent and protean process. A book this rich raises as well as answers questions: Is there, for example, a distinction to be drawn between self-declared anarchists and those who embraced some anarchist ideas without overtly identifying themselves as such? In its laudable mission of asserting a persistent anarchist presence, *Radical Gotham* does not always precisely distinguish between anarchists and those influenced by anarchism; at any rate, the book does not acknowledge that this might be a meaningful difference, although Goyens's introduction does summarize recent debates over how to define anarchism. When the authors celebrate as well as document New York anarchism, they predictably sidestep its key weakness—namely, the difficulty of achieving lasting gains through a movement wary of power, authority, and organization. And rather than being settled here, debates over the identity of New York radicalism (American? European? Euro-American? Atlantic?) will no doubt continue to be argued.

Yet Goyens and his contributors are to be thanked for producing a rewarding guide to the recurrent collision of two fascinating forces—the modern world's signature city and utopian dreams of a better world. In Gautney's words, as "state and corporate power holders shape the city in the image of Wall Street" (237) ever more relentlessly, *Radical Gotham* may well become a Baedeker to a usable past.

Reviewed by Steven Jaffe. Jaffe is curator at the Museum of the City of New York and author of Activist New York: A History of People, Protest, and Politics *(New York University Press, 2019) and* New York at War: Four Centuries of Combat, Fear, and Intrigue in Gotham *(Basic Books, 2012).*

Selected Speeches and Writings of Theodore Roosevelt

Edited by Gordon Hutner. New York: Vintage Books, 2014. 365 pages. $16.95 paperback, $16.95 e-book.

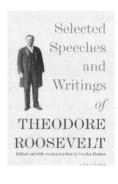

No one who ever occupied the White House has been a more prolific writer than Theodore Roosevelt. His collected works encompass many volumes, among them nearly thirty books. His works also include essays, articles, and speeches, not to mention the approximately one hundred thousand letters he wrote. What makes his written work even more remarkable is that he wrote knowledgeably on such a wide range of topics. Compiling a book that is a representative selection of the writings of this son of New York is a formidable, seemingly overwhelming task. Professor Gordon Hutner of the University of Illinois accepted the challenge to winnow the massive quantity of Roosevelt material into a single volume. The result is *Selected Speeches and Writings of Theodore Roosevelt,* a well-organized and readable gem that provides a perceptive glimpse into this multilayered figure.

Among our presidents perhaps only Thomas Jefferson matches the intellectual curiosity of Theodore Roosevelt. While Jefferson's journeys into the cerebral world generally took place in the comfort of his beloved Monticello, Roosevelt was a man of action whose journeys involved travel, observation, and adventure. He was the man in the arena, to use one of his better-known phrases. After all, no one else has been the recipient of both the Congressional Medal of Honor and the Nobel Peace Prize. To capture the essence of this man in just over three hundred pages of prose is no easy task. With so many words attributed to Roosevelt, where does one begin—what is to be included and what is to be excluded?

Wisely, Hutner has organized this collection by category. These include culture and society, national politics, campaigns and controversies, observations and travels, biography, history, and arts and letters. Each section includes between two and seven selections taken from Roosevelt's written work. These include speeches and essays as well as excerpts from his books. Each selection is preceded by solid synopsis of the material that invites and encourages the reader to delve into the documents themselves to experience the richness of Roosevelt's fertile mind.

Some of the choices are widely known by Roosevelt devotees, such as "The Strenuous Life." That selection, perhaps more than any other, provides an insightful look into his nature. Yet, Hutner also includes an essay titled "The American Boy," which was written for young people, in which Roosevelt articulates the themes of hard work, self-discipline, and physical exercise that were so integral to the development of his own character.

To remind us that no one is perfect, Hutner includes some material that today's audiences might find disconcerting. Roosevelt's last public speech was to a group known as the Circle for Negro War Relief. Although, in many ways, he was progressive on civil rights issues, this speech is rather uncomfortably patronizing and paternalistic. By including these words, Hutner reminds us that we should not be guilty of reverse moral projection by judging Roosevelt based on present-day moral values rather than those of his era. The inclusion of a document such as this one presents a more complete picture of Theodore Roosevelt the man.

Some may quibble about what has not been included. For instance, nothing from his autobiography is presented, although it is debatable whether that work was one of his more compelling literary efforts. The only account from his trip to the Amazon (which nearly led to his death) is a description of a rodeo he observed in Chile. The writings based on his personal experiences, however, are revealing and descriptive. In "Hunting the Grisly" he writes of being "lulled to sleep by the stream's splashing murmur, and the loud moaning of the wind along the naked cliffs" (186).

Roosevelt was at his best when he was passionate about a subject. An ardent conservationist, he connects conservation and democracy by stating that national parks like Yellowstone preserve the nation's majestic beauty for everyone, not just the affluent. In fact, his prescient vision was clear in an address to the nation's governors when he warned that using our nation's natural resources too rapidly would lead to a time when the public would become aware of how important it is to protect the environment.

An enthusiastic imperialist, he was also a great believer in democracy—concepts that today seem to be in conflict. In "The Colonial Policy of the United States" Roosevelt argues that such a policy benefits the peoples being colonized because the United States can help them develop through its imperialistic influence. Again, while this also smacks of paternalism, he sees a greater purpose in colonialism than just sheer exploitation of other peoples. It is a means to spread democratic values, at least in his eyes.

His most zealous writings are those that focus on his embrace of progressivism. Although he grew up in affluence, he had great compassion for those who worked hard but were less fortunate. He believed that a guiding principle for government should be fairness, and thus was born the "Square Deal" for all Americans. Only the government was powerful enough to stand up to the entrenched forces of big business. His goal for the Progressive Party was to wage war against privilege on behalf of the common man. Although denied the Republican Party nomination for president in 1912, he presented himself as the champion of the people in "The Case against the Reactionaries," a speech made to the party convention.

There are also passages from his historical and biographical works. His work on the naval side of the War of 1812 was long recognized as the seminal work on the topic. Hutner points out that much of the work in these categories lacks the vividness of most of his other writings, but reminds us that this material was intended for a scholarly audience, not a general one. Wisely, Hutner includes some of this writing as an example of Roosevelt's ambition to be taken seriously as a historian.

Professor Hutner has compiled a rich harvest of the work of this extraordinary figure. Like TR himself, the appeal of this book is broadly based. This book is suitable for a general audience seeking to plunge deeper into the larger-than-life figure that was Theodore Roosevelt, yet even those who are aficionados will find the fullness of this collection to be affirming and enlightening. Scholars will find documents that elucidate this complex and engaging individual. This work is an essential component of any library that embraces Theodore Roosevelt and his legacy.

This work reminds us not only that Roosevelt was a sportsman, historian, conservationist, biographer, adventurer, and, of course, a politician but also that he was a writer. Upon his graduation from Harvard he set his sights on supporting himself and his bride as a professional writer. In one of his introductions, Hutner speculates that Roosevelt may have been frustrated at times about having to give up his goal of being a professional writer. However, in this important collection Hutner shows us that Roosevelt always wrote like a professional, even if he is remembered primarily for other reasons.

Reviewed by T. J. Vaughan. Vaughan is an emeritus professor at Aurora University, Illinois.

EXHIBIT REVIEWS

Hodinöhsö:ni Women: From the Time of Creation

Ganondagan Seneca Art and Culture Center. Temporary Exhibit.
March 24, 2018—December 2020.

The exhibit team includes
Site manager: Peter Jemison; Curator and exhibit design: Michael Galban;
Exhibit design and fabrication: Sally Johnson and Hadley Exhibits; Public interpreter
and Seneca cultural consultant: Veronica Reitter; Native American Educator and
Mohawk cultural consultant: Tonia Loran-Galban.

Ganondagan's Seneca Art and Cultural Center opened *Hodinöhsö:ni' Women: From the Time of Creation,* in March 2018. Curator of the exhibit Michael Galban and Site manager G. Peter Jemison sought to explore the prominence and importance of Hodinöhsö:ni' women in the indigenous culture through narratives such as creation of this world, the Great Law, collaborative efforts with the women's suffragist movement, and modern Hodinöhsö:ni' women navigating two worlds. The importance of Hodinöhsö:ni' women has long been known within the indigenous cultures and communities, but their role has been far more muted in Western culture and the modern world. Hodinöhsö:ni' women have long been a source of the Good Mind, influencing diplomacy, and raising families since time immemorial—and remain steadfast examples of equity and justice that are ongoing examples for the rest of us.

The Good Mind perhaps is best understood through the lens of Creation, which is the beginning panel of the exhibit. Galban judiciously chose quotes from his vast knowledge and research that highlight the role women have played since the beginning of this physical world we as humans now reside within—on this island that rests on the back of a turtle. Women as life-givers and caretakers is a universally understood concept (though often oversimplified), but what sets this exhibit apart is that it focuses on how one culture understands the role of women within Creation, within the Great Law, and navigating modernity. The Good Mind is a belief that peace is a state of mind, of a reciprocal relationship with other humans, the natural world, and our spiritual connections to the cosmos.

The exhibit explores the role women played in helping form the Hodinöhsö:ni' Confederacy through the Great Law. The Peacemaker and Ayonewenta (sometimes called

The full wall installation of the exhibition in the Seneca Art and Culture Center.
(PHOTO BY HANNAH PADULO)

Hiawatha) journeyed together, bringing a message of peace and the resolution of human conflict using reason among the warring Hodinöhsö:ni' nations. But these two men met and collaborated with Jigöhsahsë'—The Mother of Nation, who ultimately helped form the venerable frameworks of the Confederacy itself—and cemented women's roles within the Confederacy. It was Jigöhsanhsë's words and songs that helped restore the mind of Tadodaho to establish the Great Law and Confederacy. The events shown in these sections of the exhibit are to be understood as having happened long before contact with European peoples.

Another part of the exhibit explores the understudied conversations Hodinöhsö:ni' Clanmothers had with women's rights leaders like Matilda Joselyn Gage, Susan B. Anthony, and Elizabeth Cady Stanton. During the women's rights movement in Seneca Falls, these leaders and others had ongoing conversations and contact with Hodinöhsö:ni' women and culture—where women were treated as equals, owned property such as the cleared lands and villages, and raised up leaders (chiefs) for the good of the People, Clans, and Nations of the Hodinöhsö:ni'.

Near the end of the exhibit a visitor explores and contemplates what it means for Hodinöhsö:ni' women to walk in our traditional worlds and live in and among the U.S. and Canadian cultures. This part of the exhibit features seven women who balance walking in the two worlds while remaining firmly rooted in culture, in the Good Mind, and choosing

A traditional Onöndowa'ga':
(Seneca) women's outfit.
(PHOTO BY HANNAH PADULO)

to make a powerful difference in the modern world. These women are Clanmothers, inspirational speakers, mothers, sisters, aunties, writers, and artists.

This exhibit in the new Seneca Arts and Culture Center is worth the visit to Ganondagan State Park. When visiting the center, one is greeted with friendly, knowledgeable staff and volunteers. There is a gift center where one can purchase books, Iroquois White Corn, and other items that will ensure lasting memories of visiting Ganondagan and the Seneca Arts and Culture Center. One can also hike the trails of Ganondagan, which link up with other trails throughout the area. A visitor can also visit the Bark Longhouse and Creator's garden to see what it would have been like to live at Ganondagan before 1687.

Ganondagan was a main Seneca village of approximately five thousand people that was destroyed in 1687 by a French force of nearly three thousand militia and Indian allies of the French. But much like the women of Hodinöhsö:ni' Nations and culture, the Seneca were resilient the face of the French attack in 1687. Visiting Ganondagan's Seneca Art and Culture Center, the Bark Longhouse, and the trails is wonderful way to spend the day—immersing oneself into the complexity and constancy of Hodinöhsö:ni' culture and history.

Moose antler carvings of the spirits of the Three Sisters by Stan Hill.
(PHOTO BY HANNAH PADULO)

Hodinöhsö:ni' Women: From the Time of Creation is an inspiring exhibit to explore the roles and balance of women through history, through art, and through stories. It underscores the use and lived reality of the Hodinöhsö:ni' Good Mind as a peaceful state of mind.

Reviewed by Kevin J. White. White is the former director of Native American studies at the State University of New York College at Oswego.

Black Citizenship in the Age of Jim Crow

New-York Historical Society, New York, NY. Temporary Exhibit. September 7, 2018 through March 3, 2019.

The exhibit team includes
Co-curators: Dr. Marci Reaven and Lily Wong. Research historians: Dr. Amanda Bellows and Dominique Jean-Louis. Writer: Marjorie Waters. Exhibition design: Brianne Muscente-Solga. Graphic design: Marcela Gonzalez and Julia Zaccone. Harlem installation: Ivar Theorin, Austin Muller, and Severn Eaton. Fabricators: SmallCorp, Top Notch Graphics, and New Project.

The year 2018 marked 150 years since the ratification of the Fourteenth Amendment, which guaranteed birthright citizenship to all Americans. In honor of this important anniversary, the New-York Historical Society presented *Black Citizenship in the Age of Jim Crow*, a six-month exhibit at the museum, which takes a sweeping look at the struggle for citizenship for African Americans starting with Reconstruction (1866–77) and ending around World War I (1914–18). With the passage of the 13th (1865), 14th (1868), and 15th Amendments (1870), African Americans both free and formerly enslaved, faced new prospects as they wrangled with centuries of oppression that denied them the rights of citizenship, even as they were born on U.S. soil and their labor had built this nation. Within the context of Jim Crow, a word so familiar in the American lexicon, *Black Citizenship* expertly demonstrates that racism and segregation were not just products of the South, but ubiquitous in the North too. As this impressive exhibition shows, African-American citizenship was fraught with possibilities and setbacks, and frames some of the debates on race and citizenship today.

Black Citizenship* adheres to many of the curatorial, organizational, and visual features that visitors have now come to expect and associate with the New-York Historical Society's history exhibits. Visually stunning oversized graphic panels are accompanied by smaller text panels, infographics, visual timelines, various objects that highlight the museum's own collections, and a few interactive elements. With such a vast topic to cover, the exhibit is divided into three thematic and chronological sections: "Reconstructing Citizenship, 1865–77" asks in the aftermath of the federal abolition of slavery, "Would black people be accepted as equals?"; "The Rise of Jim Crow, 1877–1900" examines the rise of segregation ("Although named for a comic minstrel character, Jim Crow was deadly serious"); finally, "Challenging Jim Crow, 1900–1919" crystallizes African American resistance that had emerged in much earlier periods of U.S. history, as the "government abandoned the cause of black equality."

Entry graphic for *Black Citizenship in the Age of Jim Crow.*
(PHOTO BY PRITHI KANAKAMEDALA)

But before visitors enter the gallery, they are greeted with a more familiar visual of African American protest—a blown-up photo featuring numerous picket signs and people from the 1968 March on Washington. It is an interesting curatorial choice, given that it is outside the exhibit focus, and its connection to the Civil War (the first thing visitors do see once they enter the exhibit) is not immediately apparent. But the opening sign—a purple photo with bright yellow, red, and white lettering—offers a visual hook that did appear to attract visitors from the museum's darkened mute corridor into the gallery space.

A portrait from the historical society's own collections of Dred Scott, who was denied his freedom by the U.S. Supreme Court on account that black people were not American citizens, opens the exhibit. But it is Thomas Waterman Wood's *A Bit of War History* (1866) that crystalizes many of the show's concerns. The painting offers three vignettes of a black man in which larger chapters of U.S. history intersected with his life: the first as an enslaved person, the second as a Civil War soldier, and the final scene as an impoverished and disabled veteran. The exhibit makes clear that for African Americans, citizenship has never been a given. Instead, it has been a right that generations of African Americans have been required to prove themselves worthy of, even as they have built this nation through their labor, demonstrated their patriotism, and consistently been rewarded with little in return. Another object highlight, a family Bible belonging to the Ellis Family on loan from the National Museum of African American History and Culture, offers an intimate glimpse into the ways in which the political intersected with the personal. The exhibit also makes use of the historical society's now familiar copy of slave shackles—on prominent display during the museum's groundbreaking *Slavery in New York* show, and even a replica of an early Ku Klux Klan gown, both terrifying and strangely domestic in its use of adorned daisies and plain brown color.

It was the final section, "Challenging Jim Crow," that was the strongest part of the entire exhibit. Covering the Great Migration, the section makes use of timelines, vertical vignettes, text panels, and objects, much like the rest of the show. But models of Confederate monuments that were built during this historical period demonstrate how this history continues to plague the American landscape today. Figures in the exhibit such as W.E.B. DuBois, Ida B. Wells, Maggie Walker, and Meta Fuller solidify how the United States has never reconciled its slaveholding past. Finally, tucked into the corner of the room a small, charming 3D model installation of Harlem's buildings and neighborhood institutions that brings together people, space, and place-making, stood out from the entire exhibit. As black women were denied from participating in the formal body politic, they found ways to grow and celebrate their communities, and, of course, remain at the center of grassroots politics and protest. And then the exhibit ends, where it began, on the advent of war again with the display of a soldier's uniform from World War I. By World War I, although African Americans had been free for over four decades, they would have to once again demonstrate their readiness and patriotism to take up the rights and responsibilities of citizenship.

Harlem artifact installation as part of the exhibition's "Challenging Jim Crow" section.
(PHOTO BY PRITHI KANAKAMEDALA)

The exhibit's reluctance to end on a hopeful note seems absolutely right and timely. At a time when white supremacy, nationalism, and citizenship attacks are on the domestic and global rise, the exhibit implicitly asks more questions about its resonance than it explicitly answers. It was in beautiful dialogue with the Betye Saar retrospective on the floor above in the museum.

Black Citizenship in the Age of Jim Crow brings together an impressive scholarly advisory board, and some of the best elements of New-York Historical Society history exhibits—dense, scholarly research that supports broad chronological reflections on the past that affect our present with exquisite glimpses through myriad objects and lives. My only regret was that the space was too small for such an important topic and it therefore felt overwhelming at times. The six-month exhibition at the New-York Historical Society has become a traveling exhibit and is also accompanied by an impressive K–12 curriculum.

Reviewed by Prithi Kanakamedala. Kanakamedala is an assistant professor of history at Bronx Community College. She is currently a faculty co-leader for the Mellon Seminar on Public Engagement and Collaborative Research at CUNY Center for Humanities, Graduate Center.

ROBERT DAVID LION GARDINER
FOUNDATION

The Robert David Lion Gardiner Foundation, established in 1987, primarily supports the study of Long Island history. Robert David Lion Gardiner was, until his death in August 2004, the 16th Lord of the Manor of Gardiner's Island, NY. The Gardiner family and their descendants have owned Gardiner's Island since 1639, obtained as part of a royal grant from King Charles I of England.

The Foundation is inspired by Robert David Lion Gardiner's personal passion for Long Island and New York history, and its role in the American experience.

Applicants must be a non-profit, history driven entity qualifying as an exempt organization under Section 501(c)(3) of the Internal Revenue Code.

The Foundation is looking to support impactful projects that can serve as model for the advancement and sustainability of regional historic organizations.

The Robert David Lion Gardiner Foundation, Inc.
148 E. Montauk Highway, Suite 1
Hampton Bays, NY 11946

Email | gardiner@rdlgfoundation.org
Website | www.rdlgfoundation.org

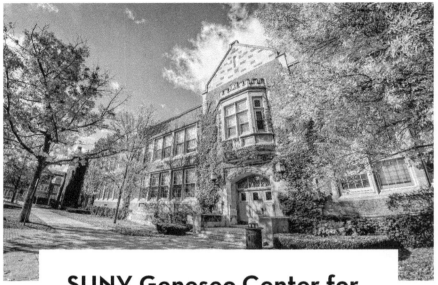

Preserving, protecting, promoting, and presenting the rich history of the Empire State through the heritage of its communities

The **Association of Public Historians of New York State (APHNYS)** is incorporated by the New York State Board of Regents. It is the official professional development organization for New York State's government appointed historians.

The Association consists of a Board of Trustees, five of whom are officers: President, 1st Vice President, 2nd Vice President, Secretary, and Treasurer. The officers make up the Executive Board.

APHNYS is divided into 12 regions and each region has a Regional Coordinator (RC) and a Deputy Regional Coordinator (DRC). Each region is encouraged to hold at least one meeting a year, preferably in the spring.

The Annual State Conferences (held each fall) offer a wide-range of sessions on the preservation, protection, and promotion of local history, as well as informative field experiences showing off the "historical jewels" of the hosting county and region. Participants learn from fellow practitioners and experts in the field from across the Empire State. The Annual Conferences offers an opportunity to network with other NYS Local Government Historians. Find out what projects others are working on that may also be beneficial for you to take back to your community as a project idea. You can contact the APHNYS President at **aphnys@yahoo.com** Find out more and keep up-to-date by checking our website: **www.aphnys.org**

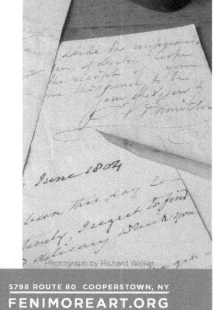

GOVERNMENT APPOINTED HISTORIANS
OF WESTERN NEW YORK
"Historians in Pursuit of Excellence - Building a Legacy"

The Government Appointed Historians of Western New York (GAHWNY) is dedicated to the promotion, research, interpretation and preservation of history related to the western portion of New York State.

The purpose of this organization is to provide educational training and programming for all officially appointed local government historians and representatives appointed by the Seneca, Tonawanda or Tuscarora Nations within western New York comprised of the counties within the Niagara, Southern Tier and Finger Lakes Regions of New York State.

To become a member or to learn more about our annual meeting, student history award program, and much more contact us at: GAHWNY, PO Box 204 Panama, NY 14767 or check us out on Facebook and at GAHWNY.ORG

SAVE THE DATE
The GAHWNY annual meeting will be held Saturday, September 28, 2019 at Mount Morris, Livingston County, NY.

HUMANITIES
NEW YORK

OUR MISSION
Humanities New York strengthens civil society and the bonds of community by using the humanities to foster engaged inquiry and dialogue around social and cultural concerns. Humanities New York offers grants and discussion programs to support history in your community:

GRANTS
Awards are made by application to nonprofits that inspire New Yorkers to explore what it means to be human: Quick Grants offer small organizations $500 for in-person public humanities programs; Vision Grants provide $1,500 to develop your ideas for public humanities programs, built in partnership with your community; Action Grants provide up to $5,000 to execute meaningful public humanities programs.

COMMUNITY CONVERSATIONS
Facilitated discussions that encourage participants to reflect on the importance of civic participation through shared reading on contemporary issues, including immigration, Martin Luther King, Jr. Day of Service, and Democracy.

READING & DISCUSSION
Facilitated reading and discussion series using texts on important humanities themes, in which participants can reflect on local issues with national relevance. Invite a group to your historic home or museum to discuss the Civil War, James Baldwin, Muslim Journeys, True Crime, Growing & Aging, and many more.

CONTACT US
(212) 233-1131
humanitiesny.org
info@humanitiesny.org
@humanitiesny on all social media

"Dan Peck's treatment of Thomas Cole's Catskill pictures is a gem of a book. It is compact yet substantial, dense in detail yet lucid in exposition."
—John Wilmerding, Princeton University, author *of Signs of the Artist*

"From socialite to saint, it was an extraordinary journey for Seton, one gracefully chronicled in Catherine O'Donnell's richly textured new biography. . . . A remarkable biography of a remarkable woman."
—*Wall Street Journal*

$36.95, HARDCOVER, 524 PAGES, 29 B&W IMAGES

$36.95, HARDCOVER, 524 PAGES, 29 B&W IMAGES

ITPS
INSTITUTE FOR THOMAS PAINE STUDIES

Founded in 2011 to preserve and develop the rich archive of the Thomas Paine National Historical Association, the Institute for Thomas Paine Studies has expanded is mission to support the broader interdisciplinary research of early American studies. Building on the TPNHA collection, which includes writings, material objects and other items by and about Paine and his world, the ITPS focuses on archival studies, public history, and digital humanities efforts. This includes undergraduate research and education initiatives, conferences, seminars, workshop series, and archival exhibits.

Highlights of ITPS initiatives, past and present, include the Gardiner Archival Fellowship program, the October 2018 conference "Revolutionary Texts in a Digital Age," the Text Attribution Project, and several forthcoming publishing partnerships. Collaborations include participation in the McNeil Center Consortium, sponsorships with professional organizations like the Society for the Historians of the Early American Republic, the Omohundro Institute, and the "Ben Franklin's World" podcast. The ITPS is also developing a vibrant digital presence through its social media and blog, ITPS Updates.

www.iona.edu/itps

itps@iona.edu

 @TheITPS

THE SEWARD HOUSE MUSEUM PRESENTS

culinary
EXPEDITIONS

SATURDAY, JULY 6, 2019 FROM 6 PM - 9 PM
IN THE SEWARD HOUSE GARDENS

THIS SUMMER, EXPLORE
THE INTERNATIONAL JOURNEYS OF
WILLIAM H. SEWARD
WITH FLAVORS FROM AROUND THE WORLD

REGULAR TICKET $38 | VIP TICKET $50

LIVE MUSIC ◆ GOURMET FOOD TASTINGS
◆ BEER & WINE TASTINGS ◆ RAFFLE ITEMS

FOR MORE INFORMATION OR TO
PURCHASE TICKETS CALL **(315) 252 -1283**
OR VISIT **SEWARDHOUSE.ORG**

 # MUSEUM ASSOCIATION OF NEW YORK

The Museum Association of New York is the only statewide association of professionals speaking with one powerful voice serving New York's museums, historic sites, wildlife centers, and cultural institutions.

MANY inspires, connects, and strengthens New York's cultural community statewide by advocating, educating, collaborating, and supporting professional standards and organizational development.

Join MANY and add your voice as a member of our growing museum community.

Connect with us

@nysmuseums | #nysmuseums

265 River St. Troy, NY 12180
(518) 273 3400 | info@nysmuseums.org
nysmuseums.org

SIENA COLLEGE'S McCORMICK CENTER FOR THE STUDY OF THE AMERICAN REVOLUTION

A community engaged teaching and learning program rooted in the traditions of liberal learning, service and advocacy

The McCormick Center partners with nonprofits and the public sector to develop and share educational programming about the history of New York State and colonial and Revolutionary America. The Center provides Siena students with personally meaningful leadership and learning opportunities that advance history education and prepares them for life, work, and active citizenship.

SIENA*college*™
McCormick Center

For more information, contact Jennifer Dorsey, Ph.D.,
Professor of History - mccormickcenter@siena.edu; 518-783-2319

UNIVERSITY AT ALBANY
State University of New York

CAHR
Center for Applied Historical Research

The mission of CAHR is to facilitate broad democratic access to historical resources and knowledge. CAHR accomplishes this by applying historical scholarship to projects outside the academy through partnerships and collaborations among public and academic historians, corporate and governmental agencies, and public and private historical institutions. CAHR fosters and preserves community and institutional historical memory; advocates the application of historical understanding in policy formation; expands the skills of historians; and utilizes information technology to make the fruits of historical research widely available to teachers, students, and the general public.

CAHR is seeking manuscript proposals for the SUNY Press series, "Public History in New York State." For this and other inquiries, contact: Ivan D. Steen (isteen@albany.edu).

Lightning Source UK Ltd.
Milton Keynes UK
UKHW011823130422
401523UK00003B/152